The Aesthetics of Freud

The Aesthetics of Freud

A Study in Psychoanalysis and Art

Jack J. Spector

PRAEGER PUBLISHERS
New York · Washington

BOOKS THAT MATTER

Published in the United States of America in
1973 by Praeger Publishers, Inc., 111 Fourth
Avenue, New York, N.Y. 10003

© 1972 by Jack J. Spector

Library of Congress Catalog Card Number:
70–168347

Printed in the United States of America

Contents

Sections of illustrations follow pages 82 *and* 146.

Acknowledgements

I am indebted to the American Council of Learned Societies for funds which I applied to my trip to London and to the Rutgers Research Council for a grant helping defray incidental costs. In London Anna Freud and the amiable Paula made Freud's library and study at Maresfield Gardens accessible to me. The Rutgers Library staff, but especially my colleague Roger Tarman, Art Librarian, constantly cooperated with me. John Hochmann, my editor, offered steady and invaluable encouragement, and Nora Conover, my reader, improved the manuscript in a number of ways. My wife Helga and my children Robert, Elisabeth and Erik have alternately enjoyed and suffered with me as this new child took shape and life.

The publishers wish to thank the following for permission to reproduce illustrations:
Alinari Art Reference Bureau, Florence (5, 6, 7, 9, 10, 14)
Princeton University Library (15, 16)
Cambridge University Press (21, 32)
Kupferstichkabinett und Sammlung der Zeichnungen Berlin (27)
ADAGP, 1971, French Reproduction Rights Inc. (29)
Arts Council of Great Britain (30)
Museum of Modern Art, New York (33-4)

Introduction

Freud's importance for contemporary Western culture is evident from the continuing impact of psychoanalysis on such diverse fields as anthropology, sociology, art and literature, religion, philosophy and biography, as well as on his own special discipline of psychology. In evaluating his stature as a powerful innovator, critics have placed him beside those Olympians of the nineteenth century, Darwin, Marx, and Nietzsche, who were also thinkers on a grand scale.

While his genius has maintained its luster for the seventy years since the publication of his masterpiece, *The Interpretation of Dreams*, the book has never escaped from the controversy that initially greeted it, so that few of his conclusions remain uncontested even today. Despite the abundance of his insights, Freud failed to produce an all-embracing and consistent theory of personality. The absence of consensus among psychoanalysts has led to a see-saw of opinions and evaluations of Freud's achievement among neo- and anti-Freudians; in fact, despite several competent surveys of the schools of psychoanalysis (Mullahy, Munroe, D. Wyss), the student unattached to any dogma who seeks to understand Freud's views on the unconscious, the libido, the role of the ego, or the death instinct, can easily become bewildered. The multi-plication of Freudian re-evaluations continues. While a firm core of orthodox Freudians (led by Jones and Reik) have with moderate success attempted to assimilate some of the heterodox opinions into an expanded interpretation of Freud's original statements, more daring writers (notably Marcuse and Brown), who affirm Freud's continuing relevance and who counterattack Freud's critics, have gone much further, proposing solutions to critical problems of our culture based on ideas found in his work. This confusion of viewpoints is no less striking in aesthetics.

Freud's views on art and the artist have been similarly obscured by an array of commentators. A large part of the difficulty in understanding his views is due to Freud himself, for he never wrote systematically on art and approached aesthetic questions mainly for their bearing on his psychoanalytic work. Apparently with the modesty of a scientist eschewing questions beyond his proper domain, Freud left the subject of genius or technique to aestheticians and to the artists themselves. Yet Freud wrote on art with an intimacy that suggests that it meant to him something more than a scientific problem; unfortunately, just where one wishes for clarification, Freud remains silent or unclear, or speaks contradictorily, as in his opinions of artists. It is understandable that Freud's insights into the artist and the brilliant hints about the psychology of art he dispersed through his writings have had so much influence on writers, artists, and critics. This influence, while pervasive, has also proved elusive, so that it has stimulated those numerous but unsuccessful attempts since Freud's death in 1939 to review and revise his ideas on art in order to synthesize a psychoanalytic aesthetics. Essential questions implicit in a psychoanalysis of art remain—and perhaps must remain—wholly or partially unanswered: How does form evolve from its origin in the chaotic unconscious, and how does it provide us with its pleasures and satisfactions? What role does the ego or controlling consciousness play in relation to unconscious or repressive forces, and to what extent can the insights of psychoanalysis guide us to an understanding of the productive processes of the artist, on the one hand, and the appreciation of the spectator, on the other? The impact of Freudian ideas on a broad range of disciplines has led to challenges by experts within each field not yet satisfactorily answered. The art historians question the significance of nonartistic experiences (especially in childhood) on the mature style of the artist, and the relation of unsuccessful productions, whether infantile, preliterate, or neurotic, to good art; art historians and critics have demanded the formulation of psychoanalytic criteria for quality in art; and many anthropologists, relinquishing the old assumption of the superiority of Western culture, which Freud shared, have demanded recognition for each "primitive" art and literature on its own terms and with its own values, an attitude hard to reconcile with orthodox psychoanalysis.

However incomplete Freud's views on art may be, they have sustained an interest equal to that of his psychoanalytic theories. A major conclusion of this writer is that aside from some fruitful implications of his ideas for criticism and art, no final system can ever be built out of Freud's views; but in any case, the appeal of Freud's *The Interpretation of Dreams* rests on other than systematic grounds. The continual patchings and scrapings, the pastings and smearings of Freud's followers, with their claims to updating or to greater accuracy or system, have proved ephemeral, while "the house that Freud built" (as Joseph Jastrow sarcastically called it) has endured. Freud's book has indeed become a classic, with the constant appeal of the work of art or philosophy, rather than the transitory interest of the scientific treatise.

In considering Freud an artist or philosopher, and his major work as an artistic masterpiece, this book does not intend to criticize the validity of Freud's scientific findings. Freud, although aspiring to produce a "metapsychology," and aware that his impact had been greater on nonscientific than on scientific circles, bristled at Havelock Ellis' apparently complimentary comparison of him to an artist. Still, the source of the work's constant, broad appeal obviously cannot be found in its scientific accuracy; on the other hand, even its initial capacity to seduce the idly curious or the prude for whom honesty in matters of sex meant pornography has diminished or become irrelevant in a world in which the public media are bound by few inhibitions. Increasing numbers of Freud's readers return to *The Interpretation of Dreams* as they would to Saint Augustine's or Rousseau's *Confessions*, or to Goethe's *Dichtung und Wahrheit* for the deep riches and fine complexities that great autobiographical literature has always offered. In the same sense, Freud's writings on artists and writers can profitably be considered not only as contributions to aesthetic studies, but as reactions to his own emotional and intellectual experiences and as *attempts to cope with these experiences*;[1] furthermore, these works generate their own excitement and should be read with the same attention as would be given to *Finnegans Wake*. Like the dream cosmos Joyce conjures up, they can perhaps best be interpreted with the aid of the very principles of psychoanalysis Freud describes.

To call autobiographical Freud's collections of case histories with their theoretical apparatus sounds mistaken or far-fetched. A major task of this book will thus be to explore the subjective and personal aspects of Freud's apparently objective studies of art, and reveal the man beneath. One might do the same thing with *The Interpretation of Dreams*, examining Freud's own dreams and his analysis of his patients' dreams, and one would find that the center of these dream fragments, with their partial interpretations, is always Freud himself, whose personality provides a ground for the mosaic of impressions and confessions. Here, the parallel is not to Joyce, whose dreamer H.C.E., the center of *Finnegans Wake*, seems factitious, but to Proust, whose person is felt throughout *À la recherche du temps perdu*, a work that retraces the author's childhood and creates a living presence by retrieving from the memory long-forgotten experiences.

At the end of the century, biographical novels of a most revealing sort became popular in German literature. Quite in harmony with this mode, the famous essayist Leo Berg, a naturalist turned antinaturalist and Nietzschean, wrote in an essay of 1895 ("Zur Geschichte und Charakteristik der modernen Literatur," in *Neue Essays*, Oldenburg, 1901) that German literature was essentially personal and subjective as compared to the impersonal objectivity of the Latin countries. He considered such great but intimate works as Luther's *Table Talk*, Goethe's *Conversations with Eckermann*, Schopenhauer's *Parerga*, Heine's journalistic pieces, and Hebbel's *Journals* (from which he quotes: "No one writes without writing his autobiography") to be grounded in a cult of the person, and to be the outstanding examples of subjectivity among great writers, guideposts for psychologists wishing to gain access to the minds of the authors. He finds that these works constitute "a literature which ... despite the immediacy of its expression, affects us with the force of true art." More specifically with reference to the late-nineteenth-century novels, Bithell has pointed out that many of these works "are, since they describe the development of the hero from youth to maturity through weal and woe, *Bildungsromane* or *Entwicklungsromane* more or less in the old sense, but the best of them are so intensely personal that they have been classified as *Bekenntnis und Bildungsromane*: in their pages the author reveals himself."[2] Freud, too, constantly probed and researched his own past, as though he were retracing the roots of his own astonishingly rich cultural development, indeed as though *The Interpretation of Dreams* (complemented by the later writings) were a *Bildungsroman* in reverse.

If this interpretation is correct, then one would expect to find in even his most objective case studies some reflections of Freud's own personality, a facet, one might say, of his life-long self-analysis. One might even try to apply to the investigation of all of Freud's writings Karl Popper's remark in his book *The Open Society* that psychoanalysts are the best subjects for psychoanalytic study. While such a monumental project is beyond the more limited intent of this book, it has seemed to me valuable and clarifying to divide the psychoanalyst's writings on art into three major phases, dependent on apparently major changes in Freud's attitudes and interests: an early prepsychoanalytic period in which problems of death, power, and identity were submerged in his medical and scientific studies; a middle period, from the *Studies on Hysteria* (1895) to the *Leonardo* (1910), a "romantic," "artistic" period in which Freud explored his own dreams and unconscious with loving enthusiasm, and discovered the erotic as a major force in the mind; and a late period, from the *Leonardo* and the first studies of religion in *Totem and Taboo* (1912) to the final allusions to art in *The Future of an Illusion* and *Moses and Monotheism*, in which Freud, having ceased to analyze his own dreams, turned increasingly toward the problem of the death instinct and toward organizational and theoretical studies. A key work in this scheme is the *Leonardo*, in which Freud implicitly expresses his anxieties about having reached a turning point in his own life, through his identification with the genius whose life he divided into an artistically rich early period and the drier scientific one of his maturity, when the unresolved problems of his childhood interfered with his artistic production. On a deeper level, it will be seen that some of Freud's most important ideas about art and the artist remained unchanged throughout his life despite changes of theme and method of approach.

The distinctive quality of Freud's genius can perhaps best be appreciated when his works are studied in relation to their intellectual and cultural background. Obviously, the formation of Freud the Viennese Jew's outlook on art depended very much on his earliest home and school experiences. As he matured, the educational and emotional influences of home and the circle of family and friends yielded to an ever-widening circle of contacts with school-mates and teachers in the elementary schools and the *Gymnasium* in Vienna, and the wide reading of literature in several languages, including Greek and Latin. Little documentation remains from those years. Curiously, Freud, on the one hand, destroyed most of his early writings, notes, and bits of evidence of the first period of his life, while on the other, he spent his whole mature professional life in the quest to recover memories of his earliest childhood experiences. But, despite this difficulty, the study of his later recollections of his infancy casts much light both on his personality and on his mature thought. The few important events from Freud's earliest period uncovered by Bernfeld and others, which Ernest Jones presents in his extensive biography, will be discussed where relevant to Freud's discussions of art.

Freud's childhood experiences shaped not only his mature retrospective writings, but his encounters with the romantic writers and artists, with the romantic classicism that enthused over the glories of vanished Rome and Greece as well as of the Near Eastern Biblical lands, and with the Jewish humor and wisdom to which especially his father exposed him. The directions of Freud's artistic tastes and literary preferences must have developed in response to the whirlwind of cultural activity of the *fin de siècle* Viennese milieu in which he matured; consequently, our discussion of this milieu can help us understand the seeming paradox that despite his expressions of distaste for Impressionist and later art, Freud's ideas about art and even his taste (as evidenced by his collection of books and art) show surprising affinities to contemporary currents of thought and to the advanced literature and art of the turn of the century. Freud, who readily acknowledged a long list of scientific forerunners, in his discussions of art also alludes to an extensive bibliography of nineteenth-century literature and art theory. We will surely be better able to grasp the historical importance of such aesthetically relevant techniques as dream interpretation and free association by studying nineteenth-century anticipations; we will be able more clearly to understand Freud's theories of beauty and pleasure in art if we are aware of earlier debates between upholders of morality, enthusiasts of art for art's sake, and advocates of materialist and sexual explanations; we can more easily comprehend his emphasis on the biological origins of art, and its persistent link to childhood, in relation to the evolutionist views of Darwin and Spencer; and, finally, we will be better able to fathom the theory of unconscious determinism central to Freud's analysis of art through seeing its relation, on the one hand, to the biological and physical models of causality taught in the Viennese schools and, on the other hand, to those unscientific speculations of romantic poets and philosophers about irrational occult forces hidden within the mind of the creator.

Freud's ideas on art and the artist, apart from the subjective and personal considerations so far indicated, seem also to have a value in themselves, above all, for interpreting works in the symbolic mode. To appreciate their value as well as to define their limits, we will do well to consider the impact of those ideas on later art and literature. To this end, I will, after analyzing Freud's own essays on specific works—especially on Michelangelo's *Moses*, Leonardo's *Virgin and St. Anne* and the *Mona Lisa*, and Wilhelm Jensen's story *Gradiva*—attempt to apply techniques gleaned from psychoanalysis to the appreciation and understanding of two modern works: the Surrealist artist René Magritte's painting *Le Viol* (*The Rape*), and a line from James Joyce's *Finnegans Wake*.

The varied attempts to synthesize from the writings of Freud a new socially oriented literary criticism, especially in Surrealist and post-Surrealist circles, the efforts to apply psychoanalysis to art history and to produce a psychoanalytic criticism relevant to modern as well as to older periods of art and literature—all reflect upon and even illuminate his ideas and help to test our own analysis of them. As already noted, Freud's influence has seemed to many writers so pervasive as to be everywhere felt to some degree; but in fact, two important qualifications must be made: first, many of the master's ideas, especially in the areas of art and culture, were considerably revised in the systems of former disciples such as Rank, Adler, and Jung, and thus reached the public modified and diffused; second, Freud's own ideas, insofar as they derive from powerful trends of nineteenth-century thought, to some extent serve as links in a continuous development from the nineteenth to the twentieth century, and share a common origin with analogous contemporary ideas, rather than inspiring them.

Freud's identity has survived intact to this day. By examining in detail Freud's concerns with art and artists, I hope in this book to open one more access to the complex mind and personality of the great psychoanalyst; for, nowhere in the massive achievements of his writings does he seem to me so clearly to reveal that elusive combination of the remote, sternly professorial intelligence and the warm, imperfect man.

The Aesthetics
of Freud

One

The Background of Freud's Taste and His Views on Art: Vienna and Freud's Education

The Interpretation of Dreams has often been considered a work of inventive genius appearing independent of tradition or even in open defiance of it. So viewed, one might not look for anticipations or expect that influences would help explain much of the significance of Freud's great innovations; yet, as Freud himself acknowledged, his psychoanalysis was not only inspired but actually prefigured by earlier thinkers; in retrospect, we might consider it to have been Freud's greatest contribution to digest, combine, and transform materials and ideas already current when he began to reflect on the nature of human motivation. The dependence of Freud's ideas upon the past has been extensively studied in relation to his psychoanalysis[1] but not in relation to his views on art.

Like all his earliest activities, Freud's first exposures to art are somewhat obscure. He systematically destroyed all his diaries and papers relating to the early phase of his life, leaving scholars to rely on the memory of the family, and his published works (including the analyses of his own dreams), autobiographical notes and letters. Ernest Jones, in his useful biography, *The Life and Work of Sigmund Freud,* has put together some of the research into Freud's preadolescent years by scholars such as S. Bernfeld, S. C. Bernfeld, and E. Rosenfeld, allowing us to gain some knowledge of the early period of Freud's life. But we must be cautious in approaching Freud's own writings, for even his partially published self-analyses and his *Autobiography* (1925) on careful examination turn out to leave many riddles unresolved. Applying to Freud his own comment (1930b)* on Goethe, who had claimed that his works were "fragments of a great confession," we may say that Freud concealed as much as he revealed, even in his self-confessional works. In his great writings, even in his "confessional," *The Interpretation of Dreams*, Freud often stops far short of completeness, leaving us with technical insights based on self-observation on the one hand, and an outline of intellectual development on the other, with little of the *emotional* man Freud showing through. Should not this reticence be respected, since we have the best of Freud in his work? My own feeling —in disagreement with all orthodox Freudians and writers such as Rieff[2] who felt that Freud's work becomes "exemplary only as it becomes impersonal"—is that it is precisely the personal side, albeit veiled and not easy of access, that gives compelling power to Freud's work, making it so much more attractive to readers than the dry emendations of his critics and followers. Thus, in his greatest and most influential works, Freud not only combined personal experience and clinical observation, but organized the parts of his presentation by the subtle, pervasive tone of his voice, his language, as though his writing were a metaphor for the working of his mind. Even works that seem objective become intimately linked with Freud's likes and dislikes the more one studies them. Thus, while *The Future of an Illusion* and *Moses and Monotheism* or his essays on Leonardo and on Michelangelo's *Moses* appear to be solely studies of an objective character, with personal opinions carefully distinguished, it can also be shown that they are highly personal expressions, products of Freud's evolving intellect. The quality and scope of Freud's views on art were, in addition, powerfully conditioned by emotional and educational experiences, not all of which were directly connected with art.

The first important allusion to Freud's formal education concerns

* Parenthetical citations such as these throughout the text refer to dates and works listed in the Bibliography.

his seventh year. "You were seven when the spirit of learning awoke in you," Freud's father wrote in a book given to his son, Sigmund, years later as a memento of that event. This book, which dominated the early development of the emerging genius and which furnished images for his later dreams and for some of his writings on art, was one of the three volumes of an illustrated Bible edited with notes by Ludwig Philippson, *Die israëlitische Bibel* (1858). Although, as he pointed out in his preface to the Hebrew edition of *Totem and Taboo* in 1930, Freud did not understand Hebrew, and in his infrequent references to the Old Testament (for example, his essay on Michelangelo's *Moses*) he ridiculed its inconsistencies and exaggerations, one senses the Bible's importance for him as a formative influence. In a sentence added in 1935 to his *Autobiographical Study* (1925), Freud wrote of the "enduring effect upon the direction of my interest" that his "deep engrossment in the Bible story (almost as soon as I had learnt the art of reading) had." Not without reason, Hermann Keyserling called Freud "an Old Testament Jew" who "spent the last years of his life writing a psychoanalysis of the Bible." In the deepest sense, Freud identified with the great figures of the Bible, above all Moses, but also Joseph, the dream interpreter. Behind these great figures stood Jakob Freud, a man who doubtless inspired and terrified the discoverer of the Oedipus complex as a small child, but who was a tender and devoted father. Freud, whose ambition must have been awakened early, found many ways to deny and ridicule and finally—in *The Interpretation of Dreams* (preface to the second edition)—to erect a monument over his father, a not very successful merchant with little formal education. Freud believed himself to be " the duplicate of his father physically and to some extent mentally,"[3] a fact that must have occasioned uneasy feelings in the proud young man. In a well-known episode related in *The Interpretation of Dreams*, the father is revealed as a man who placed survival above heroism: "What did you do when a stranger knocked your hat off and called you dirty Jew?" asked young Freud. "Why," answered his father, "I picked it up from the gutter." This is the language of Joyce's pusillanimous Bloom, not of the Biblical hero Moses.

The Bible to which Freud's father exposed his young son was a product of liberal Jewish scholarship and contained not only footnotes with a rational-scientific intention, but numerous woodcut illustrations drawn, among others, from Christian masters such as Raphael and Domenichino (*Fig. 1*). Moreover, in early infancy (before coming to Vienna at the age of three), Freud underwent a deeply impressive encounter with Christianity, when he was placed in the care of a devout nanny, who brought her charge to church with her and exposed him to the rituals of her faith. Her powerful influence (sustained by anecdotes repeated to him by his mother and others in the family) remained with him throughout his life, and his dreams blend memories of her with those of his own mother. The significance of Rome for Freud can easily be demonstrated: he combined the idea of a Jewish homeland and Rome, the capital of Catholicism, in a dream he had after seeing, probably in 1897, Theodor Herzl's play *Das neue Ghetto* when it was first performed in Vienna; like his boyhood hero, the semitic Hannibal, he yearned to go to Rome as a conqueror; and he called his first visit to Rome in 1901 "a high point of my life."[4] It was on that visit that he found the embodiment of an even greater hero than Hannibal with whom he could identify: the Moses of Michelangelo in S. Pietro in Vincoli. Freud's ambivalence toward his father, his pride in his Jewishness and his wish to be released from its burden, are echoed in conflicting attitudes toward the statue of Moses, expressed in an important essay on the sculpture, to be discussed in Chapter 2.

Freud's complex views of Moses transcend the stimuli offered by the liberal atmosphere of his father's home, and point to the great enrichment gained from his school years in the Viennese *Gymnasium*, which he entered at the age of ten. Like many bright middle-class Jewish children of the period, Freud received a *gelehrte Bildung*, a classical education (his free-thinking Jewish teachers never taught him Hebrew), which terminated in the *Matura*, a degree similar to an academic B.A. In a joyful letter he wrote in 1873 upon completing his *Matura* examinations at seventeen, a year earlier than usual, Freud indicated that he received almost entirely outstanding grades for such work as translating Vergil and *Oedipus Rex* (an unidentified passage he knew well), and for writing an essay on his choice of vocation, of which his professor (using a phrase of Herder's) said, " You have an *idiotic* style," intending the epithet to constitute the highest praise for a style at once correct and original. As part of his *Gymnasium* education,

Freud had read a wide selection of great literature, naturally including Goethe and Shakespeare (whom he read from the age of eight). Evidently, he satisfied his omnivorous curiosity with extracurricular reading on a less elevated plane, including nineteenth-century novels.[5] While in the *Gymnasium* he read and was impressed by Henry Thomas Buckle's Comtian *History of Civilisation in England* (1857), a work characteristic of its period in that it claimed, "the most accurate investigators of the human mind have hitherto been the poets, particularly Homer and Shakespeare,"[6] a view Freud was to repeat years later. All of Freud's readings, classic and modern alike, might have been professionally useful for making rhetorical points had he chosen law for his field, as he had considered doing while in the *Gymnasium*,[7] but they would seem irrelevant to the concrete tasks of the scientist or doctor, aside from private entertainment, or as illustrations of points made in his letters or conversation. Nevertheless, Freud's education was designed not only to produce scholars and writers in the humanities, but in the sciences as well; in fact, it was the education of the best scientists among his models (Helmholtz, Fechner) or among his teachers (E. Brücke, who could write both on the physiology of urine—in collaboration with Helmholtz—and the fine arts). Thus, it was not entirely a rhetorical gesture for Freud to tell the French playwright Henri-René Lenormand in the mid-1920's, "These are my masters,"[8] while pointing to his bookcase containing Shakespeare and the Greek tragedies. It should be remembered that in this epoch, when Renaissance concepts of education continued to flourish, the humanities still seemed the best preparation for the sciences, and Latin a valuable model for the study of logic. But it must be emphasized that while these scientists were interested in the arts and humanities, and cultivated a literate prose all but extinct in twentieth-century scientific writing, they wished their science to be limited to the quantitative standards of physics.

Most of the scientists who influenced Freud's early work were united in opposing romantic *Naturphilosophie*, which sought to interpret meaning in the structure of nature, as in Goethe's scientific writings. S. Bernfeld (1949) has noted that since in Austria *Naturphilosophie* never attained the strong following it had in Germany, where a strong reaction against it occurred, the Brücke Institute of Physiology in

Vienna, which Freud attended, was not dogmatic in its opposition to it. It seems highly indicative that Freud, whose initial interest in science was aroused by the *Fragment on Nature* attributed to Goethe, finally rejected even the Brücke Institute, and attempted to go beyond its narrower empirical restrictions, while still preserving many of the institute's precepts (he tried at first to establish a scientific and quantitative psychology).

Freud straddled two worlds: the empirical, skeptical, and rational world of the scientist was natural to him, and as noted by Brückner (1962), in his readings of literature as an adult, Freud tended to prefer the empirical and pragmatic eighteenth-century English writers (Fielding, Sterne), nineteenth-century realists like Dickens and Thackeray, and ironic skeptics including Multatuli,[9] "the Dutch Voltaire" (as Anatole France called him), Anatole France, and Mark Twain. This aspect of his taste is displayed in his "Contribution to a Questionnaire on Reading" (1907) in which he listed the following "good" books (not great, magnificent, or significant, as those of Sophocles, Shakespeare, Goethe, Copernicus, and Darwin): Multatuli, *Letters and Works*; Kipling, *Jungle Book*; Anatole France, *Sur la pierre blanche*; Zola, *Fécondité*;[10] Merezhkovsky, *Leonardo da Vinci*; Gottfried Keller;[11] C. F. Meyer, *Huttens letzte Tage*; Macaulay, *Essays*; Gomperz, *Griechische Denker*; and Mark Twain, *Sketches*. But Freud reveals another side of his personality through his attraction to the Victorian melodramas of George Eliot, and the suggestive mixture of dream and reality of the Danish novelist Jens Peter Jacobsen. At fourteen, he had already been deeply impressed by the romantic writer Ludwig Börne, and later by Börne's great contemporary Jean Paul. Under the guise of preparing a historical survey for *The Interpretation of Dreams*, Freud indulged this taste by reading immense quantities of dream literature. These links to the unusual or fantastic in his reading barely hint at Freud's preoccupation with the strange and the abnormal, an interest that led him to plunge into the world of neurosis and nightmare and to seek in the dark side of man the key to the lighted, rational mind.

In all this miscellaneous reading, Freud attempted to use each book for his own intellectual needs: sooner or later he would cite from them illustrations of points he wished to make. His library, preserved in London, clearly reveals this. Many works important to him received numerous underlinings,[12] whereas works he was uninterested in[13] were left uncut. Other works he must have used received few or no markings,[14] but often these were second or later editions, perhaps replacements of copies lost even before his flight from Vienna. As one might expect, the works of his favorite writers fill the greater part of his shelves: a cabinet full of Goethe's *Werke* in the Weimar edition of 1890 and later (Freud had been reading Goethe long before 1890), Dostoievsky's works in German in fourteen volumes, and, unexpectedly, Gogol's *Werke* in five volumes. Almost all of the books he cites in his writings on art can be found on his shelves, and many more that relate to his interest in archaeology, for example, Perrot and Chipiez's *Histoire de l'art dans l'antiquité* (1898) and books on Egypt and the Egyptologist Champollion. The importance Freud assigned to his collections of art and books is summed up in a letter to Stefan Zweig of February 7, 1931. In it, Freud criticized Zweig's essay on him[15] for ignoring "that despite the modesty of my personal needs (as was well known), I made great sacrifices for my collection of Greek, Roman and Egyptian antiquities and in fact have read more Archaeology than Psychology, that up to the war and once after, I felt I had to be in Rome at least once a year for days or weeks." On his trip to Paris in 1885, Freud satisfied his interest in art mainly by visiting the Antiquities division of the Louvre.

The archaeological viewpoint was essential to Freud's approach to art. Like his teachers, scientists with humanist education, he sought a pathway leading from his science to art and culture.[16] For him, this bridge was provided in part through the psychology of art, and in part through the science of archaeology, which applied scientific methodology to the study of ancient art. One of his old friends, the archaeologist Emmanuel Loewy, used to visit Freud annually in Vienna, bringing with him news of that archaeological paradise, Rome; and Freud enthusiastically greeted announcements of excavations while acquiring such classics as Schliemann's *Ilias*. But the importance of archaeology extends back much further, to his childhood and the period when he was discovering in Philippson's Bible a whole world of ideas and images, through the book's many illustrations of Egyptian and classical antiquity.

Archaeology, both as a subject and as a metaphor of scientific investigation, held for Freud a special meaning, one that touches upon a characteristic aspect of his mind. Even before the strong impressions of the *Gymnasium* led him to feel the importance of classical culture, certain early experiences may already have stimulated his interest, first, in his own past and then in broader humanistic traditions. The most impressive single event in his life may have been the family's move from his birthplace, Freiburg, in Moravia, to Vienna, when the three-year-old lost the coveted status of being his mother's only child, and also had to separate from his nanny, a figure of immense interest to him who became part of the family mythology. In Vienna began the new life of the metropolis in which his first sibling rival, his sister Anna, was born, followed by others, and leading to the feeling of loss and hunger for affection, which, as he was to note amusingly, took the form of a voracious appetite. It has been suggested that much of Freud's mature intellectual activity constituted an attempt to recover the paradise of his early infancy.[17] This retrospection can only have been intensified through his academic experiences, including not only his classical education, but the publications of Jakob Burckhardt, a cultural historian much admired by Freud, who taught that the Renaissance flourished through emulating antiquity. Since the publication of *The Renaissance in Italy* in 1860 (a book that thrilled Freud, who found in it "prehistoric" parallels to modern behavior), Burckhardt's heroic *Renaissancemensch*, a powerfully influential image, dominated the dreams of young minds filled with the humanities, and was an important source for Nietzsche's superman. Freud himself, perhaps dreaming of the Renaissance *condottiere*, had youthful ambitions to become not an artist or scientist, but a *conquistador*.

Freud's fascination with the cultural past is nowhere so vividly illustrated as in the collection of art objects that he acquired over several decades, and which, along with his library, he brought more or less intact from Vienna when he fled the Nazis. After his death in 1939, Martha maintained the house as when her husband was alive, and his daughter Anna has continued to preserve it unchanged since her mother's death twelve years later, with the assistance of Paula, the Viennese servant who has worked over forty years for the family. The guiding principle by which Freud put his collection together was personal taste rather than any systematic interest in the objects. This becomes clear not only from the almost random heaps of objects, but from the surprising gaps and jumps from period to period and culture to culture; indeed, one soon senses that what many of these works have in common is their apparent great age and the remoteness of their origins. Anna Freud was quite annoyed to learn in our first conversation that I specialize in modern art, and emphasized the virtual absence of objects later than the Renaissance. She told me that her father began collecting Egyptian and Greek pieces, and only later turned to Oriental art, a point confirmed from Freud's early letters, such as one to Fliess of August 6, 1899, in which he remarks, "the last time I was there [Salzburg] I picked up a few old Egyptian things. Those things cheer me and remind me of distant times and countries." According to Miss Freud, much of this collection was acquired from dealers who visited the extremely busy man and displayed their wares to him, mostly pieces that had probably passed through the Paris shops.[18] Although many of the objects bear numbers (apparently catalogue numbers of the dealers or of their former owners) Miss Freud knew of no systematic classification of them. While Freud knew the value and background of most of his pieces, he was not driven by a narrow interest in one area, nor by the expert's compulsion to gather all of the types in his special field. Rather, Freud most enjoyed his collection when he could use his pieces to illustrate points he wished to make to colleagues or patients; moreover, he was in the habit of fondling pieces when he was talking (but not while listening).[19] A former patient of Freud's corroborates this observation:[20] "To elucidate his system of dream symbols, he once led me into his study to show me samples of old sculptural symbols from his little private collection of antique bronze miniatures and figurines." Miss Freud, in our conversation, agreed that the collection was subordinate to Freud's psychoanalytic interests. But we must not underestimate the importance for Freud of collecting as an activity in itself. The famous French psychoanalyst René Laforgue (1954) speculated that "Perhaps these collections [of Freud] were also the embodiment of a part of Freud's own personality, e.g., of his super-ego, as he may have inherited it from the old Orient." Freud himself once compared the artistic creator to a paranoiac in whose illness occurs "the detachment of the libido from the objects (a reverse course is taken by the collector who directs his surplus libido onto the inanimate objective: love of things)."[21] The favorable light in which Freud views the collector, in comparison to the creator, is striking, since he might have balanced accounts by comparing the collector to the anal-retentive character. We thus may surmise that Freud, obsessed by a need to hold on to his own past, applied his literary talents in two directions: as a collector (of memories and objects), and as an interpreter of the objects collected.

In attempting to define Freud's taste, one might assume that the setting of the collection in the house at Maresfield Gardens where he spent the last year of his life would be no less significant than the collection itself. This assumption, however, would not be wholly justified; for the house in London, though pleasing to Freud, was chosen not by himself but by his followers, who presented it to him as a gift after his flight from Vienna. Its beautiful and secluded garden, and its clear-cut division of stories, allowing Freud to install a large office on the ground floor, must have been very attractive to the sick and aging man. But of greater interest and relevance are the contents of the house, the precious collections and furnishings rescued from the Nazis. Judging from Anna Freud's personal photographs of the Vienna apartment, Freud liked to fill up the space about him with many things, and to cover walls and floors completely. Max Eastman, who visited Freud in Vienna in 1926, remembered Berggasse 19 as a "big roomy house, full of books and pictures, the whole mezzanine floor padded with those rugs in which your feet sink like a camel's in the sand."[22] Freud's taste seems always to have been highly conservative, to such an extent that—as his son Martin (1958) notes—he resisted such innovations as the bicycle, the radio, even the telephone, and never used a typewriter or any pen other than a broad-nibbed type.

Freud's taste seems at first almost identical with that of his old mentor Brücke,[23] who had been an instructor in anatomy at the Academy of Art in Berlin, and had written a book on beauty and imperfection in the human form (third edition, 1905). In it, he points out that "everyone, with the exception of some living artists, is agreed that the plastic arts—especially painting—have fallen from their earlier height," which he locates in antiquity and the Renaissance, when an "ideal art," with an emphasis on line, was dominant. He decries " the realism now dominant," since it copies "everything, whether beautiful or ugly," and he reproaches "modern art as compared with that of the ancients" for having lost "the feeling for the beauty of line." (One wonders what the Viennese professor, who died in 1892, would have thought of the sensitive line in Art Nouveau, or the work of Seurat and Gauguin. Probably, he would have been repelled even more than Freud by all this newfangled art, for not reminding him of his classical paragons.) Freud certainly shared Brücke's biases against modern art and his appreciation of classic art, but he departs significantly from his teacher in his love of Egyptian and archaic Greek art. Even Martha's taste (she was born and raised near Hamburg, and remained somewhat alienated from Viennese society) seems to have conformed to the then current fashion of covering the floor and sofas with those sumptuous-looking Persian rugs easily available in Vienna, and the walls with richly colored and textured hangings. The couple's conservative taste in interior decoration unexpectedly skirted Art Nouveau (they appreciated some of Tiffany's products, apparently) but its Viennese counterpart, *Jugendstil*, fashionable in the 1890's, generally passed them by; of course, the austerely simple *Sachlichkeit* of such important Viennese architects as Otto Wagner and his pupil Adolf Loos never affected them. They chose the least startling examples even within the sphere of Oriental art; for, while they could be charmed by the refined decorations of the Chinese, so often suggesting the fantastic arabesques of Austrian Baroque (a Catholic style at once attractive and repulsive to Freud), they could never swallow the bold simplicity of Japanese prints, among the brilliant sources of modern art in the nineteenth century. In two respects, however, Freud's home was unusual: its overflowing collections, which amounted to a small museum of antiquities (not all of them original), and the dominance in those collections of the theme of death and burial.

Freud's collection, as preserved in London, contains an unexpectedly large number of objects, which fall into a few main categories, and are exhibited in cases along the walls of the long rectangular ground-floor room. Except for the bookcases, the interior resembles those old-fashioned provincial museums housing collections of local specimens, both geological and historical (collected for their cultural and historical rather than for their aesthetic value), such as one can see in parts of Austria even today. The large rectangular space is divided equally into a sitting room and a consultation room by a pair of sliding doors. Near the entrance to the sitting room, next to the sliding door, hangs a cast of the *Gradiva* (a gift, according to Anna Freud), about which Freud wrote; on the other side of the door is a cabinet surmounted by a Chinese terra-cotta horseman and two vases (one filled with many small bones), and containing on its three shelves, from top to bottom: Chinese jade; gold foil, scarabs, and rings; objects in bronze and terra-cotta. On the wall above is an engraving (about 24 inches by 20 inches) by H. Ulbrich, dated 1905, of the sphinx at Giza. Next, there is a long bookcase in three sections, topped with a marble relief (about 1 foot by 4 feet) that looks like an ancient sarcophagus lid, but whose eclectic style suggests a forgery, perhaps done as late as the nineteenth century. The family, said Miss Freud, thought it represented the death of Patroclus, but the blend of different subjects is closer to the death of Meleager.[24] This relief is flanked by a Persian horse on one side and a terra-cotta camel (Chinese) on the other. The last cabinet contains many small vases and jars as well as Egyptian figurines, and above it are placed a small sculpture of a camel and an archaic Greek sphinx. At this point stands the patients' couch, above which hangs an engraving of Charcot in his clinic standing beside a hysterical female patient, executed by Pirodon after the painting of Pierre-Albert Brouillet, *La Leçon clinique du Dr. Charcot* of 1887 (*Fig. 2*).[25] This engraving was extremely important to Anna Freud; her father used to lecture the girl on the dangers of emotional repression, illustrating his point by indicating Charcot's hysteric. At the far end of the couch, which is covered by a richly patterned reddish Persian rug not unlike the carpet covering the floor, is a stuffed armchair in which Freud would sit unseen beside his patient's head. Beyond this point, and terminating the wall, is a shallow alcove containing, first, six portfolios with Freud's manuscripts for his writings between 1906 and 1939, and then, a series of nine small statuettes with and without pedestals, carefully arranged by height: six busts (Chinese and Egyptian), a Chinese dog, a black Egyptian scribe, and a standing wooden figure. On the wall just above the row of sculptures, an unsigned engraving (about 24 inches by 30 inches) with a view of the Roman Forum looking toward the Colosseum, done after the excavations began there.[26] On a small octagonal table in the corner is a glass case containing a lovely white

head of a woman, apparently Coptic, lying face up, as though em-
balmed, and resembling its counterpart, a head of a man (irregularly
fractured along the top and left sides) in a glass case on a stand near
the entrance. Both heads are about ten inches long and have glass eyes.

At a little table on the right, and slightly lower than the desk, lies a
section of a richly gilded Egyptian sarcophagus cut below the shoulders;
beside it on the same table, a figure of a seated Chinese, perhaps a
philosopher, his tilted head resting on his right hand. This piece often
led the changing list of Freud's favorites, and was frequently ensconced
in the middle of his desk, where (according to Paula) Freud would bid
it good morning before he started work. The end wall contains two
large glass doors facing the intimate and well-cultivated garden. In the
corner on the wall behind the octagonal table hang several portraits: a
photograph of Freud's famous teacher in Paris, inscribed "à Monsieur
le Dr. Freud bon souvenir de la Salpêtrière. 1885–6. M. Charcot";
below this, a photograph of Freud's Viennese teacher, inscribed
"Ernst Brücke"; and, next to the latter, the largest of the three, a
portrait of Philip Melanchthon (1497–1560), Luther's colleague, celebrated for his learning as "Praeceptor Germaniae." On the narrow
wall just around the corner from this group is an engraving of the
celebrated Helmholtz whom Freud admired. Two Roman portrait
busts (late republican or early imperial), a male and a female, mounted
on narrow pedestals, are placed at either side of the glass doors opening
onto the garden. On the wall in the far corner hangs one of Wilhelm
von Kaulbach's engravings from the *Totentanz* series, showing death
tauntingly displaying a globe labeled "Cosmos" to a well-dressed
bourgeois. It may be noted that Freud liked the Munich artist so well
that, as he put it in a letter to Martha of 1883, he had in his room at
the General Hospital of Vienna, where he was an intern, "pictures by
Kaulbach over the writing table."[27] Perhaps Freud had several of the
Totentanz series in addition to the engraving just mentioned. Freud's
early taste for Kaulbach, far from representing what would have been
an anomalous interest in contemporary advanced painting, stemmed
from a conventional acceptance of this conservative artist, whose work
was placed above Leonardo's in the 1870's by his appreciative public
in Munich and Vienna. A cabinet with many bronze objects (including
Buddha figures) also contains Egyptian papyri set upright against the

back wall, and Roman and Greek statuettes; in the bottom section, there is a collection of bronze harpoons. Beyond a bookcase is a fireplace with a bear rug; on the wall above is a color lithograph (about two feet by three feet) by Ernst Koerner, dated 1906, showing the colossal seated statues of Rameses II at Abu Simbel. Another bookcase extends to the sliding door, and in the corner are several Faijum portraits on the wall. Continuing along this wall into the next room would lead you to Freud's desk and the patient's couch, already described.

Returning to our starting point: if, on coming through the waiting room, one moves left past the *Gradiva*, one passes a six-inch-high terra-cotta female bust, an archaic Greek sculpture intended to be placed against a wall (judging from its flat back), and enters the consultation room. Here, immediately to the left, is a cabinet with black-figured vases, above which hang a pair of framed facsimiles of Pompeian-style fresco fragments, bearing the numbers 837a and 837b. Against the main wall, set between both bookcases, is a cabinet with five shelves on which are set numerous tiny artifacts (mainly Egyptian), including jars, a manned boat, a Cycladic idol, a shelf filled with small wooden tomb figures standing side by side (many of them Ushabti, or statuettes of servants—characteristic of antiquarian collections in the 1880's, according to Professor Brendel), and a pair of Cypriot terra-cotta horses. Above this cabinet, several Egyptian statuettes stand stiffly, too tall for the shelves, and on two shelves behind are smaller brown-skinned Egyptian workers in a variety of postures. Further along this wall, a bookcase holds the massive edition of Goethe's works, and before the shelves are displayed photographs of several women Freud knew and admired: Lou Andreas-Salomé, the author and student of psychoanalysis and friend of Nietzsche and Kafka; Marie Bonaparte, scion of a famous family, author of an important psychoanalytic study of Poe; and Yvette Guilbert, the celebrated singer and actress, whose performances so moved him. Beyond this bookcase is a cabinet with many figurines, including some very fine pieces from Tanagra. At right angles to this wall, on a narrow area next to the doors leading to the back garden, hangs an engraving after Ingres's painting of 1808, *Oedipus and the Sphinx* (Louvre). On a second narrow area adjacent to this and facing the Helmholtz engraving are two Rembrandt etchings, the famous *Jews in the Temple*, and below it, a portrait of a Dutch burgher of 1656; to the right, an engraving by Dürer, *The Kiss of Judas* of 1508;[28] and below these three, a group of four Wilhelm Busch drawings: a donkey looking at an artist painting; a fish spitting at a fly; a rhinoceros staring at a Negro; and a chick breaking out of an egg, beside which the date "1 Jan. 1894" was written. Busch was a childhood favorite of Freud's, and his skeptical humor probably affected certain aspects of the psychoanalyst's views on art and the artist. Freud's pessimism, evolved in a climate that also produced Nietzsche's philosophy, found a comforting and amusing parallel in the superb humor of Busch, whose cartoons were known to every German child of the late 1860's and 1870's.[29] Busch's dissection of a pretentiously pious woman (*Die fromme Helene*) and of an unfulfilled artist (*Der Maler Klecksel*) whose desires swell to abnormal dimensions, amusingly prefigure the sharp observations of the disillusionizing Freud. Dominating this part of the room is, of course, Freud's desk, which stands only several feet from the wall, and on which was placed an array of about twenty (mostly standing) statuettes, facing his chair and with their backs to the row of nine figurines in the niche. When Freud moved to London, Paula placed the statuettes in the same order they had occupied in Vienna. She explained that while dusting them daily, she had become so familiar with them that she had assigned to each a nickname, and she remembered exactly where each "individual" belonged. Freud gave to each a different personality and, according to Anna Freud, compared one of them, with its somewhat regal air, to Queen Victoria. He once remarked of a Coptic Egyptian portrait: "It has a nice Jewish face."[30] Included among these pieces are works of Egyptian, Chinese, Greek, and Roman origin, all excellently preserved, a consideration of great importance to Freud, who was especially attracted to ancient pieces without imperfections. One cannot help associating this group of figurines with the sculptured ancestor-figures of primitive religions. That he seems, in fact, to have felt about them ritualistically is clear from his having once "sacrificed" (as he put it) one of his little statues by "accident."[31]

Collecting such as Freud's was not uncommon among doctors in the Vienna of his time and was avidly pursued even by some *nouveau riche* businessmen interested in exhibiting a veneer of culture. The remarkable thing about Freud's collection is its size and (considering his modest means) its better-than-average quality, both the result of years of gradual and well-advised acquisition. Freud collected mainly from the turn of the century through the 1920's, a period before nationalist efforts at conservation closed the traffic in art exports, so that Greco-Roman and even Egyptian objects (many, admittedly, forgeries) were still turning up on the art market at reasonable prices. The fashion to collect antiquities, even among the less-educated middle classes, appears less extraordinary when we consider that Vienna in the last half of the nineteenth century fostered a rich cultural life whose complexities and nuances favored the production of fresh ideas in diverse intellectual areas.

It would be simplistic to regard Vienna, in the pejorative sense, as the site uniquely fitted to be the birthplace of psychoanalysis, as some of Freud's critics have maintained, adducing its chronically debilitating atmosphere of overstimulation. Still, this aspect of Viennese life provoked even one of its greatest sons, Franz Grillparzer, to call the city a "Capua of minds," and enabled Arthur Koestler to explain caustically "the pessimistic, antihumanistic bias" of psychoanalysis as a product of Freud's "lifelong work on neurotic patients with infantile fixations and regressive tendencies against the background of the decaying civilization of the Austro-Hungarian Empire." [32] In his autobiography (1925), Freud recounts indignantly how Janet attempted to characterize Vienna as a breeding ground for neurotics, hence as a city whose psychic need engendered an appropriate mental therapy. [33] Of course, Paris, like Vienna, has had its notoriety as a pleasure capital and as a breeding ground of eccentrics and neurotics. Paris has, moreover, been the site of splendid advances in psychiatry: the Salpêtrière at the beginning of the nineteenth century provided the setting for Dr. Georget's more humane treatment and improved classification of the mentally ill, and was later the place where Freud's teacher, the great Charcot, carried out his investigations on hysteria through the use of hypnosis; in addition, several psychoanalytic themes such as infantile sexuality and the sexual etiology of neurosis were frequent topics in psychiatric circles of *fin de siècle* Paris. [34] It should not be forgotten that Freud actually felt great tenderness for the city where he had learned and enjoyed so much; in a letter to Wilhelm Fliess of September 21,

1899, written during a dark moment, he bravely cited "the coat of arms of our dear city of Paris: *Fluctuat nec mergitur.*" Thus, it probably was by no unconscious irony that Freud placed at the head of his *History of the Psychoanalytic Movement* (in which he compared Paris and Vienna) this very emblem, intending to apply it to his own controversial movement, which is also "tossed by the waves, but does not sink." We see, then, that except for the presence of Freud (and a few colleagues) the contemporary Viennese "climate" might seem no more suited for the emergence of psychoanalysis than the Parisian; nevertheless, there were special conditions in Vienna at the time that probably made Vienna unique in this respect.

Socially and culturally, the situation in late-nineteenth-century Vienna was complex.[35] Previously, there had been no independent middle class to counter the submissive and parochial attitude both of the rural proletariat that flocked to the city throughout the nineteenth century, and of the numerous anxious public servants who worked in the administrative center of the empire. Toward the end of the century, with increasing social mobility, a self-reliant, materialistic, and skeptical middle class began to form and to challenge the entrenched positions of both church and state, with their aristocratic and feudal values. In these confusing conditions, Vienna became the home of the sensitive but weak-willed *Nervenmenschen* and a city of grandiose illusions. Late-nineteenth-century Vienna thus offered golden chances to subtle observers of the psychology of the middle class; and especially to Jewish intellectuals (as most of the early Viennese psychoanalysts were) who stood slightly away from the mainstream, partly by choice, partly by necessity. The Jewish writer Artur Schnitzler, who had been trained as a physician, found rich material for his novels and plays among the Viennese he saw daily. To these men, who counted themselves among enlightened liberals, the orthodox Jewish culture seemed almost alien in its conservative "old-fashioned" bias. Gottfried Just, in his book on the writer (1968), multiplying the literary parallels and influences upon Schnitzler in order to cancel them out, observes that

... one can ... cite, aside from Freud's emerging theory, the philosophy of Ernst Mach or Vaihinger's theory of fictions, as historical background, and Neo-Kantianism and Helmholtzian materialism as

special spheres of influence, the Young-Vienna movement with its
orientation toward France (Barrès, Paul Bourget) ... Hermann
Bahr (journalist of the *Neue Freie Presse*) ... One can point to the
ideas of Nietzsche or Schopenhauer or Weininger in Schnitzler's
work, can show a relationship to de Maupassant and an affinity to
the Danes (Bang, Jacobsen), or to the quietist tradition of Austrian
poetry from Stifter to Grillparzer ... and to ... Ibsen.

Just calls Schnitzler an "exceptional case," but the writer's international
erudition was not uncommon among Viennese Jewish intellectuals,
whose horizons often extended to the borders of the polyglot Austro-
Hungarian Empire. Thus, we are not surprised to learn that for Freud,
who has been compared to Schnitzler, humanism and scholarship meant
a cosmopolitanism transcending parochial nationalism and narrow-
minded religious orthodoxy (like his father, he supported enthusiastically Bismarck's *Kulturkampf* against the Roman Catholic Curia). The
problem of identity felt by the "adolescent" middle classes of Vienna
must have seemed familiar to Jews struggling with questions of assimilation, patriotism, and anti-Semitism. In such a melting pot, Freud and
his colleagues could find the ingredients for a lifetime's work.

The interplay of psychology, culture, and politics in Vienna at this
time has been well described by Carl E. Schorske.[36] He shows that in
the first half of the nineteenth century the haute bourgeoisie produced
throughout Europe a uniform moral and scientific culture that was
secure and righteous. These men were committed to the rule of mind
over body, to Voltairian skepticism, and to the Enlightenment ideal of
social progress through science, education, and hard work. After the
mid-century, an amoral culture based on sentiment (*Gefühlskultur*)
dominated the educated bourgeoisie. In Austria, unlike England and
France, this class failed to fuse with the aristocracy, and instead remained, like the Jews, outsiders seeking assimilation. The legalistic,
puritanical culture shared by the bourgeois and Jew was utterly different from the culture of the aristocracy, which remained "profoundly
Catholic ... sensuous and plastic." Apparently as part of their effort to
achieve assimilation through emulating the aristocracy, many bourgeois during the first half of the century (and middle-class Jews a little
later) had become patrons of the arts, and had made actors, artists, and

critics their culture heroes; but by the end of the century, with liberalism defeated and anti-Semitism resurgent, the goal of assimilation seemed ever more remote. Despite their relative success in certain professions and the tolerant atmosphere of the Habsburg monarchy, which admitted Jews to significant posts, the age-old fear of oppression had never been wholly extinguished among Austrian Jews.[37] While in the 1860's and 1870's Freud, like other Jewish boys, could still dream of entering the government ministry, by the 1880's the pan-Germanic movement in Austria and the utterances of the fanatic Karl Lueger, urging Christians to combat "liberal Jewish materialism," led to serious confrontations and increasing difficulties.

It is understandable that for Jews as well as for non-Jewish members of the bourgeoisie, art became "a refuge from the unpleasant world of increasingly threatening political reality."[38] As a substitute for the life of action, art became almost a religion; moreover, as the bourgeois sensed the slipping away of the world, he became increasingly preoccupied with his own psychic life. In Schorske's words, "The disaster of liberalism's collapse further transmuted the aesthetic heritage into a culture of sensitive nerves, uneasy hedonism, and often outright anxiety." Given their political impotence, the Viennese Jews could respond to economic and social pressures either with the escapism of art patronage or collection (hardly feasible for the poor), or with the age-old ghetto response of humor—now ironic, now touched with sadness. It was this quality that enabled Jakob Freud to compensate somewhat in his son's eyes for the cowardice and weakness his son had perceived. Freud never forgot this aspect of his father's personality, and throughout his life retained an interest in Jewish jokes.[39] Thus, his father's death in 1896 probably triggered the renewal of a strong interest in jokes; for he began to collect Jewish jokes intensively after this date. Freud was fond of relating Jewish jokes and anecdotes, but as with his collection of art he used them to illustrate a point, and "never for their own end or for mere amusement," as Theodor Reik observed.[40] As a Jew, Freud had even more important things to derive from jokes. In conversation with Reik, he agreed that "the self-irony and sometimes even self-degrading character of Jewish humor was made psychologically possible under the premise of . . . a concealed national pride."[41]

The cultural life of the Vienna Freud grew up in was characterized by the same tensions of growth and change seen in its economy and politics. Of great importance for all Viennese from 1870 to the end of the century was the *Burgtheater*, in which *Oedipus*, *Hamlet*, and *Faust* were performed for large audiences representing a cross-section of Viennese society. As opposed to the *Volksoper*, which staged the frivolous comedies of men like Lehar and Offenbach, the *Burgtheater* always produced tragedies by the great writers. The break with naturalism of the Berlin *Residenztheater* in 1887 directly affected its Viennese counterpart, and heralded a new era "officially" expounded in Bahr's famous book *Die Überwindung des Naturalismus* of 1891. In retrospect, Bahr recalled how Max Burckhardt helped to overcome the wave of Berlin *Naturalismus* in Vienna by bringing Ibsen to the *Burgtheater*, which he directed from 1890 to 1898. But, as he further noted, the more serious German naturalist approach was bound to succumb in the light-hearted and frivolous atmosphere of Vienna. The opposition to naturalism does not seem to have extended to the French naturalists led by Zola, who aspired to produce a scientifically precise description of society, and whose writings influenced many Viennese, especially the writers of magazine series. The vivid but sordid pictures of big-city life, the strong antireligious sentiment, the appeal to intense emotions as solutions to life's problems, and the absence of strong, self-willed heroes (*Heldenlosigkeit*) were dominant characteristics of the naturalists.

Many Symbolists, rejecting what they considered a mere record of obvious and unpleasant facts, turned inward, to listen to "what the wishes of dreams strangely report." [42] Bahr has well characterized these "Romantics of the nerve" [43] with an example reminiscent of moralizing fairytales like Wilde's *The Happy Prince*:

A father's child dies. Let his savage pain, his utter bewilderment be the theme . . . The realistic writer will simply say: "It was a cold morning, frosty and foggy. The parson was frozen. We went behind the little sarcophagus, the sobbing mother and I."—briefly, a precise and clear report of all external things. But the symbolic writer will tell of a little fir tree, of how it grew straight and proud in the woods, and the great trees rejoiced, because never had one stretched its top toward heaven more boldly: "Then came a lean, wild man who had

a cold ax and cut down the little fir tree, because it was Christmas"
—he will tell of quite different and remote things, but things capable
of awakening the same feeling, the very same mood, the identical
state of mind that the death of the child awoke in its father . . . Such
is the method of the Symbolists, who produce an art which is inaccessible to the broad public, for whom it must remain enigmatic.

Not all of the antinaturalists saw the world through the rose-tinted
glasses of Bahr's hypothetical Symbolist. Some of these "Romantics of
the nerve," given to subtle psychological analysis, in a sense continued
one side of naturalism—its interest in the underside of life—by transforming the frank scrutiny of the ugly and brutal into an investigation
of the unusual and perverse in human psychology. Freud, who pursued
his medical studies during the 1870's and 1880's, was exposed to both
tendencies, but obviously inclined toward the naturalists. He especially
admired Zola, who aimed to produce a new form of writing based on
the scientific models he found in the writings of the biologist Claude
Bernard. However, Freud was familiar with the work of Schnitzler,
Hofmannsthal, Thomas Mann, and Rilke, and certainly must have
followed the shifts in style and content of the plays performed at the
Vienna *Burgtheater* as its emphasis changed from naturalism to Symbolism. His visit to Paris from October, 1885, to March, 1886, to work
at the Salpêtrière would have offered Freud opportunities to savor the
new trends in the theater, literature, and art just at the time he was
turning from the strict biological research for which he had been trained
to the field, then so excitingly cultivated in Paris, of psychiatric research,
especially Charcot's and Bernheim's investigations into hysteria by
means of hypnosis. In German-speaking countries, artists and writers
such as Oskar Kokoschka (*Die träumenden Knaben*, 1908) and Alfred
Kubin (*Die andere Seite*, 1908) produced works involved with dreams;
and earlier, the psychology of the dream and the unconscious were
discussed in books by men such as Theodor Lipps, a writer whom
Freud was to cite frequently. Perhaps Lipps's ideas influenced Freud
as early as the mid-1880's; Freud's copy of Lipps's *Grundtatsachen des
Seelenlebens* (Bonn, 1883), which unfortunately lacks an inscribed date
or signature, has numerous pencil marks. A sentence beside which he
drew a double line seems especially important: "unconscious processes

underlie and accompany all conscious ones." The impact of these and other innovations in psychology seems to have given rise to a literary fad, which in some respects adumbrates psychoanalysis. Thus, by 1890, the widely read Viennese Hermann Bahr was able to report ironically on "Die neue Psychologie" (1891), then being discussed in Paris, and in vogue among many young writers. The critic considered the trend an extension of naturalism, which has brought "a method . . . with a modern way of thinking, which is deterministic, dialectical," in the sense that feelings constantly come to life and die, turning into their opposites, and "decompositive" in that feelings can be rejected from consciousness and returned to their "primitive appearance prior to consciousness." It is worth noting that although Freud alluded to the "so-called psychological novels" of the period in the essay "Creative Writers and Day-Dreaming" (1908), he did not think very much of them, nor did he acknowledge any indebtedness to them; but one cannot help wondering whether Freud had absorbed more than he knew.

Freud seems steadfastly to have ignored the exciting and controversial developments in art and literature then occurring in Paris, as the naturalism of Zola yielded to the Symbolism of Moréas, and as Impressionism was transformed in the art of Seurat, Pissarro, and Cézanne. Admittedly, he left Paris before he had a chance to see the last great Impressionist exhibition in May, 1886, but he nowhere refers in his letters from Paris to the much talked about and rather accessible works of these artists, nor about the burgeoning Symbolist movement. If he had any opinion about the Impressionists, it would surely have been less sympathetic than the one expressed by Georg Brandes (an admired literary historian whose ideas about Shakespeare he followed) after first viewing their works in Berlin in 1882: "pure Impressionism . . . is too close to dilettantism. Its main principle throws open the gateway to preciousness and slovenliness; one must fear that the works of its masters will drown in the flood of its amateurs." But Freud had plenty to interest him in Paris apart from the new art: he was deeply impressed by Sarah Bernhardt, attended performances of the classic plays of Molière, and was awed by the towers of Notre Dame.[44] As he customarily did when travelling, Freud looked up Egyptian and other antiquities, and thus spent much time in these sections of the Louvre.

The fixed boundaries of Freud's taste suggested in his letters, and in the contents of his collection—which contains no primitive, child, or psychotic art, nor any landscape—suggests the very personal significance of art for him: apart from his beloved antiquities, one finds only a few scattered works from later periods. Freud, who respected Böcklin's art, was surely on the side of that large German public that Julius Meier-Graefe[45] castigates for preferring Böcklin's "modernity" to that of great nineteenth-century French artists like Monet and Cézanne. (That a new dimension of Böcklin's painting was to be discovered by de Chirico and the Surrealists may signify more than a historical coincidence.) Thus he was utterly indifferent to the furors concerning the powerful movements of Fauvism and Cubism, or of German Expressionism, and he followed his disciple Oskar Pfister, who in his book on modern art, *Expressionismus in der Kunst* (1923), lumped together all these diverse movements under the term Expressionism. Probably his caustic remarks about a portrait representing Karl Abraham, written to his disciple on December 26, 1922, best epitomizes his unfriendliness toward modern art:

> Knowing what an excellent person you are, I was all the more shocked that such a trivial weakness of character as your tolerance or sympathy for modern "art" should be so horribly punished [as in the portrait]. I hear . . . that the artist explained that he sees you this way! That sort of person should be the last ones to have access to analytic circles, for they are quite unwished-for illustrations of Adler's statement that precisely those with congenital defects in their eyesight become painters and draughtsmen.

His dislike for contemporary art is matched by his indifference to contemporary architecture (for example, in his published correspondence he nowhere refers to the newly erected Eiffel Tower, the talk of all of Paris during 1889, in his second visit to the city). Freud's turn to the past seems very like Burckhardt's historicism; but although he steeped himself in the great historian's *Cicerone, The Civilization of the Renaissance in Italy*, and *The History of Greek Culture* (seeking in the latter "links to the prehistoric past"), and shared Burckhardt's pessimism toward the modern age, he did not, as Burckhardt did, blame science for the feebleness of modern culture. Drawing upon his own scientific training, he attempted to explore the great cultures of the past with psychoanalytic methods he believed scientifically valid. (Freud's aversion to the products of modern technology such as the telephone and airplane had no effect on his constant faith in the science of his youth.)

Freud's primary interest in art, apart from his collecting, was for its themes related to the dream, the unconscious, sex, and neurosis. While the main discussion of these aspects of Freud's approach to art will be the topic of the next chapter, here it will be germane to describe some of the main themes implied by the works in his collection, and to in- quire briefly whether these may not reveal a kinship, in spite of Freud's apparent indifference to the contemporary, to prevailing themes of the late nineteenth century in Europe.

None of the works in Freud's collection obviously illustrate any of the above themes, unless the engraving of Charcot's hysteric can be interpreted as an instance of a neurotic with a malady whose sexual origin lies hidden within the unconscious. However, even were we to grant this interpretation, we could not so easily match the remainder of the collection to these themes. Yet connections do exist in Freud's mind, which, while not immediately obvious, pervade the objects and images Freud chose to live with. To understand these connections more fully, we must first learn how those themes work in Freud's own mind, as we will do in the next chapter. Here it will be sufficient to note that many, perhaps all, of the objects in Freud's collection are associ- ated with ideas and desires rooted among his earliest experiences. Like his passion for archaeology, his enthusiasm for collecting antiqui- ties originated in events that occurred during his second and third years, but which influenced him through dreams and memories for the rest of his life.

Beneath the quietly academic surface of Freud's house, with its books and antiquities, one detects the professor and perhaps the doctor, but it is not easy to discern the psychoanalyst who explored the daring themes of sex or the unconscious. However, the topic of dreaming or sleeping was certainly illustrated; for an engraving, probably of Fuseli's well-known *Nightmare* (*Fig. 3*), once hung in the entrance to Freud's office at Berggasse 19 in Vienna.[46] It shows a sleeping woman twisting on her bed as though to escape the demonic incubus squatting on her chest and leering down at her. Painted in 1783, in the midst of the limpid planarity and unambiguous arrangements of the neoclassical period, the work (despite its strong neoclassical elements, especially in the woman), sounds a harsh and dissonant note out of tune with the dominant style. Although nowadays critics may not be quite convinced by Fuseli's ogre, and may regard as histrionic, the intrusion of a romantic emotionalism into a neoclassical context, Freud might well have found these qualities nicely suited to his own views on art; in fact, with its murky background, from which a pop-eyed horse bursts upon the spotlighted figure coquettishly sprawled in the foreground of the boudoir, even as a print the work may have spurred the psycho-analyst's imagination to some bold surmises,[47] especially if considered in the light of erotic caricatures (*Fig. 4*) of the theme known to Freud. A picture of the disturbed dreaming of a nightmare might have seemed odd in any nineteenth-century physician's office, except one like Freud's in which a couch was the chief apparatus, and the free associa-tion of a reclining patient the main therapeutic procedure. However, he also displayed the conventional *Anatomy Lesson* by Rembrandt;[48] and another engraving hung in Berggasse 19 sustains the theme of the healer more prominently exhibited in the engraving of Charcot's clinic, already mentioned: the fresco by Masolino and Masaccio in the Brancacci Chapel in Santa Maria del Carmine, Florence, executed between 1424 and 1428, showing *The Healing of Aeneas* on the left and *The Raising of Tabitha* on the right (*Fig. 5*). Both scenes come from the same passage in the New Testament (Acts IX) describing the works of St. Peter. A certain man in Lydda named Aeneas was palsied. "And Peter said unto him, Aeneas, Jesus Christ healeth thee . . . And straight-way he arose." The group at the right shows the disciple at Joppa named Tabitha, a woman full of good works, who fell ill and died. Peter is called, and when he came he saw all the widows weeping, and showing the coats and garments Tabitha had made; whereupon, he "kneeled down and prayed; and turning to the body, he said, Tabitha, arise. And she opened her eyes; and when she saw Peter, she sat up." Freud could have used the illustration of these episodes to explain his concept of neurosis and its therapy; for he considered both palsy and cataleptic sleep to be hysterical symptoms whose treatment usually did not so much demand medicines or instruments, as the dialogue of patient and psychoanalyst. In a curious way, the role of Saint Peter can be compared to Charcot's, with his hysterical patient shown in the engraving, a comparison that gains relevance from one of the psychiatrist's last works[49] in which he concludes that hysterics are among the best subjects for treatment by faith healing.

Although the subject of sleep rarely appears among the works exhibited, it can be found implicitly in many places: in the supine figure depicted on the mummy case and in the immobile seated figures of the pharaoh in the engraving of Abu Simbel; in the reveried world of the Egyptian laborers or sailors in their ships of death; and, even in the plaster cast from a reduced copy of Michelangelo's *Slave* (*Fig.* 6).[50] Placing the Renaissance genius' sculpture in the same context as the somnolent Egyptian is not so incongruous for this period as might be assumed. At almost the same moment in France, the late romantic Gustave Moreau found in Michelangelo's allegorical figures an example of his principle of inertia: "All of these figures," he told Ary Renan,[51] "seem to be fixed in a gesture of ideal somnambulism; they are unconscious of the movement they execute, absorbed in revery to the point of seeming to be transported to other worlds." Of course, what Moreau appreciated in Michelangelo was not wholly there: the Renaissance master had conceived his figures as spirits trapped in matter, within the framework of Christian Neoplatonism, although they could also be interpreted not as characters in a religious drama, but in terms of pure dreaming. The same kind of secular reinterpretation occurs throughout the thinking of Freud, who analyzed the great works of old masters not as icons, but as manifestations of human psychology.

Perhaps more significant than any of the themes so far discussed is that of death. This subject, partly hidden, partly obtrusively visible, pervades almost the entire collection, and has intimate links with the theme of sleep. One can easily list the more obvious instances: all of the Egyptian works, the little marble name plaques from a Roman sarcophagus, the Greek and Etruscan burial urns, especially one containing ancient bones, the Kaulbach engraving from the *Totentanz* series, and an engraving after what the poet Hilda Doolittle[52] called "some nightmare horror, a 'Buried Alive' or some such thing"—probably the well-known *Burial Alive* of Antoine Wiertz, painted in 1854. The latter painting is half-filled with a coffin whose heavy lid has been slightly raised by a man within who pushes up with one hand, and gropes sideways toward his liberation with the other. This subject, so fascinating to romantics like Jean Paul and Victor Hugo, also haunted Freud, who wrote to Martha in a letter quoted by Jones[53] about his destruction of diaries and quantities of his early writings, explaining his fear of accumulating such material with the image of drowning in sand like the Sphinx, with only the nostrils showing above the mass of paper. (The fact that Freud was also a collector of art objects he firmly held on to is a paradox which may point to the most significant, but also obscure, aspects of his personality; can his collecting have compensated for self-inflicted losses and reminded him that his little gestures of destruction were not, after all, catastrophic?)

For Freud, the dead were by no means static figures in repose, but rather were filled with an energy sometimes sexual, sometimes anxious. This connection of death and sex helps us to understand his strong emphasis on buried objects of antiquity, which he insisted should be preserved as perfectly as possible. Perhaps also the connection can elucidate the implicit sexuality of those twisting, struggling figures of Michelangelo and of Fuseli, which seem situated midway between the ecstasy of sexual release and guilty restraint, between sensual immediacy and the moral phantoms of memory. Even the calmer ancient pieces probably seemed to him more vital, even sexual, than one might at first assume, and in regard to the latter, we will find his essay on Wilhelm Jensen's story *Gradiva* particularly revealing. Freud's feeling that the "dead live" in his collection is nowhere more clearly expressed than in his underlinings in a copy of Burckhardt's *Cicerone*: "What the eye perceives in this and in other Greek edifices, are *not mere stones, but living beings*"[54] (Freud's underlining in green pencil). Interestingly, Freud not only believed that the past can seem as alive as the present, but sometimes the converse, that the most exciting of contemporary things ought to be compared to the vital past. Thus, on a visit to Brussels, he admired "a building so massive and with such magnificent columns as one imagines an Assyrian Royal Palace to have had, or as one finds in the Doré illustrations."[55] A poignant expression of the great atheist's sentiment for the preservation of the dead in art is embodied in the Grecian urn in Golders Green Crematorium, containing Sigmund and Martha Freud's ashes. Freud once told Marie Bonaparte, who had given him the vase, that "it is a pity one cannot take it into one's grave." [56]

Freud's taste for Egyptian and Greek sculpture, and his sense of their "vitality," resemble the attitudes of certain artists among his contemporaries who turned to ancient art in rejecting realism or Impressionism in painting. Evidently to Freud, as to the Post-Impressionist artist, a painting had to offer more than a bright and pleasing "feast to the eye"; consequently, both sought for the symbol latent within the immediately visible. Rejecting the fleeting moment of the Impressionist sketch, Neo-Impressionists like Seurat looked to the "primitive" styles of Egyptian, Greek, and early Renaissance art, with their greater sense of permanence and stability; and a similar mood already characterizes the formulations of Konrad Fiedler [57] and of his follower, the artist Adolf von Hildebrand, [58] who preferred the unity and planarity of classical and Renaissance art to the fragmented spatial illusionism of nineteenth-century realist art. To the mystical artists who called themselves the Nabis (Prophets), Egyptian art seemed to possess just the qualities demanded by an ideal modern religious art: monumentality, mystery, gravity, and repose.

For some ironical thinkers of Freud's generation, the mystery of the symbol, which once pointed skyward to God, now pointed to the bedroom. Nietzsche, who castigated the Germans for their psychological "uncleanliness," stated in *Ecce Homo* that "what is called 'deep' in Germany is precisely this instinctive uncleanliness in relation to oneself of which I am speaking: one does not want clarity about oneself." (These seem prophetic words anticipating the psychoanalytic "confessional" therapy for repressed "filth," which indeed might be compared to a "mental bath.") Many European artists and thinkers in the 1880's believed that symbols could provide clues to the hidden aspects of man and his culture, especially when those symbols could be linked to the "classics" from the Greeks to Shakespeare. [59] The classics were no longer regarded as remotely Olympian. On the one hand, they formed the models of the modern bourgeois tragedy (the *bürgerlisches Trauerspiel*), in which for the first time so generally middle-class characters have tragic emotions, as in Arno Holz's *Papa Hamlet* (1889); and on the other hand, the Goethian idea of a healthy, simple classicism is reversed in von Hofmannsthal's *Elektra* (1903), a one-act drama of "feminine hysteria," whose heroine has been called a "female Hamlet." The movement of Symbolism forms a curious and interesting backdrop to the emergence of Freud's dream theories, with their emphasis on the symbol in memory; and a host of tempting but unreachable *femmes fatales*, including Salomé and Mona Lisa (see Spector, 1968), and the alienated artist hiding behind a comic mask, joined with the hysteric and neurotic as attractive subjects of study. The themes of the Sphinx (von Hofmannsthal's *Oedipus and the Sphinx*, 1906) and of the indecisive Hamlet (Paul Bourget's novel *André Cornelis* of 1887 concerns a new Hamlet who kills the slayer of his father) irresistibly attracted a generation that included Ibsen and Mallarmé among the writers, and Redon, Moreau, Munch, and Ensor among the painters. "The parabola of the sexes during the nineteenth century," noted by Mario Praz,[60] in which the "male, who at first tends towards sadism, inclines at the end of the century towards masochism," is well illustrated in the literature and art of the period, in which the woman appears as powerful and domineering—Freud would say castrating—whereas the man appears increasingly nervous and sensitive. The androgynous figure dominates decadent literature and art during these decades, when the sexually neutral charm of Leonardo's figures becomes no less fascinating than the great man himself, and when faded and sensually exhausted characters like Huysmans's Des Esseintes make their debuts, along with the illustrations of Beardsley for Wilde's *Salomé*. In Paris, Moréas, leader of the Symbolist movement, issued a manifesto in 1886, declaring the death of naturalism and the birth of the Symbolic-Impressionist novel, which will "only seek in the *objective* a simple . . . starting point" for its "work of *subjective deformation*"; and somewhat later, the pompous mystic Sar Peladan proclaimed Symbolism to be hieratic, religious, and mysterious.[61] The leading Symbolists, whose writings would soon be called sentimental distortions by Jules Romains, considered their art and writings (as Coleridge and the romantics had already) to be guides to the truth, and Gauguin told the Symbolist poet Charles Morice in 1890 that "truth is to be found in a purely cerebral art, in a primitive art . . .—in Egypt,"[62] while the same poet considered literature to be optimally "the dress of the true." As late as 1904, the important but neglected Symbolist Tancrède de Visan (*Paysages introspectifs*) suggested that the Symbolists were in search of truth, seeing oceans of mystery behind sensory perception.

While such writers were pouring truth into their poetic dreams—a group of Symbolists even founded a review, *Le Rêve et l'Idée*, which was to link the dream to truth [63]—another generation searched for clarity (Proust, Valéry); and Freud, who also emerged in a generation whose literature was dominated by Symbolism, at the very outset of his career, had sought to analyze a story by C. F. Meyer, the Swiss who has been called "the great German forerunner of European Symbolism." [64] Like the Symbolists, Freud would take nothing at face value; however, in his depth psychology he would aim not to cultivate occult mysteries, but to bring to light the elemental and biological essence of truth secreted in dream, poetry, and art. The positivist Freud's snooping out mysteries like a Sherlock Holmes, and his attempt to label and classify mental states, was precisely the sort of activity the late Symbolists like Royère detested as suppressing the enjoyment of the poem and vulgarizing its meaning. Moreover, Freud's minimizing of formal values and his association of dynamic vitality to the ancient and Renaissance art he collected, resulted in a very personal appreciation of older art, as distinct from that of contemporary artists. Although the most advanced artists among the Post-Impressionists also appreciated Egyptian and some classical art, their taste had matured—as Freud's had not—from an avant-garde assimilation of Impressionism followed by a reaction toward older art. But this convergence of Freud's taste with the Post-Impressionists can help elucidate the profound bearing of Freud's ideas on the later art he apparently rejected.

Two

Freud and the Artist

Freud was continually drawn to the subject of the artist and his work, about which he wrote intermittently throughout his career, sometimes with exquisite sensitivity and penetration. Close examination of these scattered remarks, however, suggests provocative unanswered questions, even paradoxes, about Freud's relation to both art and the artist: he expressed contrary opinions about artists, at one time admiring them and advising a hands-off policy toward their unfathomable gifts, while at another, disdaining their infantilism and calling their achievement a form of sublimated sexuality; and he "psychoanalyzed" a dead genius, but no living artist. Freud's insecurity about the artist may have extended far back to his youth, and seems to be tied to the mixed emotions of admiration and envy, judging from his responses first to Max Meyer, a musician cousin of Martha's, and then to Fritz Wahle, an artist friend of Martha's, both of whom he considered rivals for her affection. Ernest Jones[1] recounts Freud's views about the abilities of artists (particularly Fritz) to please ladies, and quotes Freud's remark: "I think there is a general enmity between artists and those engaged in the details of scientific work. We know that they possess in their art a master key to open with ease all female hearts." Jones describes the intriguing evolution of Freud's passionate suit of Martha and his rivalry with Fritz, who he insisted to Martha was unconsciously in love with her. In a letter to her summing up his feelings about artists, Freud comments on the contradictory feelings we all may experience at a given moment, but particularly artists, "people who have no occasion to submit their inner life to the strict control of reason."

These problems and biases tantalize anyone seeking clues for a deeper understanding of Freud's ideas. In the following pages, an attempt will be made to analyze Freud's thought and personality in relation to his views on art. But, to analyze the greatest of psychoanalysts is obviously a delicate and risky enterprise: orthodox Freudians are not alone in questioning what there is to see that he did not perceive more clearly and deeply about himself. Still, it ought to be possible for an observer outside Freud's own frame of reference to see things he may have overlooked about himself, a possibility implied by his own psychological theories; for Freud was self-analyzed, a pioneering achievement which nevertheless hampered his ability to gain perspective on himself.

It has often been noted that Freud, in his efforts to arrive at universal principles to explain human motivation and feeling, went beyond the scope of a scientifically valid and testable psychology and arrived at a philosophic or speculative system. While this is sometimes meant as an unfriendly criticism of Freud's incompetence as a scientist (Jung, John Dewey), other writers intend it more neutrally to describe Freud's abilities in both areas (Havelock Ellis, at first), or even as high praise of a genius comparable to Goethe's (Wittels, Mann). Certainly, Freud's fecund genius produced a series of beautiful and fascinating metaphors and images, which in sum could be regarded as a mythology of the unconscious, night side of the mind. But we must not forget that Freud the clinician, with the rational and empirical alertness of the scientifically trained mind, usually avoided the fantastic excesses of men like Wilhelm Stekel or of some of his own followers.

While Freud avoids wholesale surrender to self-centered fantasies, he did approach many questions with an intuitive certitude and an unshakable conviction of rightness that brooked no opposition, and that avoided correction. Thus, in his preface to the third English edition of *The Interpretation of Dreams*, he noted that thirty-one years after its appearance, and despite numerous changes in psychology, the book "remains essentially unaltered" (a praise repeated by his disciple Jones). This highly subjective attitude is especially prominent in the aesthetic field; thus, with regard to his studies of art and artists, it will be shown presently that Freud's choices of subjects had less to do with central aesthetic questions than with his own personal needs and obsessions, and that in some instances when critics proved him incorrect, he not only failed to correct his errors, but he refused to modify his theses, or even to mention his critics' views. The underlinings in his books prove that in at least one instance Freud knowingly selected facts supporting his theory, while rejecting (without discussion) others that did not fit; similarly, he obstinately adhered to Lamarck's position against the best biological opinion of his time, simply because it suited his own needs.

The point is that Freud's truth, rather like Nietzsche's or Bergson's, includes a dimension that is not quite testable or subject to the same criteria as more limited scientific hypotheses, which can be rejected or subsumed into new syntheses after crucial experiments are performed; instead, one seeks richness of imagery as well as insight, dramatic interest, and above all, consistency, as in literary or some philosophic productions. If there is one thread that connects the complicated turns and changes of Freud's theories, it is his continuous preoccupation with himself; briefly, Freud is the hero of his own work. He makes himself into the central character of the Oedipus myth and the tale of Hamlet, he identifies with the problems of Leonardo and the genius of Goethe, and he responds with a romantic intensity to Michelangelo's *Moses*. But, just as he allows us to perceive the reality of his patients beyond his theoretical superstructure, so he grants to the series of great men and characters with whom he identifies enough of their intrinsic qualities to convince us of his objective perception. Thus, Freud is a complex hero, behind the scenes, emerging only at certain critical points of contact between himself and his subject. In all of Freud's writings, there are interspersed passages that bear on his personal life; but they are distributed in a way that lacks obvious coherence and connection, and sometimes were published without his revealing that he was writing about himself.[2] One requires the whole of Freud's work, one is impelled to seek in ever wider circles of his production for the man behind the writings. Still, one book above all others may provide us with a most intimate view of this great mind—the record of Freud's self-analysis contained in *The Interpretation of Dreams*, of which he said in a letter to Fliess of May 28, 1899: "None of my works has been so completely my own as this; it is my own dung-heap, my own seedling, and a *nova species mihi*."

The Interpretation of Dreams remains Freud's most imposing and celebrated work, regarded by its author and the public alike as the foundation of his abiding reputation. Despite the rather jejune view of the editors of the Standard Edition,[3] who call it "a scientific classic with little amusement to be had from it," it has been constantly sold to an audience composed less of scientists than of interested and curious laymen. Its fascination for the public must surely have less to do with questions of scientific validity than with Freud's personality as seen through his literary expression. We can glimpse some of this in the enchanting, even compelling, titles he gave to some of the over fifty dreams discussed: Irma's Injection; "*Autodidasker*"; Bird-beaked Figures; Botanical Monograph; Castle by the Sea; The Forgotten Church-tower; Cliff in the Style of Böcklin; "Close the Eyes"; The Outhouse; A Revolutionary Dream about Count Thun; Dissecting My Own Pelvis; Etruscan Cinerary Urn; Father on His Deathbed like Garibaldi; Goethe's Attack on Herr M.; Keeping a Woman Waiting; "My Son, the Myops"; The One-eyed Doctor and the Schoolmaster; The Pope is Dead; Riding on a Horse with a Boil on His Buttocks; The Three Fates.

Freud's sensitivity to form is recognizable in his attitude toward his writing, as expressed in a letter of September 21, 1899, criticizing his work on *The Interpretation of Dreams* as lacking form, and so implying "an incomplete mastery of the material"; and stylistic criticism is carried even further with a reference to Boileau at the end of chapter 5 of *The Psychopathology of Everyday Life*. In its self-analysis, together with its searching insights into the human mind in general, the work has the appeal of a domestic drama that rises to the level of great poetry or philosophy. Throughout the book, in numerous guises, Freud's presence is felt (we sense his burdens of responsibility, as scientist and man); we confront a powerful and cultivated mind in its domestic, even in its bathroom intimacy; and we follow him through obscure intellectual adventures, until we stand beside him, sharing the exhilaration of his insight. In this respect, he towers above other contemporaries such as Havelock Ellis, who similarly approached the problems of sex and the dream through the case study, but who treated them more abstractly and with less of Freud's gift for the dramatic and for suggesting untouched depths. Stanley Edgar Hyman sensed the artistic quality of Freud's masterpiece when he praised the book for being held together by the "great organizing metaphor" of Freud's passage from scene to scene as though in a Dantesque search for illumination and the right direction.

While some analysts insist that Freud's self-presentation is not complete since, despite his apparent frankness about himself, he hides his warmth and love from us, still we glimpse parts of his personality vividly. Moreover, his concealment of some aspects of himself, while unhesitatingly exposing others, lures us to search deeper and to discover, as we study him, truths pointing to his essential integrity (like the unfolding of Joyce's meaning through the lifetime's study he demanded of his readers). The references to literature and art that stud the work manifest a culture at once humane and animated, counterbalancing and in contrast to the intimate but rather mundane data of daily life offered by the dreams and case studies. Indeed, it is this culture and the high moral tone of his prose when treating banal or offensive matter, that sets his work off from both the scientific treatise and vulgarly attractive exhibitionism. His vigorous prose, with its "idiotic style" (as his *gymnasium* professor called it), transcends the prudish inhibitions which led aristocratic Victorians to the curious split between public moralizing and private pornography.

In considering *The Interpretation of Dreams* as autobiography, we must keep in mind that many apparently personal revelations were meant primarily to illustrate theories, and are imbedded in the context of their exposition. Freud intended to give us no more than the indispensable data necessary for his explanation, and stops short of revealing embarrassing details about himself or his intimates. In fact, there occur not infrequently obscurities that Freud acknowledges himself unable or unwilling to fathom. In 1935, he wrote, "in self-analysis the danger of incompleteness is particularly great."[4] Usually, he frankly admits his difficulties, but sometimes (showing a common enough human failing) he purposely but without acknowledgment concealed embarrassing information, such as the disguised autobiographical material attributed to a former patient in the "Screen Memories" of 1899; in fact, it is a challenging enterprise to piece together a coherent picture of Freud from the fragmentary and unconnected probings of himself that the book offers. Still compared to the prosaic and polemical *Autobiography* (1925) and the apparently clear but impersonal tone of his periodic summaries and expositions of his theories, *The Interpretation of Dreams* offers a richness suggesting that somehow we can come to grips with the elusive and genial spirit inhabiting its pages. The less this quest for the "real" Freud succeeds, the more his will-o'-the-wisp personality tantalizes us. Careful reading of his writings in the Standard Edition, or of Jones's wide-ranging and often intimate biography, can elucidate the adult personality, but the youthful Freud's development remains forever obscured by the absence of data: Freud destroyed all of his early diaries and letters, leaving little for his biographers except the allusions to early experiences filtered through his later memories.

The theoretical base and the coolly analytical tone of *The Interpretation of Dreams* set it apart from great confessionals such as Saint Augustine's, with its polemical soul-baring, and Rousseau's, with its stagy emotionalism. If Freud's personality, together with its reflections in the problems of his patients, is his subject matter, he approaches himself somewhat in the spirit of the naturalist novels of Zola, an author he much admired, but without Zola's panoramic vision of man in society, his political sloganizing, or his long, sensitive descriptions of things. In these respects, Freud reminds one rather of late-nineteenth-century Viennese personalities such as Schnitzler, whose writings, like Freud's, combine skepticism and humanity, clinical knowledge and culture, presented in a familiar conversational tone that masks the real drama beneath. Freud's genius as a lecturer and conversationalist— which his perceptive friend Lou Andreas-Salomé placed even above his ability as a writer—enabled him to conduct his readers gradually into intimacy and depth, as though familiar ground were never lost sight of, and to address his readers in a mental dialectic so personal that they seem to share directly in the thought processes of the author.

The best qualities of Freud's style are displayed in the first and central dream of the book, "The Dream of Irma's Injection." Its interpretation constitutes a landmark in Freud's intellectual development: he half-jokingly proclaimed its importance by asking his friend Fliess, in a letter of June 12, 1900, whether he thought that one day a marble tablet might be placed on the house where he had this dream, inscribed with the words: "In this house on July 24, 1895, the Secret of Dreams was revealed to Dr. Sigmund Freud."

The dream, which is easily accessible and widely known among students of psychoanalysis, contains two essential passages. At the beginning: "A large hall—numerous guests, whom we are receiving.— Among them was Irma. I at once took her on one side, as though to answer her letter and to reproach her for not having accepted my 'solution' as yet." And, at the end: "We were directly aware, too, of the origin of the infection. Not long before, when she [Irma] was feeling unwell, my friend Otto had given her an injection of propyl, propyls . . . propionic acid . . . trimethylamin (and I saw before me the formula for this printed in heavy type) . . . Injections of that sort ought not to be made so thoughtlessly . . . And probably the syringe had not been clean."

In explaining this dream, Freud applied his basic principle for dream interpretation; namely, that they are the fulfillment of a wish. Freud had been feeling uneasy about the success of his work with a patient named Irma (he had cured her of hysterical anxiety, but not of all her somatic symptoms), and he expressed in the dream the wish to be exculpated from responsibility for the incompleteness of her cure, while reproaching Otto, also a doctor, for causing Irma's pains through an injection of an unsuitable drug with a dirty needle. Other ideas in the dream, apparently unrelated to the main wish, can in fact be collected, says Freud, "into a single group of ideas and labelled, as it were, 'concern about my own and other people's health—professional conscientiousness.'" Freud acknowledges that he has not explored all the possibilities of the dream, nor even offered all that he has actually uncovered (out of demands of privacy). Later students of the dream have not been so secret, and have exposed the essential sexuality of the injection (doubtless following Rank and Sachs's interpretation of the ejaculatory symbolism of the word *Spritze*) as well as the lingering feelings, not only of rivalry, but of homosexual attraction toward Wilhelm Fliess. Still, a lingering doubt remains as to why Freud considered this the most important, the founding dream of psychoanalysis, since, as Grinstein (1968) points out, the wish-fulfillment idea had already been discovered before this dream.

In my view, the dream is important not because it "provided him a certain intellectual and esthetic appeal,"[5] but because it marked (as sensed by Erikson, 1954) a fundamental break with Fliess, who functioned as a father figure. Up until this point, Freud had shared with Fliess the biologically—and chemically—reductive perspectives on the mind entertained by the circle of Helmholtz, which had shaped both men. Freud's word *Lösung*, meaning solution or explanation of, unites two distinct meanings: the chemical solution of Fliess, and Freud's psychological puzzle of hysteria. Up to now, Freud had tried hard to accept and integrate the "solution" Fliess continually offered for problems concerning neurosis, which would place the mental phenomena on a chemical foundation.[6] But at this point, Freud began to give up his awe of Fliess. In a letter of May 25, 1895, two months before the decisive dream, Freud had written to Fliess, "I have found my tyrant . . . My tyrant is psychology." The desire to come to terms with physical-scientific dimensions of psychological phenomena induced him to write in September, 1895, "A Project for a Scientific Psychology," which, once completed, no longer obstructed his imaginative and insightful work in clinical psychology. In the same letter, Freud greets the claim of an important discovery by Fliess with the remark, "The only thing left for you to do is to make up your mind what kind of marble you prefer," a compliment he was to apply to himself five years later, in referring to his own marble plaque. Freud's "solution" for the widow Irma, the implications of which he would explore during the rest of his life, not only alludes to sexuality (Fliess also emphasized sexuality, but always looked for a chemical "solution" to psychic problems, using substances such as trimethylamin), but to his discovery that the nature of mental problems is frequently psychological rather than organic. Henceforth, Freud was to shift his attention from the region where psychiatry shades off into biology, to where the abnormal makes contact with the normal mental processes. From this new vantage point, Freud could incorporate materials drawn from art and literature into his work; whereas the equally cultivated Fliess, aspiring much too precociously to the discovery of the mathematical basis of psychology and biology, arrived at a number mysticism as fascinating and as impractical as astrology or numerology.

The dream of Irma's injection concerns a theme that directly or indirectly runs throughout *The Interpretation of Dreams*; namely, the attempt on the author's part to prove his powers through the successful application of his novel ideas to his own dreams, and thus, in a sense

to triumph over his feelings of inadequacy retained from his own childhood. One could link with it a number of secondary topics also in the
dream: spatial symbolism (the hall, the Munich Propylaeum, the
woman's chest, mouth and genitals); the voyeuristic "examination
dream" (the name of the house, *Bellevue*, the medical examinations,
including palpating the woman through her clothes and looking down
her throat, a subject remotely linked to his guilt at seeing his "*matrem
nudam*" when he was between two and two and a half); male hysteria
and pregnancy (from the intestinal troubles of a male hysteric he passes
to the excretion of albumen—the nutrition of the embryo—by a female
hysteric and later to his wife's current pregnancy); memories of deaths
due to injections he blamed himself for, especially concerning the use
of cocaine; a series of chemical associations perhaps ironically mimicking Fliess's "mental chemistry" (amyl, methyl, propyl, proprionic
acid—the latter made from propyl alcohol, a substance often mixed
with fusel oil in perfumes); and, the sexual chemistry proposed by
Fliess, which is associated with Freud's fears of homosexual attraction
("*ananas*," or pineapple, a gift of Otto, stinks of fusel oil and is
"poisoned"; Otto's habit of giving the Freuds presents suggests a
latent homosexual attraction, doubtless recalling his friend Fliess's
repeated offers of warmth; and the uneasy dreamer expresses the hope
that Otto's habit will be "cured" by a wife). Immediately behind the
characters arrayed in the dream can be discerned, on the one side,
strong male competitors or models and, on the other, a series of female
patients whom he examines, probes, and injects, and more remotely, the
figures of his father and mother. These figures would inevitably dominate a book that plumbs the depths of the author's Oedipus complex,
precisely through developing the themes of love and hate for his parents,
of the desire for warmth and the fear of being little, weak, and inadequate.

Freud's concern with ultimate problems, his willingness to face
within his self-analysis questions of love and hate, life and death, and
his discovery of the world within himself and himself within the world,
led him to treat more than the abnormal and psychopathic: his ambition turned toward the psychology of the normal person, toward
understanding the motives for the behavior of persons untroubled by
neurosis. In making normality the center of his system, Freud was

drawn sometimes to regard genius also in terms of normal motivations, and to find in genial works of art and literature, links to the average human being, who inevitably undergoes "birth, copulation, and death."

The Interpretation of Dreams chiefly concerns, as we have seen, Freud's endeavors to explore his own Oedipal involvements with his father as well as his mother. The harsh sides of his personality are more apparent, as he comes to grips with his dead father, in terms of his ambition, his long-buried resentments against his father's punishments and criticisms, and his smoldering rivalry for his mother's affection (which he more easily released against newly arrived sibling competitors). His passionate feelings toward his mother, who was still alive when he wrote the book, appear in veiled allusions, and intermingled with reproaches against his wife, and a distaste for sexuality itself, which "smells bad." In this book, so close to himself, he was not ready to acknowledge the attachment to his mother, but in his later writings, for example, in his discussion of Leonardo, he was able to assert that the highest and deepest satisfaction a man can have is as an infant suckling at its mother's breast.

In the course of this self-analysis, Freud discovered mechanisms and patterns of wish and behavior in himself, which he compared to those of his patients and to characters in literature. Unusual and apparently abnormal behavior Freud wished to relate to "normal" behavior, to find the common base for a wide range of human situations. In this search for the universal in man, Freud launched an unending quest in ever-wider circles of reference. This process of finding himself in great characters of the past, and in his intimately known patients (whose experience he controlled through his interpretations), is part of Freud's seemingly unlimited development as a human being, and implies—as he was ultimately to admit—that his self-analysis was an endless and never-completed task. Freud's powerful need for a figure to replace his father led him to a series of transient father figures, great men whom he could identify with, in ways dependent on the emotional needs of any given period of his life. Within *The Interpretation of Dreams* itself, the number of minor characters (literary and real) who adapt themselves to aspects of Freud's personality is staggering, although these characters can be reduced to splinters from several major heroes, above all, Oedipus and Hamlet.

The Psychopathology of Everyday Life builds on the ground of *The Interpretation of Dreams* and extends its insights and ideas both to a wider world and to other phenomena than the dream world analyzed in the earlier book. While *The Interpretation of Dreams* dwells on the problems connected with Freud's feelings about his aged father's death, and thus might be called the "Jakob" book, *The Psychopathology of Everyday Life* concerns the real daytime world of the son, and might justifiably (as we shall presently see) be called the "Joseph" book. Freud continues his self-analysis by exploring several significant errors he had made in *The Interpretation of Dreams*, and in doing so, he discloses the basic theme of the book: the feelings of mixed triumph and resentment liberated by his self-analysis, and his "growing up" from his attachment to his father and to his father substitute, Fliess. In a letter to Fliess of August 7, 1901, Freud refers to the "fact that we have drawn somewhat apart from each other," and then mentions how much of Fliess is in *The Psychopathology of Everyday Life*: "It is full of references to you: obvious ones ... and concealed ones, where the motivation derives from you. Also you supplied the motto." The freedom from Fliess is clearly seen in the expanded discussions of the significance of numbers, a subject he had already broached to his friend in 1899. Freud shows that a determinism covers the cases of apparently randomly or accidentally thought-up numbers, and in a sense throws his own brand of determinism—psychological—into the face of Fliess's biological determinism, wherein dates and time periods are determined by regular "laws."

In working toward his self-assertion, Freud once again relied on a series of identifications, mingling associations to literary characters with memories of real persons he had known. The famous introductory example of Botticelli-Boltraffio he had already cited to Fliess in a letter of September 9, 1898, in which his forgetting of the name of Signorelli, the creator of the great *Last Judgment* frescoes at Orvieto, is shown to involve several unpleasant memories that Freud wished to repress concerning death and sexuality. The diagram that he published, outlining the pathways along which the repression operated, reminds one of his vivid image of the trimethylamin formula, which he saw so vividly in the dream of Irma's injection. This diagrammatic interpretation was probably suggested earlier, in a letter of April 28,

1897, in which Freud, annoyed that he did not have Fliess's address, wrote:

> I had a dream last night which concerned you. There was a telegram giving your address: (Venice) Via Villa *Casa Secerno*. That way of writing it shows which parts were obscure and which appeared in more than one form. Secerno was the clearest ... your telegraphing your address was a wish fulfillment. All sorts of things lie behind the wording: memory of the etymological feasts you set before me ... Also the wording conveys other things as well:
>
> Via (Pompeii streets which I am studying)
> Villa (Böcklin's Roman Villa). In other words our talks of travel ...

The major contribution from Fliess seems to be derived from Freud's attempt to absorb and then transcend his ideas in the fields of chemistry and etymology. Freud combined the representations of chemical formulas with diagrammatic analyses exhibiting the "genealogy" of words probably like those that Fliess discussed with him; but, for Freud, such analyses were transformed into tools for exploring the mind. The genetic relation of unconscious (often archaic) thoughts to conscious expression seemed to him analogous to the linking of older forms of words to their later descendants, usually shown in tree diagrams.

The explanation of his forgetting of Signorelli's name makes use of this famous diagram:

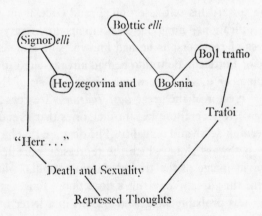

In his brilliant analysis Freud traced his forgetting of the familiar name of Signorelli—and its replacement by the names of Botticelli and Boltraffio—to the connections between these names and painful repressed thoughts. Thus, Bosnia and Herzegovina, linked verbally to the innocuous artists' names on one side, are linked on the other to a sentence beginning "Herr," which the fatalistic Turks, when faced with death, address to their physicians: "Sir, what can I say? I know that if he could be saved, you would save him." Boltraffio was linked to Trafoi, where Freud heard of the death of one of his patients who was faced with an incurable sexual ailment; thus this sentence of the Turks, showing complete confidence in their physicians, embodied an obvious wish with regard to Freud's own patient. He had also been thinking of the central place of sexuality in the Turks' lives: when this pleasure ceased, life for them lost its savor, and they often preferred to die. Death and sexuality are fitting themes for this book, which represents Freud's final separation from Fliess.

The turn from Fliess, and thereby from his father, is best seen in the series of errors of memory that Freud found in *The Interpretation of Dreams* and that he analyzes in chapter 10 of the *Psychopathology*. In some respects, this analysis may be considered the core of the entire book, marking it as a continuation of *The Interpretation of Dreams*. The three errors concern, first, calling Schiller's birthplace Marburg instead of Marbach; second, naming Hannibal's father Hasdrubal (his brother) instead of Hamilcar Barca; finally, stating that Zeus emasculated his father Kronos, thus carrying the atrocity one generation forward, since Greek mythology speaks of Kronos committing this act upon his father, Uranus. Freud shows that all three errors derive from repressed thoughts connected with his dead father: Marburg was the name of a business friend of his father's; the substitution of the brother Hasdrubal's name for the father's corresponds to his dissatisfaction with his father's cowardice in the hat-in-the-gutter episode, and the wish to be the son of his much older half-brother, a child of his father's first marriage; finally, the same brother was linked to the generation-error, since he had once admonished Freud "that you must not forget that . . . you really belong not to the second but to the third generation in relation to your father." Thus, Freud's Oedipal wish against his father was appropriately advanced to his own generation.

All of these threads leading from *The Interpretation of Dreams* to the new situation of *The Psychopathology of Everyday Life* meet in the fascinating material related by Freud with regard to an error he had made in his first manuscript while writing the later chapters for the dream book, but which was published correctly. The error, discussed in chapter 7 of the later book, concerned the daydreams narrated in Alphonse Daudet's novel *Le Nabab* by a poor bookkeeper named Joyeuse as he walked the streets of Paris. Freud not only misnamed the character M. Jocelyn, but ascribed the following fantasy to him, which does not in fact occur in the book: M. Jocelyn while unemployed and walking the streets of Paris had the fantasy that he threw himself at the head of a carriage with a runaway horse in the street, and brought it to a stop; whereupon the carriage door opened and a great personage stepped out, pressed M. Jocelyn's hand, and said, "You are my savior. I owe my life to you. What can I do for you?" Freud explains his false recollection or paramnesia as derived from identifying Joyeuse's situation with his own experience of walking the streets of Paris when he first arrived there and was "lonely and full of longings, greatly in need of a helper and protector." The identification with Joyeuse was made easy by the equivalence between *Freud(e)*, the German for joy, and *Joyeux*, *Joyeuse*, its French counterpart. Freud remarked in a passage (removed in editions after 1924): "But the irritating part of it is that there is scarcely any group of ideas to which I feel so antagonistic as that of being someone's protégé . . . I have always felt an unusually strong urge 'to be the strong man myself.' " In place of this passage, Freud added a footnote that points out that as a child he probably read a story with a rescue scene just like the one he attributed to M. Jocelyn: "The phantasy which, at the age of 43, I thought I remembered as having been produced by someone else, and which I was subsequently forced to recognize as a creation of my own at the age of 28, may therefore easily have been an exact reproduction of an impression which I had received somewhere between the ages of eleven and thirteen." Thus, it really signified a fantasy of his own rescue, his "longing for a patron and protector."

What is of great interest here is precisely what Freud did not disclose (or repressed) and which his critics have not even attempted to explain: why Freud should have revived just this fantasy, with its identification with Daudet's character, at this moment of his life; and why Freud chose to distort the name Joyeuse in just the way he did. The key, it seems to me, is in Freud's new mood of independence of Fliess, and the anxieties and angers accompanying this breaking of the old friendship, with its overtones of paternal domination. If we regard the "great personage" saved to be the father of Freud, then we can understand Freud's underlying attitude in terms of an essay of 1910 ("A Special Type of Object-Choice"). This essay explains the fantasy of rescuing one's own father:

> When a child hears that he owes his life to his parents, that his mother gave him life, the feelings of tenderness in him mingle with the longing to be big and independent himself, so that he forms the wish to repay the parents for this gift and requite it by one of like value ... He then weaves a phantasy of saving his father's life on some dangerous occasion by which he becomes quits with him, and this phantasy is commonly enough displaced on to the Emperor, the King, or any other great man. . . .
>
> The phantasy of rescuing the father will also occasionally have a tender meaning. It then expresses the wish to have the father for a son, that is, to have a son like the father.

We may add to these points the great significance Freud attached to names; as he put it in *Totem and Taboo* (1912), "A man's name is one of the main constituents of his person and perhaps a part of his psyche."

Freud's ambition is summed up in his choice of the name Jocelyn, which not only contains the syllable "Jo" (used by Freud in both French and German, as in Joseph) but "ce," which in French would sound like "se" in German; thus, the name is close to the sound of "Joseph," and this is the other name, along with "Freud" that is repressed. Years later, in a letter dated November 29, 1936, to his friend Thomas Mann, Freud, commenting on Mann's *Joseph in Egypt*, published that same year, analyzed the behavior of Napoleon I in terms of a "Joseph-phantasy," which was "the secret demonic motor behind his complex biography": "He was a Corsican, a second son in a bunch of siblings. The oldest, the brother before him was called— Joseph . . . In the Corsican family, the privilege of the oldest child is guarded with quite special awe. (I believe that A. Daudet once depicted this in a novel, in *Nabab*?)" Freud apologized for bending Mann's ear by explaining, "I don't take my efforts very seriously, but it has a certain charm for me, rather like a crack of the whip for a former carriage-driver." Freud seemed to be attached to this analysis, and had to be reminded by his daughter that he had already told it to Mann.

Bits of Freud's analysis link up to the Jocelyn discussion, even including an allusion to a carriage-driver. Years before the Mann letter, in the dream of Count Thun, analyzed in *The Interpretation of Dreams*, Freud had spoken of the aristocracy as occupying the driver's seat, while he belonged to the plebeian middle class; now, the long-powerful man Freud compared himself to an old coachman, thereby remaining a worker, but occupying the envied seat of the driver. The identification with Joseph, emphasized already in *The Interpretation of Dreams*, fulfills his life-long wish to absorb his father's power; for, as he surely knew, Joseph, after saving the Pharaoh through interpreting his dream correctly, achieves so much power that when he discloses his identity to his brothers, he can tell them that he is like the "Pharaoh's father."

The evolving struggle against his "father" Fliess led Freud in 1905 to assert his new independence, as already suggested, in the first of the *Three Essays on the Theory of Sex*, where he disputed the originality of Fliess's theory of bisexuality in men and women. Again, referring to the key term of the Irma dream, Freud asserts that only the psychoanalysis "discovered by Joseph Breuer and me" can offer a "solution" to the problems of sexual disturbance. While acknowledging the roles of anatomical and chemical factors in determining sexual behavior and its abnormalities, Freud based his own analysis on the distinction between activity (regarded as masculine) and passivity (regarded as feminine). The central problem of the *Three Essays*, to show essential links and continuities between "normal" and "abnormal," "male" and "female" sexuality, in part also characterizes the book *Jokes and Their Relation to the Unconscious*, written at precisely the same time. The subject of jokes was to provide Freud with an arena in which to express simultaneously his reverence for his father and his superiority to him. Freud had long been fascinated by his father's gift as a raconteur, and he had begun collecting Jewish jokes and anecdotes even before writing *The Interpretation of Dreams*. His book, therefore, represents one more point of identification with his father, of taking over his father's admired qualities. Another facet of his relation to his father through Fliess is also present, however, and is alluded to in chapter 6, where Freud indicates that his "subjective reason for taking up the problem of jokes" was the similarity between the dream and jokes. In this instance, too, he is answering the criticism of Fliess, who had remarked in 1899 that *The Interpretation of Dreams* was too full of jokes. Freud took up the challenge by revealing that not only was it valid to reveal the bad jokes underlying the dream, but that the essential motivation and pleasure derived from jokes—even good ones—is closely allied to those of the dream. Here, as in *The Psychopathology of Everyday Life*, Freud, in expanding the insights of *The Interpretation of Dreams*, applies them not only to neurotics but to the world of normality.

Freud's extension of himself, his absorption of other roles by identification, can be seen clearly in his next work of consequence for this discussion, his essay of 1906, *Delusions and Dreams in Jensen's "Gradiva."* Not since his brief discussions in a letter to Fliess in 1898 on *Oedipus*, *Hamlet*, and especially on C. F. Meyer's story *Die Richterin* (*The Female Judge*), wherein he discovered that literature could be seen as a reflection of the writer's own problems, had Freud undertaken a major independent discussion of a work of art. While the analysis of *Die Richterin* begins with the notion that the story reflects the writer's problems, the analysis of *Gradiva* concludes with this idea. Freud reasserts that there is a fluctuating frontier between normal and pathological states of mind and presents the cogent idea that "there is a grain of truth concealed in every delusion." But the most interesting aspect of his discussion is his barbed remarks against scientists who would explain dreams by physiology, and his declaration that the creative artist is the ally of the psychoanalyst, "for they draw on sources not yet opened to science."

The power of Freud's insights and his stylistic merits appear nowhere so strongly as in his analysis of *Gradiva*, where he was able to rescue a trivial story by a writer nearly forgotten even in German letters, and to make a fascinating discussion of it. Jensen's original has apparently not enjoyed republication (except as a companion to Freud's essay in the rare French edition of 1931), although students of psychoanalysis might appreciate an opportunity to compare the original with

Freud's rendering of it. This exercise in the late-nineteenth-century genre of the *archaeologischer Roman* (best represented by the works of the Egyptologist and novelist Georg Ebers and by M. G. Conrad, both active in Munich) posed problems nicely suited to Freud's analytic powers as well as to his interest in the setting at Pompeii. Moreover, Freud could give free rein here to his long-time interest in archaeology. He was rather happy to have his own work corroborated by Jensen's valid example of a successful psychotherapy, for Jensen, "without knowledge of psychoanalysis, had drawn from the same sources and worked upon the same subject."

The story concerns the German archaeologist Norbert Hanold, who had so devoted himself to his profession that he had no place for a mistress of flesh and blood. In the course of his studies, he became fascinated by an ancient relief (*Fig. 7*), a plaster cast of which he owned, showing a fully grown woman stepping along with a peculiar gait, the forward sandaled foot resting flat on the ground, the trailing foot with its heel raised almost perpendicular to the ground. Obsessed, for no apparent reason, by the relief, the archaeologist assigned specific characteristics to it; thus, from her brisk step he gave her the epithet Gradiva, based on Gradivus, the surname of Mars, signifying he who walks in battle, and in his imagination transported her as the daughter of an aristocratic Roman family from Germany back to ancient Pompeii. Hanold felt impelled by an insatiable curiosity about the work, which he explained to himself as being scientific, and wondered whether the sculptor had used a contemporary model. Soon he began to roam the streets examining women's gaits, ostensibly to check whether such a posture might still be discovered. Needless to say, such girl-watching excited return glances, some pleased, some annoyed; but Hanold pursued his quest with no apparent emotional involvement, insulated from the present by his archaeology. With regret, he had finally to conclude that he could not find Gradiva's gait in reality.

Not long after, Hanold had a terrifying dream of being in Pompeii, witnessing the city's destruction in A.D. 79. Suddenly he saw Gradiva nearby (in Freud's quotation of Jensen's text): "Till then he had no thought of her presence, but now it occurred to him all at once and as though it was something natural that, since she was a Pompeian, she was living in her native town, and *without his having suspected it, living as his contemporary*." Fearing for her, he cried a warning, whereupon she stepped calmly along, turning her face toward him, and walked untroubled to the portico of a temple. "There she took her seat on one of the steps and slowly laid her head down on it, while her face grew paler and paler, as though it were turning into marble. When he hurried after her, he found her stretched out on the broad step with a peaceful expression, like someone asleep, till the rain of ashes buried her form." Now, for the first time in his fantasies, Hanold mourned for her as for someone dead. Once more impelled by an unaccountable impulse, Hanold rushed off to Italy, with the excuse of investigating the archaeological significance of the relief, but in fact dominated by his delusions about the life and death of Gradiva. All about him he noticed newlyweds, who annoyed him with their foolish and conventional behavior, and later in Pompeii, he was disgusted by the sexual couplings of the "evil and unnecessary" house flies. What, in fact, was beginning to occur was a change in Hanold to a more emotional person. After having the delusion of seeing Gradiva walk across a street, he realizes that he had come to Pompeii precisely to seek her actual historical traces (footprints in the ashes). At first, he regards her as a hallucination, but when she scares away a lizard, he considers her to be a ghost—something within the world (though not alive), rather than a projection of his own mind. Still investigating, he asks her to lie down as he had seen her in his dream, and is rebuffed by the girl, who disappears.

We soon learn that Gradiva is really a living girl, who startles Hanold by replying to him in neither Greek nor Latin, but in German. She is a neighbor from his home town, with whom he had had an intimate childhood friendship, involving affectionate "thumping and bumping." Her name is Zoe Bertgang. Zoe, in love with Hanold, purposely conforms to his delusion about her in order to find a way to cure him, and she conducts her therapy so skillfully that Freud finds her an exemplary therapist, who has the advantage over the psychoanalyst of knowing at first hand her patient's childhood experiences and of being able to use "love as her medication." Zoe's family background—her mother dead, her father an unreachable idol totally dedicated to his profession of zoology—made her increasingly dependent on her early love for Hanold, who could easily have replaced her father in her heart. In a moment of anger at Hanold, for his coolness toward her, and for his blind preoccupation with his science, she described him as "grandiose as an 'archeopteryx,' " a term for an antidiluvian reptilian bird, which Freud interprets as combining references both to her father (zoology) and to Hanold (archaeology).

The question of the role of repression enters precisely at this point: Freud uses the valuable phrase "return of the repressed" to explain how the instrument of repression, archaeology, elicited the childhood memories of Zoe while simultaneously screening them. Thus, beneath the manifest content of Hanold's dream of the burial of Pompeii and the loss of Gradiva, lies the latent, true content: his passionate longing for the Zoe he had known. Freud compares Hanold's unsuccessful repression and distortion of his erotic feelings for Zoe to the motto: "You may drive nature out with a pitchfork; but she will always return." Freud cites as an insightful illustration of the process, Félicien Rops's etching of an ascetic monk wracked by sexual temptations (*Fig. 8*). Upon appealing in desperation to the crucified Christ, he discovers to his horror the image of the savior transformed into a voluptuous nude woman. Even mathematics, that seeming refuge from the "impurities" of life, can become the vehicle for the return of repressed material, as in the case cited by Freud of a boy whose repressed sexuality breaks out and is betrayed by two particular problems: " 'Two bodies come together, one with a speed of . . . etc.,' and 'On a cylinder, the diameter of whose surface is m, describe a cone . . . etc.' "[7]

Freud's interpretation of the lizard that appears in Hanold's second dream raises some problems. Freud's account is strikingly meager with regard to this most obvious of sexual symbols. Freud shows that the lizard-catching theme originates with Zoe's father and that she in turn uses the technique for man-catching. According to the psychoanalyst's interpretation, Hanold's dream reveals the archaeologist's awareness that Zoe was wooing him, and the "slipping through narrow gaps and disappearing in them" recalled to the dreamer "the behavior of lizards." In contrast to the powerful image of Zoe-Gradiva, Hanold appears as a very weak creature to Freud, whose concluding remarks point out that the archaeologist wished to be subjected to her, "for we may construe [that] the wish behind the situation of the lizard—catching was in fact of a passive, masochistic character." Inasmuch as Hanold's delusion is described as hysterical (Freud's paper of two years later on "Hysterical Phantasies" relates them to bisexuality) and since Hanold's absorption in his science led to his sexual frigidity, we can see the stage being set for the discussion of the question of bisexuality. This next phase of Freud's continuing though subterranean contest with his father and Fliess, is evident in his book on *Leonardo*, which he admitted to be one of his most subjective works. But there is some of this subjectivity in his essay on *Gradiva*, too. Freud's analysis of the book, so far beyond the original work in some respects, has made of Jensen an unwitting oracle for Freud's ideas. Adolph Wohlgemuth, in his generally unfair critique of Freud's theories, *A Critical Examination of Psychoanalysis* (1923), makes at least one valid point about the essay on *Gradiva*, namely, that much of the dream interpretation came from Freud and not Jensen. Freud's tendency, in his search for self-knowledge, to find personally significant aspects in art or literature might well be dubbed the "*Gradiva* principle" of his criticism, since, especially in his analysis of this story, Freud exceeds the quality of his subject matter by projecting himself into it.

Before turning to Freud's book on Leonardo, published in 1910, it might be useful to fill in the four years following the *Gradiva* essay of 1906. In 1908, Freud wrote "Creative Writers and Daydreaming," in which he developed ideas that emerged ultimately from the preoccupations of the earlier works, and once more treated the question of finding transitions between apparently unrelated aspects of the human mind. In the *Psychopathology*, he had linked errors and slips to unconscious drives not far from the neurotic's, and in the present essay, he compared the child's play or the idle daydreaming of the average man to the fantasy and imagination of the writer. In aspiring to extend his own experience to all spheres of human feeling and motivation, Freud sought a gradual approach to the seemingly inaccessible mystery of the creative writer. Preoccupied with his own problems of identification, he asserted the importance of this process for the novelist, whose hero, like the daydreamer's, he calls "His Majesty the Ego." In contrast to the *Gradiva* essay, the artist here is not treated as a colleague, whose insights are fully equal to the psychoanalyst's, but in terms of the unreal or illusory aspect of his productions. In the *Leonardo*, the problem of the relation of art to science becomes a central concern.

In some ways, the *Leonardo* marks a turning point in Freud's life: the "heroic" days of *The Interpretation of Dreams* and its several brilliant follow-ups had brought with them a new sense of independence from Fliess, but also a new sadness at his being isolated and alone, having lost, as he wrote to Fliess in 1902, his "only remaining audience" (a point more melodramatically than actually true). From this point forward, the reporting of his dreams became much less frequent. His turning to the more systematic working-out of rough ideas already introduced, was like the turn from the path of artistic fantasy to the logic of science, which he observed in that great genius Leonardo. Years later, in 1930, on the occasion of receiving the Goethe Prize for literature, he noted that Goethe and *not* Leonardo had successfully harmonized the scientist and the artist in himself. One wonders how he viewed his own work at this moment, when his writings, which he regarded as science, were honored for their literary merit.

The ideas already hinted at in *The Interpretation of Dreams*, the *Psychopathology*, and *Three Essays* had cleared the ground for the deeper discussion of the role of the mother in Freud's life; but, instead of continuing his own self-analysis, he chose the fateful path of projecting his analysis onto Leonardo, who had already come up as a major personality in his talks with Fliess, and who was especially attractive for two reasons: a striking phrase, understood by Freud to be a memory of Leonardo, was accessible for analysis; and Leonardo's most celebrated works, including the Mona Lisa, presented characters whose "enigmatic" smiles teased the interpreter Freud as much as the riddle of the sphinx had previously enticed him to investigate the Oedipus complex.

Freud developed his study of Leonardo's character formation, including his homosexuality, out of a single "memory" of his childhood, and explained the master's turning from warm and creative art to dry science as an outgrowth of his neurosis, which even inhibited the realization of his homosexual urges. The history of Freud's interest in Leonardo goes back at least to October 9, 1898, when he wrote to Fliess: "Leonardo, of whom no love-affair is recorded, was perhaps the most famous case of left-handedness. Can you use him?" The question referred to Fliess's interest in a speculative connection between bilaterality and bisexuality, one to which the *Leonardo* study alludes, as we shall presently see. Nothing is heard again of Freud's interest in Leonardo before 1907, when Freud, naming the ten "good books," listed Merezhkovsky's *Romance of Leonardo da Vinci* (1902) in the German edition of 1903. According to a letter of October 17, 1909, to Jung, Freud had a patient with some of the characteristics of Leonardo, without his genius. There are reasons for believing that Freud's feelings toward his brilliant and independent emulator Jung recalled some unresolved homosexual feelings toward Fliess, and stimulated his working out of these problems in terms of his study of Leonardo. Characteristically, treating this patient must have helped Freud to face some of his own problems, which could now surface as identification with the Renaissance genius.

Freud's thesis is that Leonardo's problems as an adult—his incapacity even for homosexual love, his indifference to his artistic productions, and his ultimate turning from the rich, imaginative life of the artist to the colder one of the scientist—can be traced to childhood experiences: while lacking his father as a model during his earliest years, he was overwhelmed with the tenderness of his unwed mother's starved sexuality, a situation terminated through his eventual adoption by his prosperous father and his kindly (and childless) stepmother. Leonardo's "childhood memory," really a fantasy according to Freud, is cited by the psychoanalyst as a clue to the mature Leonardo's state of mind, revealing those hidden or overlooked processes of his mind that ultimately surfaced as enigmatic patterns of behavior. "It seems," Freud quotes Leonardo, "that I was always destined to be so deeply concerned with vultures; for I recall as one of my very earliest memories that while I was in my cradle a vulture came down to me, and opened my mouth with its tail, and struck me many times with its tail against my lips." Freud interprets this fantasy as a wish to return to the aggressive tenderness of the mother who provided the exquisite pleasures of suckling and passionate kissing (he compared the tail in the mouth to fellatio). Freud had already, in a footnote to his book on jokes (1905), traced back the origins of "the grimace characteristic of smiling, which twists up the corners of the mouth," to the "infant at the breast when it is satisfied and satiated." The fantasy also provides an indication of a "causal connection between Leonardo's relation with his mother in childhood and his later, manifest, if ideal homosexuality." He substantiates this hypothesis by a long discussion of the vulture-headed deity Mut, an Egyptian mother-goddess who was fertilized not by a male but by the wind, and who was usually represented with a phallus. Freud reasoned that Leonardo knew these Egyptian mythological details, and was thereby enabled to compose a fantasy about the parthenogenetic mother-goddess. Leonardo's fantasy thus eliminated the hated father who had deserted him as an infant (although he later received him into his household). This construction helps Freud explain the mysterious smile of Mona Lisa (*Fig. 9*), and of the Virgin in the *Virgin and St. Anne* of the Louvre (*Fig. 10*): upon meeting Mona Lisa, Leonardo was stirred by the memory of his mother's blissful smile, and so the whole happy world of his infancy was "restored" to him. The important mechanism of the recall of the past through a later experience was first suggested by Freud in his letters to Fliess and in his "Creative Writers and Daydreaming". In the *St. Anne*, he presents two mothers: St. Anne, the tender grandmother, represented Leonardo's real mother Caterina from whom he was taken by his father between the ages of three and five; and the virgin, his young stepmother, his father's wife.

It is well known that while the sweep and elegance of Freud's presentation has always found admirers, his main theses have been sharply criticized by all but the most myopic supporters of psychoanalysis. Most strikingly, critics have shown that the "vulture," a mistranslation of *nibio*, really means kite, and so the whole argument based on the Egyptian goddess Mut falls to the ground. This error, already pointed out in the *Burlington Magazine* in 1923 by Maclagan, must have been known to some of the members of Freud's English circle, who kept him up to date on the relevant art news published in this major journal.[8] Freud introduced several changes in the editions of his work of 1919 and 1923 and a minor one even in that of 1925, and maintained an active interest in the Renaissance genius at least up to the early 1920's.[9] As late as 1931 Freud could still maintain that the *Virgin and St. Anne* in the Louvre could not really be understood "without the characteristic childhood experience [*Kindheitsgeschichte*] of Leonardo."[10] Surprisingly, Freud nowhere takes into account the most serious criticism of the book; even the most recent editors of the Standard Edition, while admitting that the whole Egyptian connection has become irrelevant, staunchly defend the validity of his psychosexual analyses in the book. These editors might understandably have overlooked the cogent essay of Edmund Wilson (1941),[11] which points to the chief difficulties in Freud's essay on Leonardo, that his method does not make any attempt "to account for Leonardo's genius," nor even to address the central question of aesthetics—value (a point repeated by Susanne K. Langer in *Philosophy in a New Key*, 1942); that in treating Leonardo as a "case history," Freud has inadequately considered nonpsychoanalytic factors in his art, and has (Wilson implies) "built a Freudian mechanism out of very slender evidence." But not to have at least noted the major and highly relevant study that goes far beyond Wilson's— Meyer Schapiro's essay (1956)—raises doubts about the objectivity of the editors, who must have known this article, in view of K. R. Eissler's attempt to refute Schapiro's thirty-page article in a book (1962).[12] The pathetic justification of Freud's error is summed up by a footnote of the editors of the *Minutes of the Vienna Psychoanalytic Society*,[13] backing Eissler against Schapiro with the argument that, anyway, "a 'kite,' like a 'vulture,' is a bird."

The subjectivity of Freud's exegesis is more than matched by his own personal involvement in the book. Freud himself called it "half-fiction," but this description completely understates the autobiographical nature of the work, emphasized by Jones in 1955. In a penetrating little study, Schapiro (1955–56) had shown that Freud erroneously thought of Leonardo as "somehow outside his father's family. It may be that in identifying with Leonardo in this biography . . . he had to separate his hero as far as possible from his brothers and sisters . . . The father, too, was minimized . . . the relation of the illegitimate child to the abandoned mother becomes the decisive fact." This attempt on Freud's part to play down Leonardo's father fits perfectly into the development of Freud's own personality, along the lines of what he called "the family romance," and as a problem of Freud's, it helps us to understand other errors and omissions of his book. Thus, Freud states in chapter 2 that the only sure fact we have concerning Leonardo's childhood is that by the time he was five he was a member of his father's household: "We are completely ignorant when that happened— whether it was a few months after his birth" or when he was about five years old. But in chapter 4, Freud, discussing Leonardo's two mothers, asserts that he was "torn away" from his first, true mother, Caterina, "when he was between three and five." Freud's willingness, even compulsion to distort the picture of Leonardo, in order to make it a projection of his own personality, becomes clearer still when we consider an omission that he knowingly made with regard to the relation of Leonardo to his parents. Freud's copy (preserved in his library) of Gabriel Séailles, *Léonard de Vinci*, in the series "Les Grands Artistes" (no place or date) is inscribed in black ink on the cover "freud/10.x.09" (before he finished writing his study of Leonardo), and the following passage on page 11 is emphasized by a green line in the margin: "Sans doute, sur les instances de son père, ser Piero rompit avec Catarina [*sic*], *prit son fils et la même* [six words underlined in green] année se maria ... Fils naturel, recueilli par son père, Léonard se passa de cette influence maternelle que doit subir tout grand homme qui se respecte." ("Without doubt, at the urging of his father, Ser Piero broke with Caterina, *took his son and the same* year married ... An illegitimate son received by his father, Leonardo missed that maternal influence to which every great man who respects himself must submit.") Since Freud accepts the fact that Leonardo's father married his stepmother "in the same year that Leonardo was born," the omitted quotation that he underlined would have contradicted Freud's hypothesis of a long period after this marriage when the young genius was alone with his doting and love-starved mother.

If the objectivity of Freud's study can be shown questionable in several instances, this does not mean necessarily that no light is cast on the character of Leonardo, but it does open the prospect of gaining valuable insights into Freud himself, and his attitudes toward art. Assuming, then, that this study significantly reflects the author's problems, we can set about uncovering where there are significant points of contact between the two men, and so perhaps come better to understand both. Freud, his study of Leonardo notwithstanding, would certainly have responded unsympathetically to any attempts to study his own personality, and he not only rejected the astute biography of Wittels, but wrote in a letter of May 31, 1936, to his would-be biographer Arnold Zweig: "Whoever undertakes to write a biography binds himself to lying, to concealment, to hypocrisy, to flummery and even to hiding his own lack of understanding, since biographical material is not to be had." I hope to avoid at least some of these draw-backs.

Perhaps the key point in Freud's unintended self-revelation concerns the vulture, which he refused to renounce even in the face of continued severe criticism. Moreover, Freud treated the vulture "memory" as serious to Leonardo and neglected to raise any questions about it, although he had marked with brown double lines the passage in the German edition of Merezhkovsky[14] wherein the fantasy is quoted, which concludes that Leonardo only intends the vulture story "half jokingly, half in earnest, in the symbolical manner of the waning middle ages." Freud also insists that Leonardo knew of the identification of the vulture with the mother, if not from the *Hieroglyphica* of Horapollo[15] then from the writings of the fathers of the church, where, Freud notes, the Virgin's parthenogenesis is used as an argument for the credibility of the Virgin birth. But Freud overlooks alternative attributes for the vulture: the *Horapollo* passage (I, 11) to which Freud himself refers, reads: "When they [the Egyptians] mean a mother, or sight, or boundaries, or foreknowledge, or the year, or the heavens, or pity, or Athene, or Hera, or two drachmas, they draw a vulture." Furthermore, while some of the church fathers allude to the vulture in terms of its virginity, later Christian accounts of vultures indicate their demonic quality; thus Peter the venerable, of the twelfth century, tells of a monk assailed in his bed by the devil in the form of a vulture.[16]

If the vulture-mother of which Freud makes so much is not, in fact, Leonardo's, then it seems not at all unreasonable to suppose that it was Freud's own, especially since one of his most remarkable dreams discussed in *The Interpretation of Dreams* involved beings with bird beaks: "I saw my beloved mother, with a peculiarly peaceful, sleeping expression on her features, being carried into the room by two (or three) people with birds' beaks and laid upon the bed." Freud associated the "strangely draped and unnaturally tall figures with birds' beaks" to illustrations of Philippson's Bible (*Figs. 11 and 12*), especially those of "gods with falcons' heads from an ancient Egyptian funerary relief," so that his mother was actually lying on a bier. Eva Rosenfeld (1956) has correctly, but in a very limited way, compared this image to the vulture of the Leonardo study: "Freud's error in calling the kite a vulture . . . and linking it with Egypt has yet a deeper meaning. It brings into the picture Freud's own childhood dream of the beak-headed gods." Freud dated this dream to his seventh or eighth year, and it is important that his father, sending Freud the second volume of Philippson's Bible on his son's thirty-fifth birthday, commented, "You were seven when the spirit of learning awoke in you." An allusion made by Freud years earlier, in a letter to Martha of 1885 from Paris, reveals his constant interest in such curious mongrel figures as those depicted in the Bible; for, after examining the obelisk from Luxor in the Place de la Concorde, he commented: "Think of it, a real obelisk, with the prettiest bird's heads [*Vogelköpfen*], and a little seated man, and other hieroglyphs scribbled on it."

The link between the Philippson Bible and the dream concerns a boy Freud knew in the Freiburg period, Philipp. Freud calls him "an ill-mannered boy . . . who used to play with us . . . when we were children . . . it was from this boy that I first heard the vulgar term for sexual intercourse, instead of which educated people always use a Latin word, 'to copulate,' and which was clearly enough indicated by the choice of the falcons' heads [*Sperberköpfe*]." Freud is alluding to the German word *vögeln*, to act like birds (*Vögel*), related to the English vulgarism "fuck." The Philippson Bible refers both to *Sperber*, or falcons, and to *Geier*, or vultures, and has illustrations of both (*Fig. 13*), though in different volumes, so that it is quite likely that the falcon-headed figures of Freud's dream were interchangeable with the vulture. The name Philipp—or even better Philippson (close to the German *Sohn*)—had another important connection with Freud's childhood, for it was the name of his half-brother, who was twenty years older than he and who he had wished were his father. It was from this brother that Freud had derived his first knowledge of pregnancy. The bird dream served, therefore, as a bridge in Freud's mind between the bird as mother, the vulture (falcon) as symbolizing the sexual act, and the wish to escape from his own father to another. No wonder that Freud, identifying with Leonardo, made these very connections the heart of his interpretation of the "vulture" fantasy, and distorted parts of it to fit his own wish to be fatherless and alone with his mother—the typical "family romance" he often discusses. The opposed contents Freud found in his mother's peaceful expression—dying and sexual craving—parallel the opposed qualities he attributed to the Leonardesque smile: tenderness and sinister menace. Even the confusion as to whether Leonardo's happy period with his real mother ended any time before five, or between three and five, parallels Freud's own experience of leaving the "paradise" of Freiburg at the age of three, shortly after losing one of his "mothers," the Catholic nanny. It is very possible that to the important experiences with this woman—who Freud considered to be "the primary originator" of his neurosis[17]—Freud owed his imaginative invention of the theme of the "two mothers" with which he tried to interpret the *Virgin and St. Anne*. This clever and elderly Czech woman taught Freud about heaven and hell, and seems so much to have impressed the infant, that he developed a lasting desire to see Rome. The meaning becomes clear in a letter to Fliess of December 3, 1897, in which he says, "the Rome of my dreams was really Prague." One might speculate that Freud's unpleasant remembrances of the nanny disguise his hostility toward his all-powerful mother felt during his earliest years, the period which he always uncritically extolled (perhaps his mother blended some suppressed aggression at males with her overwhelming tenderness directed at her "*goldener Sigi*"). Many of Freud's unresolved problems look back on this period, which Freud called the pre-Oedipal, when the mother, according to him, seems to have the power and even the genitalia of both sexes. Freud wrote in his essay on "The Sexual Theories of Children" (1908) that the earliest idea of boys "consists in attributing to everyone, including females, the possession of a penis." Since she seemed to him to possess male and female characteristics, Freud's mother must have loomed above her young son as an overbearingly powerful being. Given Freud's own profound difficulties with the mother of his earliest infancy, it is no wonder he had residual difficulties with women, not only in his married life, but in analyzing them (see, for example, "Female Sexuality," 1931).

Underlying Freud's essay on Leonardo seems to have been an anxiety about his own homosexual impulses, and his admiration of Leonardo's ability to sublimate them into nonsexual activities. A peculiar episode in Freud's life can help elucidate the homosexual content of the Egyptian bird dream as well as of the book on Leonardo to which it is linked. On November 24, 1912, as related by Ernest Jones, who was present,[18] Freud met in the Park Hotel of Munich with several colleagues, including two Swiss, Jung and Riklin.[19] Freud complained that the Swiss were ignoring his name in their writings about psycho-analysis, and in the course of a heated argument, Freud fainted. On coming to, he spoke the strange words, "How sweet it must be to die." Soon afterward, Freud wrote to Jones to explain the attack, pointing out that in 1906 and 1908 he had suffered from similar symptoms "in the same room of the Park Hotel." The room, and indeed Munich itself, Freud notes, are strongly linked to his relation to Fliess: "I saw Munich first when I visited Fliess during his illness . . . There is some piece of unruly homosexual feeling at the root of the matter." A curious aftermath of Jones's account is his second version, written several years later in his autobiographical *Free Associations*,[20] with roughly the same details except for blotting out Fliess's name. In *The Life and Work of Sigmund Freud*, Jones quoted Freud as saying that "the room was associated with Fliess," whereas in *Free Associations* Jones says that Freud had told him of fainting on only one other occasion, years before "in that very room, the dining-room of the Park Hotel, during a painful scene with a man who was perhaps his closest friend, Oscar Rie." As an intimate of the Freudian circle, perhaps Jones himself suffered from an emotionally conditioned "Freudian slip." Or did he inadvertently expose a buried corner of Freud's life suppressed in his three-volume biography? Jung's account of the curious episode (1961) complements and helps clarify those of Freud and Jones. First of all, as Jones fails to mention, a similar fainting fit had occurred once before, in Bremen in 1909, provoked by Jung's loquacity about the subject of "peat-bog corpses," mummified bodies of prehistoric men drowned or buried in certain marshes of northern Germany, where Bremen is located. Freud, irritated by Jung's talk, several times exclaimed, "Why are you so concerned with these corpses?" and later, while they were having dinner, he suddenly fainted. Jung states that Freud was convinced that the "chatter about corpses meant [to him] that I had death-wishes toward him." With regard to the Munich incident, Jung tells us (again, as Jones does not) that beforehand the conversation had concerned Amenophis IV (Ikhnaton), who had destroyed his father's cartouches. Freud's theory that "at the back of his great creation of a monotheistic religion there lurked a father-complex" irritated Jung, who insisted that Amenophis was "a creative and profoundly religious person whose acts could not be explained by personal resistances toward his father." Actually, Jung pointed out, Amenophis held his father in esteem and destroyed only the cartouches bearing the name of the god Amon, whereas other pharoahs had replaced their fore-fathers' names with their own without inaugurating a new style or religion. "At that moment Freud slid off his chair in a faint," says Jung, who picked him up. While being carried to the next room, Freud half came to, and out of his weakness looked at Jung "as if I were his father." Jung concludes that both incidents had in common Freud's "fantasy of father-murder," especially significant for Jung, whom Freud was then regarding as his successor.

The *Leonardo* contains several allusions to the ideas associated with Fliess, such as bisexuality and left-handedness, and the role of chemical factors in determining sexuality; moreover, the demonstration that numbers played an important part in Leonardo's life as symptoms was aimed directly at Fliess's occult numerological determinism. Freud's response to the opposition of a powerful and respected figure such as Fliess or Jung probably included a homosexual component, translated into the image of sweetly dying. We might speculate that for Freud there was a great temptation to "become" (identify with) his mother, the all-powerful being who sustained and nursed him, and that the homosexual component was related to his desire not to have her in the manner of the later Oedipal impulses he describes, but to be inside her as a child, fusing with her body; therefore, "dying" or going back to where you came from (the womb) would be the psychological equivalent of orgasm. The other side of this intense attraction to his mother—a deep resentment, caused by his need to survive and keep his own ego—is expressed by his aggressive image of his mother's dying, and by his fascination with the image of the Medusa ("Medusa's Head," 1922), a representation of the hairy female genitals that rouse, he says, "a terror of castration." Freud's conflicted yearning for the Ur-mother (as he called the mother of his earliest years) seems to have been so strong that he never could accept heterosexuality with full enjoyment, to judge from recent discussions of his sex life,[21] nor—like the Leonardo he describes—did he ever realize his homosexual impulses as an adult, except perhaps indirectly, as in his legendary requirement that all his close colleagues, like him, smoke cigars. Some light may be cast on the question of Freud's fears of sex and women from a footnote added to the second edition of *The Interpretation of Dreams*,[22] which was published in the same year that he fainted during Jung's talk about the mummified corpses. In the note, Freud speaks of the importance of fantasies about life in the womb, which he feels "contain an explanation of the remarkable dread that many people have of being buried alive," and also provide "the unconscious basis for the belief in survival after death." Freud also later explained in "The Uncanny" (1919) how "the idea of being buried alive," "the most uncanny of all," was based on the pleasurable fantasy of returning to the womb.[23]

The crucial conflict between his desire to lose himself in his mother and to separate from her in order to achieve individuality gave rise to Freud's Faustian restlessness, and his never quite satisfied attempt to find a father figure with whom to identify. This problem of identification may help explain how Freud came to deny the Jewishness of one of his chief heroes, Moses, through making him an Egyptian. Freud alluded to Moses throughout his adult life, and may have begun to reflect on the prophet already as a boy of seven, when his father showed him the Philippson Bible. Freud's quite secular but profound interest in Moses accounts for his fascination with the famous statue of the prophet by Michelangelo, which he saw in the church of S. Pietro in Vincoli, Rome, first in 1901 and then at various times later (*Fig. 14*). Freud's problems may also help account for certain curious memory lapses and oddities in his behavior toward the subject of Moses.

It is known from his letters that in September, 1912, Freud visited this statue often, and already planned to write something on it, but started the actual writing in the fall of 1913. Curiously Freud, in a letter written twenty-one years later,[24] gives the *month* correctly but mistakes the year when he speaks of visiting the statue during "three lonely weeks in September 1913." If we add to this the fact that Freud published the work anonymously, we begin to suspect that, like the *Leonardo*, his study of Michelangelo's *Moses* was more than an exercise in objective scholarship. In his essay, Freud noted that no piece of statuary ever made a stronger impression on him, and that while in Rome he often came alone to the church to see it. He responded to its powerful impact by regarding it as an inscrutable work whose mystery he wished to divine. Upon researching the views of art critics and historians, he felt dissatisfaction, above all, with the interpretations of the mood of Moses that the artist intended to convey. At first Freud was inclined to agree with the general opinion that Michelangelo meant to represent the great leader just as he spied his disobedient followers worshiping the golden calf, at the critical moment before his outburst of rage; but after much thought, he concluded that the artist shows us Moses *after* his explosion of rage at the faithless, and in the process of restraining himself. Thus Michelangelo created not a historical figure, but a timeless "character-type, embodying an inexhaustible inner force which tames the recalcitrant world." According to Freud's interpretation, Michelangelo has revealed the superior character of the law-giver; for Moses

> will neither leap up nor cast the Tables from him. What we see before us is not the inception of a violent action but the remains of a movement that has already taken place. In his first transport of fury, Moses desired to act, to spring up and take vengeance and forget the Tables; but he has overcome the temptation, and he will now remain seated and still in his frozen wrath and in his pain mingled with contempt.

Jones,[25] noting the resemblance between Freud's situation in 1913 and his interpretation of Michelangelo's statue, has pointed out that Freud's essay, far from being a cool and objective analysis, may have served him as a screen on which to project some of his concurrent anxieties and wishes. As Jones put it: "Was Moses on descending Mt. Sinai unable to control his anger as the Bible related, or could he attain the heights of self-control which Freud maintained Michelangelo depicted? We know that this preoccupation coincided with the time he was suppressing his own indignation at the way his Swiss followers had suddenly repudiated his work." In this context, Freud's confusion of 1912 and 1913 (not discussed by Jones) becomes intelligible: Freud was implicitly signifying that his identification with the powerful but self-restrained figure of the law-giver in 1912 really was repeated in his own experience with his followers in 1913. The explanation of Freud's behavior in terms of his identification with Moses corroborates Jones's comparison of the two men, and seems all the more convincing since this resemblance can be demonstrated to have lasted up to his old age, when he was often described as patriarchal in manner.[26] It

should also be noted here that Freud, aware of the incipient dis-
sensions among his Swiss followers, had already, in February, 1912,
published an archaeological anecdote, "Great Is the Diana of the
Ephesians," an excerpt from a book by Sartiaux, a French art historian.
The allegorical content of this excerpt has been insightfully explained
by Henri Ellenberger[27] in terms of Freud's identification with Saint
Paul, whose disciples are turned from him through the betrayal of his
once faithful follower John (Jung), a disciple of mystical tendencies.

While Jones's discussion of the Freudian identification with Moses
is on the right track, its simplistic treatment of so complex a personality
is not wholly satisfying. Freud responded to Michelangelo's *Moses* not
only as to an admired hero with whom he could identify, but also as to
the wrathful law-giver whom he feared; indeed, in the same essay, he
describes how as he stood before the statue, he "attempted to support
the angry scorn of the hero's glance. Sometimes I have crept cautiously
out of the half-gloom of the interior as though I myself belonged to the
mob upon whom his eye is turned—the mob which can hold fast no
conviction, which has neither faith nor patience and which rejoices
when it has regained its illusory idols." Here Freud, unable to sustain
his identification with the all-powerful paternal figure, reveals a secret
wish to lose himself in the tribe of the "sons," a wish that evidently
made him quite uneasy.

Freud's ambivalence toward Moses, on the one hand admiring and
identifying with the law-giver as a protective father, and on the other,
feeling uneasiness and even anxiety before him as a dangerous power,
fits clearly into the pattern Freud himself defined as the Oedipus complex, in which a son identifies with his own father as his mother's husband, and at the same time wishes to remove his father as a rival for his
mother's love. Freud's ambivalence toward his father manifested itself
in part in his mixed attitudes about being a Jew; thus, the twelve-year-
old Freud must have felt both sympathy and distress, as well as secret
satisfaction on seeing his much-admired father humiliated when the
anti-Semite knocked his hat off. Freud explains that he expressed his
feelings of disappointment and contempt by seeking father substitutes,
Semitic heroes like Hannibal and Napoleon's marshal Masséna (presumed to be Jewish). Not unexpectedly, Freud's public stance indicated
a firm pride in his Jewish heritage (whereas in private, he probably

dreamed of becoming a non-Jew as a solution to his shame and anger at his father), and in the last year of his life, on May 12, 1938, as he fled from Vienna to London to avoid the Nazis, Freud wrote to his son Ernst, "Sometimes I see myself as a Jakob [his father's name] being taken by his children to Egypt when he was very old."

The question of Freud's Jewishness may, in fact, be linked to even deeper levels of emotional involvement. Still wrestling, late in life, with his own guilt for wishing the death of his long-deceased father, a guilt he analyzed at length in terms of the Oedipus complex, Freud sought relief both from his internal self-oppression and from the external social and political oppression he was experiencing with increasing intensity in Vienna. The psychoanalyst's complex mind explored solutions in more than one direction: becoming with old age more and more like his father, the powerful and rebellious son becoming the oppressed and defeated father, Freud released some of his guilt on one level by making Moses a non-Jew in *Moses and Monotheism* of 1939,[28] thereby opening the way to assimilation; moreover, if Moses is Egyptian, then he's not the Jewish father Freud displaced (that is, killed in fantasy). It must be remembered that in the Vienna of Freud's youth, assimilation was a commonly proposed solution advanced in the liberal Jewish circles Freud's family frequented. Another, perhaps more deeply satisfying solution linked to his creative genius probably occurred to him. Freud apparently sustained throughout life the conviction that he was unique, grounding his belief not only on his ability, but on his unusual position within his family, since he was younger than any of his father's children by a first marriage, but the oldest and dominant child, and the favorite among his own mother's children. Freud apparently took a special pride and pleasure in being alone with his creations: for, although he seems to express regret at his "loneliness" in his "Address to the Society of B'nai Brith" (1926), he may have secretly exulted over his position. His explanation that "the announcement of my unpleasing discoveries had as its result the severance of the greater part of my human contacts" appears now quite questionable since Ellenberger (1970) has marshaled studies showing that, in fact, Freud's works were never ignored nor was he ever isolated. We are left to conclude that Freud *wished* to be "the only one," and so came to believe it. In his special family constellation, he was like a triumphant Oedipus, at once son to his parents and older siblings, and father to his younger siblings. No lonelier than God, and continually creating new ideas, Freud must have exulted over his good fortune; for, as he himself put it in an essay already quoted ("A Special Type of Choice of Object," 1910), "All the son's instincts are gratified by the wish to be the father of himself."

As the first psychoanalyst, father of a whole movement, and as one of the few who remained completely self-analyzed (although he recognized the limitations imposed by his self-analysis, he claimed that analysis of himself by one of his own pupils would have been impossible), Freud might well have felt self-begotten, a leader above and beyond his followers, like his great model Moses. If even this triumphant identification turned out to be unstable, and Moses had to become in his eyes a non-Jew, we must seek the ultimate reasons in the shadowy first years of his life, when the dominant relation to his awesome mother fixed in him for life an insatiable lust for power, coupled with a Faustian instability. No wonder that in summing up his personality to Fliess, he called himself a conquistador.

Freud's hunger for conquest may have originated very early, perhaps at the breast of his (for him) all-powerful and all-providing mother, and in making his father the butt of his constant rejection through mockery and the quest for bigger and better father substitutes, he may have only been looking for easier targets than his mother. Something of this condition became visible through Freud's identification with Goethe, which probably dates back to his youth, but which—as Wittels (1930) has shown—is clearly present in the dream of "Goethe's Attack on Herr M." (*Interpretation of Dreams*). With some justification, Ludwig Marcuse (1956) could say, "Freud's failure to recognize the boundaries between Goethe and himself was one of the few illusions of this very illusionless scientist." Freud's discussion of Goethe offers an important means for perceiving this terrifying relation to the mother. In concluding his study "A Childhood Recollection from 'Dichtung und Wahrheit'" (1917), Freud commented, "He who has been the undisputed darling of his mother retains throughout life that victorious feeling, that confidence in ultimate success which not seldom brings actual success with it." It is somewhat ironic that this study mainly discusses the rage excited in this "undisputed darling" by the birth of a new sibling rival, feelings Freud himself deeply shared in his own youth. An even stronger affinity between the two "conquistadors" of life can be perceived in Freud's conclusion: "And a saying such as 'My strength has its roots in my relation to my mother' might well have been put at the head of Goethe's autobiography." Freud's sympathy with Goethe extended even to associating the ironic play on his own name (Freud(e)-Joyeuse) to a similar abuse of the poet's name by Herder, who compared "Goethe" to the words *Götter* (gods), *Gothen* (Goths), and *Kote* (dung).

The allusion to Goethe's name terminates Freud's dream of "The Three Fates," also recounted in *The Interpretation of Dreams*, which contains material that can illuminate Freud's attitudes toward his father and his "Ur-mother." Freud dreamed he went into a kitchen for pudding and saw three women standing in it; one of them, "the hostess of the inn was twisting something about in her hand, as though she was making *Knödel* or dumplings." She told him he had to wait "till she was ready," whereupon he became impatient "and went off with a sense of injury. I put on an overcoat. But the first I tried was too long for me." On taking it off, he found to his surprise that it was trimmed with fur. He put on another one that had "a long strip with a Turkish design" on it. Then a stranger came up who had "a long face and a short pointed beard," and "tried to prevent my putting it on, saying it was his." When shown the Turkish pattern embroidered on the coat, he asked, " 'What have the Turkish [designs, stripes, etc.] to do with you?' But we then became quite friendly with each other." Freud's interpretation connected the three women to the three fates "who spin the destiny of man," and indeed one of the three women was his mother, the one who had given him life, and who had explained to him when he was six years old that he would one day die and return to the earth of which he is made. Freud's rich and complex associations include plagiarism and hunger (especially for mother's milk); in particular, he elaborates the detail of the stranger with the long face and pointed beard, who turns out to have been a shopkeeper from Spalato in Yugoslavia who had sold some Turkish stuffs to Freud's wife. "He was called Popović, an equivocal name." We may note that "Popo" is a word often used in Austria by children to indicate the "behind"; moreover, in its diminutive form, *Popöchen*, psychoanalysts find also an allusion to the penis.[29] The beard, too, has sexual connotations in some German literature; indeed, Arthur Schopenhauer wrote that "the beard ... is ... as an indication of sex in the fore-front of the face, obscene, and this is why it pleases women." [30]

Freud's interpretation of the dream, however, seems to omit its most interesting aspects, and I should like here to present my own interpretation, which links together a number of elements to be found in his later writings. Freud's mother was working in the kitchen making children (*Knödel*), which would produce sibling rivals, who were "plagiarizing" his unique situation. In his own desire for her (but not siblings), he put on a condom (Freud's own interpretation of overcoats in dreams), but found his penis much smaller than his father's. Then he tried again, feeling like the Turks, of whom he remarked (as we remember) in the Signorelli example, that they "value sexual pleasure above all else." Next his father—a "stranger" (compare with the previous *Leonardo* discussion), in accord with the "family romance"— with his long penis and his beard came up and claimed the condom and Freud's mother for himself, pointing out that the Turkish sentiments about sex had little to do with Freud. At this point, they apparently became friends instead of rivals. [31] Actually, of course, Freud expressed his resentment by joking about the name of the stranger, Popović, who appropriately is a merchant like his father. The insult to his own father through associating "Popo" to "Papa" closely follows the technique in a case of visual obsession that Freud analyzed during 1916. The patient used the word *Vaterarsch*, which Freud interpreted as combining patriarch and "father-ass," ideas of awe and derogation: the very feelings he must have experienced intensely during the last weeks of his father's life, when the old man suffered complete paralysis of the intestines. In many places, the contest with his father shifted ground from the behind to the penis, and is often expressed in pervasive images of urination or squirting. In his dream about an outhouse where he sprayed away faeces with his urine, Freud compared himself to Hercules cleaning the Augean stables. And he expressed megalomanic feelings through images culled partly from reading before going to bed Rabelais's text about how his superman Gargantua sat astride Notre Dame of Paris and turned "his stream of urine upon the city," and partly from looking at Jules Garnier's illustrations to the book (*Figs. 15 and 16*). The image of urinating, so important in Freud's book (the *only* illustration to it, from the fourth edition on, was "A French Nurse's Dream" on this very subject; see *Fig. 17*), is obviously linked to an experience recounted in his "Dream of Count Thun." In it, Freud associated his feelings of ambition with the famous episode in which he wet his bed at the age of seven or eight, and was reprimanded by his father with the words "The boy will come to nothing" (the whole dream book was, in a sense, Freud's ambitious reply to his father). Freud mingles associations in the dream to the sensual Paris of Zola's novels (from which he derives the appropriate name of a French flower, *pisse-en-lit*) and to the uproarious egoism and braggadocio of Gargantua, whose language of bodily functions he adopts. Freud loved Paris, and so one might wonder at his identification with its desecrater. Perhaps as a Jew, Freud felt rather aggressive in these years toward the Paris that condemned his hero, the Dreyfusard Zola, and with unconscious wit sullied the Parisian coat of arms he knew so well and admired in his letters to Fliess—*Fluctuat nec mergitur.*

It is quite likely that the experiences of the night before that provided the content of his dream had to do with the increasing difficulty Freud and his wife presumably had after the birth of Anna (their last child) in 1895, and maybe with the common practice of withdrawal as a contraceptive measure: Freud, who perhaps ejaculated prematurely after being told to wait till Martha was ready, would have felt his impotence (possibly also connected with resentment of the strong and maternal Martha) as akin to his infantile situation between the powerful couple of father and mother. He had tried to be his father to his giant mother, but had found himself too little. It is understandable that *The Interpretation of Dreams* should be filled with subtle reproaches leveled by the dreamer Freud at his wife Martha.

Freud's reproaches to Martha betray his secret suspicion that the golden childhood to which he often refers was in reality not so perfect. The resentment against his mother (fused to his image of the Catholic nanny) and against all women, supported by the prejudices of a patriarchal society, remained with him all his life; on the one hand, it inspired his invidious theory that women inevitably envy men for their penises and, on the other, prevented him from ever satisfactorily completing the analysis of a woman. His mocking of the efforts of women to achieve emancipation [32] and his excessively protective tenderness toward his fiancée Martha, his "little princess," his "gentle, sweet girl" who was unthinkable as colleague or competitor, and who belonged in the home (and was fulfilled there), all point to a Victorian dogmatism from which the otherwise deeply innovative thinker was never to free himself.

Freud's continual engagement with the memory of his father is resumed once more in his great essay "Dostoievsky and Parricide," written in 1926–27 and published in 1928, which mainly centers on *The Brothers Karamazov*. Freud's interest in Dostoievsky dates back at least to 1920; for, in a letter of October 19, 1920, to Stefan Zweig, stimulated by the discussion of the Russian genius in Zweig's *Three Masters*, Freud already suggested both the importance of hysteria in Dostoievsky's makeup, and that *The Brothers Karamazov* "treats the most personal problem of Dostoievsky, parricide." In this essay the debate with Fliess over the organic vs. the psychological explanation of hysteria, bisexuality, the Oedipus complex, and the limits of the psychoanalytic explanation of art, are intertwined in a matrix highly significant for understanding Freud. In effect, he seems to have picked up the major questions of his *Leonardo*, probably regarding them as incompletely or unsatisfactorily answered.

Freud analyzes Dostoievsky's character through the study of both his writings and his biography, and concludes that the writer suffered from neurotic epilepsy, postdating the trauma of his eighteenth year when his father was murdered. Dostoievsky's fits and death seizures represented an identification with the dead man, and expressed self-punishment for the earlier wish for his father's death. Freud characterizes Dostoievsky in terms of hysteria and traces this—as he had already done in his essay of 1908—to a constitutional factor of bisexuality: in his death seizures Dostoievsky became the father, "but the dead father." This behavior is linked to the Oedipal situation in which the "Queen-mother is won after repeating the slaying of the father by killing the Sphinx, the monster that symbolizes the father."

A scrutiny of Freud's discussion reveals subjectively motivated inconsistencies as impressive as those we found in the *Leonardo*. First of all, Freud incorrectly refers to Oedipus's sphinx as a symbol of the father, whereas the monster in Greek mythology is always female, a detail displayed on the breasted sphinx in the engraving of Ingres's painting owned by Freud, and well known to Freud's contemporaries (witness Hugo von Hofmannsthal's play of 1913, *Ödipus und die Sphinx*); however, the Egyptian sphinx is almost invariably a symbol of the king, and this must be the source of Freud's confusion. Consistent with his making the riddling sphinx a man, Freud emphasizes at the end of his article that there is nothing puzzling (*rätselhaft*) in a woman's love life. Secondly, Freud calls the fate "ultimately only a later father projection," without even alluding to his emphatically stated opinion in "The Theme of the Three Caskets" (1913) that the three fates represent for a man his relation to woman as mother, companion, and destroyer, or to "the figure of the mother as life proceeds: the mother herself, the beloved who is chosen after her pattern, and finally the Mother Earth who receives him again." To these two snubs of the woman in Freud's essay may be added a third, even more important, noted by Harry Slochower (1959), who shows that Freud does not discuss the hero's mother Katya, for whose love he and his father vie: "That the master of the Oedipus complex should have missed the major incest figure in the novel seemed incredible to me." Actually, Slochower maintains, Freud does allude, albeit unconsciously, to a mother figure in an apparent digression on a story by Stefan Zweig, analogous to Dostoievsky's, which is in fact essential for his analysis. In attempting to explain this omission, Slochower turns to Freud's relations to women, pointing out that his Oedipal scheme is patriarchal and has little to say about matriarchy "beyond noting that 'the maternal inheritance is older than the paternal one.'" Freud, Slochower says, held the nineteenth-century German conception of woman as a "soft, giving, non-competitive figure"; but, Martha was by no means weak, and actually had "'a firmness of character that did not readily lend itself to being molded.'"[33] Moreover, Freud depended on Martha, who was stronger than he in major personal issues; and resenting that dependence, he reproached her often.[34] Martha's combination of competitive masculine qualities with sweetness threatened Freud's ideal conception of woman, Slochower maintains, so that Freud failed to appreciate the historic function of the matriarchy and did not consciously recognize Katya's dominating personality as a mother figure in Dostoievsky's novel.

Freud makes much of the Oedipus complex in analyzing *The Brothers Karamazov* as one of the three masterpieces of world literature, along with *Oedipus Rex* and *Hamlet*. As a modern Oedipus who prided himself on solving for all time the riddle of the sphinx, he probably hoped secretly that a fourth masterpiece would join his select list of immortals—*The Interpretation of Dreams*. But whatever its value as world literature, we may question whether Freud, in tackling the Oedipal problem, ever got to the core of his difficulties with women. Given Freud's resentment of Martha and his more general problems with women, we can be sure that his picture of an idyllic childhood at his mother's breast contains only a part of the truth, ignoring as it does the darker pre-Oedipal mother. Some of the old terror that was hinted at in the anxiety dream of the Egyptian gods at his mother's bier, seems to hover around Freud's discussion of Dostoievsky, but in terms of the later stage of the Oedipal father fears. Actually, far from being indifferent for him, woman was a subject constantly in the back of his mind, but woman not as wife or even mother so much as the Ur-mother of his earliest infancy: the confusion of the older Egyptian (male) for the Greek (female) sphinx signifies not the triumph of the male in Freud's mind, but his preoccupation with unresolved and terrifying pre-Oedipal problems.

Freud's projection of his own problems onto his analysis of *The Brothers Karamazov* not only renders the novel unclear, but also obscures his explanation of Dostoievsky's Oedipal complex, since subtle aggression replaces desire for the woman and the confusion of mother and father complicates the roles assigned to them in the Oedipal drama. It seems that Freud was less interested in the novel than in the personality of its author, toward whom he felt a powerful sense of identification mingled with revulsion. Dostoievsky's death-like seizures, which Freud linked to a homosexual impulse, must have recalled his own fainting in Munich during the quarrels with Fliess and Jung in which the feeling of dying was mingled with a voluptuous sensual pleasure. Freud's fainting constituted, then, an inverted or passive expression of his feeling of rivalry: in "dying," he would destroy the being with whom he identified. But there is also the lingering sadistic image of intercourse with his mother that the Egyptian bird dream contained— the equation of getting into the mother's body by "dying" in her, and being "buried alive," and returning to the womb. The tall (phallic) beaked monsters would represent the frightening bisexual Ur-mother whom he dared not approach. And even deeper than these problems lay the question of Freud's identity, epitomized in the sleeping figure: who was this person—his mother? his grandfather? his father? himself? All may have slept together in Freud's mind, fused within the same image.

A central concern of Freud's life (pointed out by Wittels and emphasized by Jones)—discovering a figure with whom to identify—was never to find a final solution, although he constantly circled in thought about his father as a model. In *Moses and Monotheism*, he attributed the greatness of men like Goethe, Leonardo, and Beethoven to their being "the prototype of the father," and he explicitly indicated that "the great Goethe, who in the period of his genius certainly looked down on his unbending and pedantic father, in his old age developed traits which formed a part of his father's character." As we have seen, Freud acknowledged in himself the same tendency to resemble his father increasingly with age; but we also know that the matter is not so simple, since—aside from the problem of his relation to his mother—Freud also felt a strong need to deny his closeness to his father. His argument against the Jewishness of Moses means in this context that he was escaping from ties to his father. He also came eventually to wish a new identity for another of his models, Shakespeare.[35] Freud compared *Hamlet* to *Oedipus* as early as October 15, 1897, in a letter to Fliess, almost one year after his own father's death on October 23, 1896; and his identification with Hamlet brought him to identify with Shakespeare with whose "own psychology . . . we are confronted in *Hamlet*."[36] Freud, who must already have noted that *Hamlet* treats the relation of the son to his parents in Oedipal terms, found in Brandes's work on Shakespeare of 1896 the comment that the "drama was composed immediately after the death of Shakespeare's father (1601)." Similarly, the production of Freud's own masterpiece on dreams was written, as he said in the preface to the second edition of 1908, "as my reaction to my father's death." Just as he did with Moses, Freud years later undermined the simple identification of Shakespeare and, relying on a very weak source, questioned whether the genial creations could have been done not by the low-born and uneducated son of a Stratford petit-bourgeois but by the "high-born and well-educated . . . aristocrat Edward de Vere, Earl of Oxford." His own "family-romance" framework beautifully fits this attempted shift in the identity of the greatly admired father figure to a higher and nobler status.

The analysis in the first half of this chapter has shown how involved Freud was with questions of his own identity, and that this involvement was reflected in his choice of subjects in art and literature as vehicles for finding heroic models to emulate. Furthermore, the deep unrest and the impulse continually to seek new models that characterized his earliest childhood, is connected to his dissatisfaction with his father as a model. But, we have seen that even this is an inadequate explanation for the dynamics of his search. Ultimately, we must acknowledge that he could never rest, since he had already set the terms of his problems in the inaccessible stage predating the Oedipal; that he was already discontented somehow with his mother in early childhood, and hence sought to rationalize this discontent, and to overcompensate for it by denying it and claiming a happy infancy. That this happy state was an illusion, a will-o'-the-wisp, helps account for Freud's search, and also for the instability of his identifications with great artists and writers: they were all substitutes for a deeply frustrated longing.

Three
Freud's
Theories of Art

It is commonly asserted by Freud's critics, who usually base themselves on the well-known *General Introduction to Psychoanalysis* of 1917, that he considered the artist a near-neurotic whose instincts impel him to seek fame and fortune, honor, power, and the love of women, but who lacks the ability to attain these goals. Failing real achievement, the artist seeks other interests, often even turning aside from reality to express his wishes (mainly sexual) in creating fantasies. Starting from such a position, a Freudian would presumably seek in the work of art traces of the artist's sexual or neurotic motives, and would ignore the essential qualities of form and technique that contributed to the value of the work. This apparently simplistic position stems from Freud's earliest speculations, as in a letter of May 31, 1897, to Fliess, which asserted that "the mechanism of creative writing is the same as that of hysterical phantasies." He gives the example of Goethe's combining in his Werther "something he had experienced (his love for Lotte Kastner) and something he had heard of (the fate of young Jerusalem who had killed himself)." The fantasy of Werther, which served to protect Goethe from his suicidal urges, was drawn in part from his emotional disturbance and in part from objective knowledge of someone else's behavior. Freud's position, then, is not simple even in his early formulations; indeed, in his most suggestive writings on art, Freud associated elements of immediate perception and earlier remembered experience. At his best, Freud recognized the necessity for the good artist to maintain contact with reality and to synthesize his experience with his neurotic wishes and fantasies; but the nonproductive neurotic, the daydreamer, or the bad artist in Freud's view bypassed reality or included too small a proportion in the artistic mix of reality and fantasy.[1]

As we have seen in discussing the *Gradiva*, Freud was apparently willing to grant the artist powers similar to the psychoanalyst's, insights into the mind that were unavailable to academic "scientific" psychology (which helps explain the great fascination of the Surrealists with his work, to be discussed in chapter 4); indeed, already in *The Interpretation of Dreams*, Freud often allied himself to the artists and writers whose remarks on dreams he found so much more rewarding than the dry scholarship of academic investigators. But Freud never regarded the artist's insights as really comparable to the rational understanding of the psychoanalyst; thus, in the *Minutes of the Viennese Psychoanalytic Association* of February 13, 1907, he spoke of Jensen's unawareness of psychology, and later, in the *Autobiographical Study* of 1925, he even disdainfully described *Gradiva* as having "no particular merit in itself." Freud had already concluded that the story grew out of the author's own neurotic relationship to his sister, and he was to make comments criticizing other writers for their distorted sense of reality, which made their work interesting chiefly as reflections of their own problems. From these remarks we can see how inaccurate is the claim of S. E. Hyman that Freud believed that "all artists are analysts."[2] In a letter to Fliess of June 20, 1898 Freud analyzed C. F. Meyer's story *Die Richterin* (*The Female Judge*) as "a defence against the writer's memory of an affair with his sister," which happens, he adds, "exactly as it does in neurosis." Again, in an essay of 1908, he compares the imaginative writer to the daydreamer, and the essential technique whereby the poet pleases us to a bribe that seduces us into accepting his egotistical daydreams.

The inconsistencies of Freud's positions may perhaps be reconciled if we understand that Freud usually made a distinction in the back of his mind between the ordinary artist and the genius. Some of his views doubtless stem from the Burckhardtian tradition, which saw the artist as descended from the grand models of the Renaissance individual; thus, Freud could speak of the artist in a letter (November 7, 1914) to the painter Hermann Struck as "a being of a special kind, exalted, autocratic, villainous, and at times rather incomprehensible." Here,

Freud departs somewhat from the characterization of the artist as neurotic, and allies him more to the Bohemian type of romantic vintage, with a slight touch of the awe felt by the bourgeois gentleman before such wayward creatures on the fringes of society. The link of the artist to sex was inevitable, given Freud's general attempt to reduce, especially in his early writings, all areas of adult behavior to that of the basic drives expressed so openly in childhood. Freud's famous formula in *Totem and Taboo* (1912–13), embracing the major expressions of culture, reads, "hysteria is a caricature of an artistic creation, a compulsion neurosis a caricature of a religion, and a paranoiac delusion a caricature of a philosophic system." While Freud does not maintain the converse (that a caricature is no more than a hysterical expression), the connection between these remote areas of human behavior must have startled the world and been read as an attack upon its idols.

Freud's uneasiness about the artist—clearly visible in his remarks on Martha's artist friend and in his letter to the painter Struck, and from his never having analyzed a living artist—bears directly on his oblique approach to the work of art itself; for Freud, preoccupied with the emotional and sexual aspects of the artist's mind, concentrated on these aspects of the work produced and largely ignored the more purely aesthetic ones. This would explain his centering a discussion of paintings by Leonardo on such details as the smile and the dramatic grouping of the figures, while overlooking the artist's concerns with formal composition, anatomy and perspective, line and chiaroscuro. The paintings are thus said to be linked to one another and to hypothetical childhood experiences by certain details of motif abstracted from the paintings, whereas Leonardo's characteristic formal achievement within a traditional iconography is ignored.

Freud was not unaware of these criticisms, and carefully avoided claims to a comprehensive theory of aesthetics. He stated several times his position of coy retreat before the artist's secret of achievement: "Where the artist gets his ability to create is no concern of psychology" ("The Claims of Psycho-Analysis to Scientific Interest," 1913b); "before the problem of the poet, psychoanalysis must lay down its arms" ("Dostoievsky and Parricide," 1928). In a preface (1933) to Marie Bonaparte's study of Poe, Freud insisted that psychoanalysis attempts not to explain genius, but to study the laws of the human mind as exemplified in outstanding individuals. Yet, while nominally avoiding these forbidden and perhaps unresolvable questions, Freud kept returning to art, with numerous allusions strewn throughout his writings, allusions comparable to those he made about religion, another metapsychological subject that preoccupied him, particularly in his later years. Freud's undoubted love of art as a personal and intimate experience is apparent in his passion for collecting and handling objects, but his main writings on art concern only famous and monumental works, and his discussions likewise present Freud's public face, revealing little of the tenderness he could express in his letters and conversations. These writings exhibit, rather, the "conquistador" Freud's relentless pursuit of himself, his uncovering of ever deeper layers of meaning and of a truth he felt attainable through the rediscovery and re-experience of his childhood. This search for himself doubtless imposed on him a ceaseless demand to modify his ideas and theories as well as to seek out new heroes. Like the wandering Jew Ahasverus, to whom Freud compared himself at the end of his life when compelled to leave Vienna, Freud spent his life in solitary intellectual transit. Yet Freud was obviously far from being merely self-involved; indeed, had he been a pure narcissist, turned inward and self-contemplating, his work would have had none of the exciting tension between the subjective and objective that one can sense in it. In this context, Freud's personality displays itself as two-sided: he sought himself, but he did so with a constant awareness of and interest in the outer world, the objects (whether people or things) he contemplated being the other side of his interest in himself. He learned about himself in part through his study of others' behavior, hence his interest in clinical work; and he came to grips with important questions about his perceptions and motivations through analyzing his aesthetic responses, hence his interest in analyzing art.

Defining the balance of truth and illusion in the work of art was a nagging problem for Freud's aesthetics, which generally aimed to penetrate the apparent illusion of art to a hidden and repressed truth. Thus, for Freud even the fantasies of the adult projected back to childhood as memories have a validity in the individual's development. The art of the individual, like the myth of the race, embodies "valid fantasies," a point he makes clearly with regard to Leonardo's fantasy of the vulture, comparing it to the early legends, traditions, and interpretations of a nation, which contain "historical truth lying behind the legendary material . . . In spite of all the distortions and misunderstandings, they still represent the reality of the past."[3]

Freud's point that there is a truth to the wish, a motivational truth, which can be realized in various forms by art, is nowhere so richly and complexly illustrated as in his discussion of the Oedipus complex, the feeling of guilt (which Freud considered universal) over the wish for the father's death, a feeling that embodies a racial memory of an actual "Ur-event," the killing of the primal horde father. He describes in his momentous letter to Fliess of October 15, 1897 (ideas incorporated in *The Interpretation of Dreams*), that he had realized the generality of the love of one's mother and jealousy of one's father, and that "the gripping power of *Oedipus Rex*, in spite of all the rational objections to the inexorable fate that the story presupposes, becomes intelligible." Later dramas, such as Grillparzer's *Die Ahnfrau*, which treat the same theme, do not grip us as much because they show an "arbitrary individual fate" (an interesting attempt on Freud's part to introduce an evaluative criterion). What makes the work so powerful, then, is its essential truth: "Every member of the audience was once a budding Oedipus in phantasy, and this dream-fulfillment played out in reality causes everyone to recoil in horror." He then extends his discussion to *Hamlet*, hinting at the neurotic basis of the hesitation, and implying that both works owed their greatness to the ability of their authors to tap the unconscious, a depth only genius can sustain. Freud's treatment of Hamlet as a real person who can be psychoanalyzed (like Norbert Hanold) is by no means a modern invention, and L. C. Knights's essay "How Many Children Had Lady Macbeth"[4] offers a broad discussion with bibliography on attempts as early as the end of the eighteenth century to psychologize Shakespeare, and in the romantic nineteenth century to regard Hamlet "as a real person, a recently deceased acquaintance." But Freud's dwelling on the nonclassical aspect of *Oedipus Rex* was certainly an outgrowth of the late-nineteenth-century re-evaluation of the classics—primarily considered heretofore for their ethical or literary qualities—in a decadent spirit of psychological probing, and the fascination with revealing Greek barbarism or psychosis, as in Hoffmansthal's *Elektra*.[5]

The seminal idea of the Oedipus complex has spawned a whole school of commentators. Most notable, of course, are the writings of Ernest Jones on Hamlet,[6] explaining his hesitation in Freudian terms. If, as the sympathetic critic L. C. Knights (1951) remarks, Jones's essay "helps to explain the persistence of the Hamlet legend from early times to the popularity of Shakespeare's play," it is also true, as Knights adds, that it is "impossible to believe that Hamlet is *merely* a mouthpiece," or the spontaneous expression of Shakespeare's deepest unconscious feelings. And Albert William Levi,[7] among others, opposes Jones's explanation of Hamlet's behavior in terms of psychology: "The long controversy that has raged over Hamlet's 'hesitation'—his failure to kill Claudius at prayer (III, iii)—has been, despite its intrinsic interest, largely beside the point." The delay, he believes, was occasioned by the demands of the plot, and in the interest of complexity; in fact, he notes that *Oedipus Rex*, with its less complicated development, could proceed with great speed to unfold its own treatment of the theme. In a similar vein, Philip Wheelwright devotes a whole chapter to the guilt of Oedipus (*The Burning Fountain*, 1954), in which he criticizes Freud's interpretation as irrelevant to the story (though he seems to respond more sympathetically to Erich Fromm's interpretation). Ludwig Jekels (1952) extended Freud's views on Hamlet to *Macbeth*; and A. Bronson Feldman (1956), taking clues from Jekels, considered not only *Macbeth*, but also Zola's *La Bête Humaine* to depict Oedipus complexes. Inventors of new complexes have naturally not been lacking: the anthropologist George Devereux (1953) discovered "complementary 'Laius- and Jocasta-complexes' ignored by Freud and his followers"; and Gaston Bachelard (1938) named a "Prometheus complex," which is "the Oedipus complex of the intellectual life." In his view, if the child steals the father's matches, it has nothing to do with sexual aggression but rather with the important role of fire as a powerful and pervasive metaphor for problems of disobedience, and the child's aspirations to liberty and equality with the father. While Freud seems to have been somewhat cautious about pushing his analyses into the early childhood of his great subjects, others have not been so restrained. Warner Muensterberger (1951) pursued the creative artist back into a pre-Oedipal phase, finding that "artists temporarily abandon reality" and "retreat into the 'womb,'"

1. Engraving after Raphael's *Aaron Blessing the People,*
from Philippson's Bible.

2. Engraving after Pierre-Albert Brouillet,
La Leçon clinique du Dr. Charcot, 1887.

3. Henry Fuseli, *The Nightmare*. Goethe Museum, Frankfurt.

The Night Mare.

4. Caricature of *The Nightmare*
(eighteenth-century English print). Reproduced
from Eduard Fuchs, *Geschichte der erotischen
Kunst* (Berlin, 1908).

5. Masaccio and Masolino, *The Healing of Aeneas* and *The Raising of Tabitha.*
Florence, Brancacci Chapel. Photo: Alinari Art Reference Bureau.

6. Michelangelo, *Slave*, from the Tomb of Julius II. Paris, Louvre.
Photo: Alinari Art Reference Bureau.

7. *Gradiva* (fragment of an ancient relief).
Rome, Vatican Museum. Photo: Alinari Art Reference Bureau.

8. Félicien Rops, *The Temptation of St. Anthony.* Reproduced from Arsène Alexandre *et al., Félicien Rops et son oeuvre* (Brussels, 1897).

9. Leonardo da Vinci, Mona Lisa. Paris, Louvre.
   Photo: Alinari Art Reference Bureau.

10. Leonardo da Vinci, *Virgin and St. Anne with the Infant Jesus.*
Paris, Louvre. Photo: Alinari Art Reference Bureau.

11. Engraving of an Egyptian ship of death,
    from Philippson's Bible.

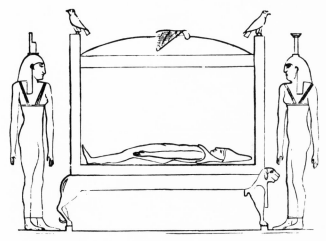

12. Engraving of an Egyptian funerary relief,
    from Philippson's Bible.

Der Sperber, Falco nisus.

13. Engraving of a
    falcon's head, from
    Philippson's Bible.

14. Michelangelo, *Moses,* from the Tomb of Julius II.
Rome, S. Pietro in Vincoli. Photo: Alinari Art Reference Bureau.

15. Illustration for
Rabelais's *Gargantua*
(Book I, Chapter 17)
by Jules Garnier.
Reproduced from
*François Rabelais
et l'oeuvre de
Jules Garnier.*
(Paris, 1897). Courtesy
Princeton University
Library.

16. Illustration for
Rabelais's *Gargantua*
(Book I, Chapter 36)
by Jules Garnier.
Reproduced from
*François Rabelais
et l'oeuvre de
Jules Garnier*
(Paris, 1897). Courtesy
Princeton University
Library.

17. *A French Nurse's Dream*. Illustration for
Freud's *The Interpretation of Dreams* (4th to 7th editions).

and that "the creative act would be a form of aggression against the phallic mother, so that the later act of killing could be interpreted as an oedipal repetition of pre-oedipal impulses."

Freud's insistence on the reality of the psychic experience in infancy, that these early experiences shape the adult—in a word, that "the child is the father of the man"—raised an interesting question in relation to the artist's identity. Freud had assigned a special role to art as the product of a singular being capable of remaining in touch with his earliest period of life and embodying those early experiences in his art. Since the adult yearns subconsciously to return to the lost world of childhood, and actually does return in dreams and neurosis, art especially interests the adult spectator as offering another pathway whereby he can return to such past experiences. Judging from the model of the study of Leonardo, the artist produces his major works and his unique contribution out of fructifying contact between a precipitating experience and a memory of childhood. This world of childhood is not at all the world of angelic innocence of the nineteenth-century Christian romantic, void of experiential impressions. For Freud, each of us carries with him into the world the burden of the whole race's experiences, transmitted somehow in the germ plasma itself, without the need for education or experience. This process of being born "guilty" closely resembles the Christian sense of guilt, and perhaps Freud himself derived some of its content from his own earliest exposures to his nanny's teachings about sin and evil; but, for Freud, the primal event is one that occurred here on earth, and is repeated symbolically daily in everyman's life, not a mystical occurrence in a higher sphere. The picaresque novel of adventure, or the novels of Dickens and Thackeray Freud so liked to read, with their heroes progressively growing up through experiencing life, have little to do with Freud's vision of the rediscovery of one's past, which I have already characterized as a *Bildungsroman* in reverse.

Freud's belief that our "racial memory" of the Oedipus events originated in real occurrences is opposed to the special "as if" reality that artists usually assign to the world of their imagination. In an interesting exchange with Yvette Guilbert, the Parisian soubrette who enchanted him, he insisted that the highly versatile actress really had had the experiences of which she sang. Freud might have gained a truer picture of Yvette's early experiences had he inquired about her vocational choice—why she *wanted* to represent so wide a variety of types, and to "experience" them in her imagination nourished by reading, the theater, and so forth. But Freud seemed rather obsessed at times about unearthing concrete experiences through his psychoanalytic archaeology.

The archaeological metaphor for psychoanalysis has been placed by several writers at the center of Freud's thinking,[8] and Freud himself, in one of his last papers ("Constructions in Analysis," 1937), returned to it in his remark that the psychoanalyst's role of construction or reconstruction "resembles to a great extent an archaeologist's excavation of some dwelling-place that has been destroyed and buried, or of some ancient edifice." This metaphor of archaeology bears strongly on his analysis of the artist, as in his *Gradiva*; for Freud always sought the early events that could serve as guidelines for better comprehending the mind of the genius, as in his studies of Leonardo and Goethe. Moreover, at a meeting of the Vienna Psychoanalytic Society on November 24, 1909, he noted that "a content has as a rule its history," and that with regard to art one could properly say that "form is the precipitate of an older content." In his emphasis on memory, Freud apparently comes close to certain aspects of Plato's thinking; actually, Jones[9] points out that Freud, who probably derived most of his knowledge of the Greek's philosophy from John Stuart Mill's essay on Plato (which he had translated in 1880), had been most impressed by a topic treated in that essay—the theory of reminiscence. Mill finds this theory epitomized in the *Meno*: "The Reminiscence Theory is maintained on the express ground that every existing thing, in itself incomplete, brings to mind a type of its own nature more perfect than itself, and as we can only be reminded of that which we once knew, we must have known the type in a former life."[10] In Mill's presentation of Plato's theory, one can find striking parallels to Freud's idea of the therapeutic role of remembering formulated in his work with Breuer (1895). The theory that joy in recognition could serve as the basis for the enjoyment of art (attributed to Aristotle) forms a link in Freud's argument in his *Jokes*,[11] and the whole theory of reminiscence provided Freud with the basis for his analyses of Jensen's *Gradiva* and of Leonardo's paintings. It is quite possible that Freud's old friend from the 1890's on, the distinguished archaeologist Emmanuel Loewy, who had developed in his works the theory that artistic patterns are based on primitive images residual in the collective memory, may have influenced the psychoanalyst's ideas about the role of memory in art.[12]

Creative inspiration depends, in Freud's view, on an ability of the artist to tap through memory and recognition the lost images and feelings of his childhood past. This ability is available to the artist and poet, who have the advantage of being less bound than most men by the repressive aspects of culture; in Freud's words, he has "flexibility of repression," meaning that the artist has access more easily to the riches of his childhood experience. Freud attempted to explain why the poet or artist would wish to offer, and the audience or spectators would wish to receive, these residues of long-past experience, in two major works *The Interpretation of Dreams* and the book on jokes.

The Interpretation of Dreams contains Freud's two major contributions to psychology that have had the greatest impact on art and the criticism of art: his conception of the unconscious, and his theory of the pleasure principle. The work of Freud's many anticipators in the study of the unconscious has often been described (most recently in the survey by Ellenberger, 1970). Characteristic was the popular work of the German pessimistic philosopher Eduard von Hartmann (*Philosophy of the Unconscious*, 1867), who, like Hegel and Schopenhauer before him, saw a tension between the ideal and the real, which he tried to overcome by declaring the unity of reason and will in an "absolute unconscious." Von Hartmann's confidence in the determination of all conscious thought by the unconscious was shared by Freud, who acknowledged the philosopher in a note to *The Interpretation of Dreams*.[13] To the frequently presented nineteenth-century ideal of an unconscious, Freud added a novel idea in distinguishing between two unconscious processes—the primary, or absolute, and the secondary, or preconscious—of fundamentally different character.

In attempting to make sense of dreams, neurosis, and irrational behavior, Freud speculated that all of these aspects of mental activity involved transfers of energy whose tensions and discharges governed the motives of men. The absolute unconscious, the one that is inaccessible to thought, operates through the primary process, in which hypothetical units of energy move freely and without restrictions;

whereas the energies within the second division of the unconscious, called the preconscious, are bound, directed, and attached to real satisfactions. The great difficulties Freud faced, and to which he devoted much of his thinking, are, first, the problem of the mechanisms whereby the two systems relate to one another, and second, of the translation of the ordinary mental operations such as perception and memory into the new terms. Freud attempted to relate the two systems essentially by a quantitative exchange of energy, with the "ego" (a vaguely defined notion of the self) considered as an organism that has a constant charge ("cathexis") of energy. Freud postulated a link from perception to memory to motor activity, and accepted the old reflex-arc theory that excitations flow from the organs of perception to the muscles where they are discharged in purposeful activity that can satisfy the drive to gain pleasure, and to avoid pain according to the pleasure (originally unpleasure) principle.

While the nature of the flow of energy in the two systems is very different, Freud considered their aim to be identical; namely, to seek the satisfaction of a wish, and in this respect, all thinking can be summed up as a path leading toward the goal of wish fulfillment. The uncontrolled primary process has the quality of infantile wish fulfillment, whereas the secondary process has the capacity to inhibit or bind the free energies of the primary process and thereby to charge the ideas with energy, which can find an outlet in motor behavior leading to real satisfactions. The two systems make use of memories in very different ways: the first, moving back further and further in time toward infant satisfactions, like the dream; while the second moves to relevant, helpful, and causally related memories that will aid in reaching the goal of finding pleasure or terminating unpleasure. Freud distinguished between a "progressive" direction leading from perception to motor responses and to the formation of a memory trace, and a "regressive" one, moving back from the memory trace toward the entering perceptions, thereby creating a hallucinatory "perception" of a satisfaction.

Freud used the notion of regression in a second sense to mean a turning back of emotions to an earlier condition. Thus, the experience of the dream is a regression both in terms of the hallucinatory perceptions involved, and in terms of the return to older, infantile wishes.

These wishes belong to the unconscious system, but are never lost, Freud theorizes, and are exposed to the adult at certain moments of his experience, such as in dream or through neurotic unfulfillment. The importance of linking up a long-buried wish with present perceptions, and the complicated interplays that can result, were traced out by Freud in the *Gradiva*, but a year later, in 1908, he turned even more explicitly to the theme of the relation of adult thinking to childish and egocentric wishes, in his essay "Poets and Daydreaming."

Before turning to a detailed discussion of regression, we should see how the workings of the dream relate to the work of art. Although Freud denied in one place that what he called the dream-work could of itself bring about such "manifestations of judgment, criticism, surprise or deductive reasoning as are met with in dreams,"[14] he clearly asserted elsewhere (1914c) that dream interpretation could help us understand poetry, and that the conception of "unconscious psychic activity enabled us to get the first glimpse into the nature of poetic creativeness." In fact, on December 11, 1907, at a meeting of the Vienna Psychoanalytic Society, Freud affirmed that whereas "pathography cannot show anything new, psychoanalysis, on the other hand, provides information about the creative process." From these hints, it seems that the curious world of the unconscious, the primary system, the buried and never-conscious world of the dream, was for Freud somewhat like the "interior Africa" of which the romantics and later Raymond Roussel spoke: a lost continent whose geography he for the first time described in its main outlines. At certain moments Freud insisted on the centrality of the unconscious, from which all the achievements of art and literature come: "We are probably much too inclined to overestimate the conscious character even of intellectual and artistic production." He believed that the most essential part of the creations of geniuses such as Goethe and Helmholtz "came to them in the form of inspirations" as a result of unconscious thinking. The unconscious is the true psychic reality whose inner nature, somewhat like a Kantian *Ding-an-sich*, "is just as much unknown to us as the reality of the external world." Because of the importance assigned to this achievement, we must now turn to these discoveries of Freud, especially in order to see their applications not merely within the dream world itself, but to the world of art and literature.

The meaning and purpose of the dream-work can best be introduced by considering its relation to repression. Freud regarded repression as the foundation stone for his whole psychoanalytic structure, and defined its function as "rejecting and keeping something out of consciousness" in order to avoid pain. Repression usually results when wishes, especially sexual ones, come into conflict with a person's ethical or aesthetic values. Such conflicts imply a dynamic and dramatic conception of the mind, one in which forces struggle to arise from the unconscious, below, and are pushed back from the conscious, above. The dream, occurring precisely on the border between these two different worlds, presents a manifest content on the surface of consciousness, which corresponds to latent dream thoughts derived from the depths of the unconscious. The problem of the interpretation of dreams meant for Freud the translation of the "hieroglyphics" of the dream content into the language of the underlying dream thoughts. Dreams are picture puzzles or rebuses, which are not to be treated like rational artistic compositions, as older interpreters of dreams had mistakenly done. Freud cites an example of a dream that included in part a house with a boat on the roof, then a single letter, then a headless figure running. He notes how absurd it is for a headless figure to run and for a landscape to contain the letters of the alphabet, probably without realizing that the art of the very next decade was to make just such elements prominent (Chagall, Picasso).

The distortion of meanings that occurs when unconscious thought becomes the conscious, or manifest, content of the dream is linked by Freud to the operation of a censor, which represents our moral and ethical resistance to the sexual and aggressive components of the unconscious. The latter components are not annihilated, only disguised. As Freud pointed out in the discussion of the Vienna Psychoanalytic Society of December 11, 1907, to which we have already referred, "The relationship between the contents of the conscious and of the unconscious" is that "the elements are the same, but the order is changed in many ways." The laws of this distortion—the dream-work —form the heart and the most rewarding aspect of Freud's whole analysis, or "archaeology," of dreams.

The far-reaching and fundamental process of condensation, whose intensity varies in degree from person to person and indeed from dream to dream, explains how the meager and patchy dream can signify the rich, extensive, and even fantastic dream thoughts. We have already seen how the sparse remembered fragments of "The Dream of Irma's Injection" indicated a whole world of unexpected and far-reaching ideas, and a similar richness underlay the apparently trivial and insignificant slips and errors such as those analyzed in *The Psychopathology of Everyday Life*. While Freud does not extensively discuss condensation in literature, his dream analyses constantly incorporate literary associations,[15] and in many places he implies that there is much more than meets the eye in any piece of literature. Little would be new in this were it not for the brilliance with which Freud described hidden meanings in apparently quite simple and obvious statements, and for the extraordinary potentials of the technique, which others were to realize. Although rarely emphasized in Freud's discussion of art and literature, condensation underlay his approach to these fields and its implications touch the other dream processes as well.

The work of displacement, like that of condensation, serves to disguise the essential content of the dream thoughts, by displacing emphasis from the important to the trivial or irrelevant. Freud accounts both for condensation and for displacement, in terms of a powerful phenomenon occurring in all dreams, overdetermination—the reappearance of every element of the dream content in the dream thoughts. As an example, the word "amyls" in "The Dream of Irma's Injection" is cited, with its reappearances in association with propyls, trimethylamin, Wilhelm (Fliess), propylaeum, and so forth. The multiple determination of one element accounts both for the condensed aspect of the dream, which is really richer in thought than it first appears, and for the shift from the main thoughts to such peripheral ones as the name of the chemical compound. In literature and art, one must seek in the periods of mannerist art for the peculiar temperament that would demand such shifts of emphasis: for more classically oriented periods would surely reject them. As we shall presently see, Freud almost exclusively chose works in which the main point is clear and central, although many of his followers have attempted to expand secondary aspects even of classical works in order to make far-fetched analyses.

A third process of the dream-work, the regard for conditions of representability, is of the utmost interest for the potential application of Freud's views to art and literature. Freud notes that in addition to the first type of displacement, in which one particular idea replaces another to which it is somehow related, there is a second, in which a verbal expression substitutes for the thought. In this case, a pictorial and concrete expression replaces a colorless and abstract one, with the advantage for the dream that a pictorial thing is "capable of being represented." This pictorial language, which is "not made with the intention of being understood," can nevertheless be translated like ancient hieroglyphic scripts, but in interpreting dream elements we must face the problem of their ambiguity: should they be taken in a positive or negative sense; historically, as recollection; symbolically; or in terms of their wording? To the question of representability belong the representation of logical relations and the role of symbolism.

Freud describes among the means of representation of logical relations some extraordinary devices of interest to writers and artists; for such relations are represented by the "formal characteristics of dreams." Thus, he notes that in dreams logical connection is reproduced by simultaneity in time, rather as in Raphael's *School of Athens* or in his *Parnassus*, which places the philosophers or poets of different epochs in one group, although they had, of course, "never in fact assembled in a single hall or on a single mountain-top." To this example from art illustrating how elements close together in the dream imply a similarly close connection between their underlying dream thoughts, he adds one from writing: the letters "ab," which are close together, are to be pronounced as one syllable, whereas a gap between them implies that the "a" is the last letter of one word and the "b" the first of the next. Causal relations may be represented either by mere sequence, in which a shorter preliminary dream may stand for an "if clause" and a longer main dream, for a "then clause," or by the transformation of one image into another. Alternatives do not exist in dreams, and for "either-or" one should substitute "and"; that is, as Freud shows in several examples, the two or more things are really additions to one another, not alternatives. Contraries and contradictories cannot be expressed directly in dreams and so are disregarded; in fact, dreams "show a particular preference for combining contraries into a unity"; for example, the flowers in a dream he analyzes were associated at the same time with sexual innocence and guilt. Contraries can be expressed in dreams both by exchanging one person for another representing an opposite trait or character satisfying the dream censor, and by the device of turning a piece of dream content that has already appeared into "just the reverse." Freud gives the example of his dream of Goethe's attack on a young man, a reversal of the fact that a young critic had attacked his much admired, "Goethean" friend Fliess. A final logical relation, and the one most frequently appearing in the mechanism of dream formation, is similarity, what Freud also calls "the relation of 'just as.' " This relation, which "constitutes the first foundation for the construction of a dream," can be represented in a variety of ways and is assisted by condensation. Similarity and possession of common attributes are represented by unification through the dream's either using materials already present ("identification" with persons) or freshly constructing new syntheses ("composition" of different things).

Through identification, several persons linked by a common element will appear in the manifest content of the dream under the guise of one covering figure, but since, as Freud remarks, "every dream deals with the dreamer himself," this figure is really a disguise under which the dreamer himself is hidden. In "Creative Writers and Daydreaming" (1908c), Freud extended this point from the dream to a broad class of modern literature, in which the writer splits portions of his own ego into several characters for his novel.[16] While identifications can be extended to other than persons—for example, proper names of localities, as in Freud's identification of Rome and Prague in a dream— the process of composition seems to be more frequent with things. Freud compares the composite images constructed in dreams to imagined centaurs and dragons, with the important difference that the production of the imaginary figure in waking life is determined by the effect on spectators intended by the new structure; whereas the formation of the composite structure in a dream is determined by a factor extraneous to its actual shape—the dream thoughts represented. As an example of a composite structure, Freud cites a dream of a woman patient in which a thing resembling a bathing hut at the seaside, an outhouse, and an attic appears. Observing that the first two elements were both linked to people being naked and undressing, he notes that "their combination with the third element leads to the conclusion that [in her childhood] an attic had also been a scene of undressing."

A fourth factor in dream construction, the secondary revision (mistranslated by Brill as secondary elaboration), results from critical feelings "in which the dreamer is surprised, annoyed or repelled in the dream." To make the dream tolerable to the never-sleeping censorship that had inadvertently let it through and can no longer suppress it, the dreamer thinks, "This is only a dream." This contribution to the dream comes not from the dream thoughts, and resembles the psychical function of waking thought; indeed, this function of dream censorship occurs regularly at the moment before waking. A more important aspect of the revision concerns the additions and interpolations made in the dream in order to fill in the lapses in the story or to make sense out of some of the dream's illogic. Although these connecting thoughts were not in the original dream, they nevertheless lead back to material in the dream thoughts, and usually do not make new creations. Freud does not deny that this factor "has the capacity to create new contributions to dreams," but he emphasizes that it acts "principally by its preferences and selections from psychical material in the dream-thoughts that have already been formed." This possibility of contributing something new is of importance, for Freud calls this element of dream thought "fantasy." Freud compares fantasy to the daydream, a phenomenon that is not only of interest to imaginative writers such as Alphonse Daudet (in *Le Nabab*), but which is itself allied to the writer's own imaginative production, as he pointed out in "Creative Writers and Daydreaming."[17]

The relation of the whole process of the dream-work to creative and imaginative thought was recognized by Freud and his followers, and in the fourth to the seventh editions of *The Interpretation of Dreams*, the chapter on dream-work was followed by essays of Rank on "Dreams and Creative Writing" and "Dreams and Myths." That they were later removed from editions of his collected works does not diminish their significance for Freud, who had once wanted them included. It must be observed that for Freud, the dream-work belongs together with neurosis, the psychopathology of everyday life, and the pathology of genius rather than in aesthetics as an explanation of the creative process. When, at the meeting of the Vienna Psychoanalytic

Society on December 11, 1907, Freud asserted that psychoanalysis "provides information about the creative process," he was more sanguine than in later, more modest disclaimers about the ability of psychoanalysis to penetrate the mysteries of art.[18] It is certain that Freud never would have subjected art to an analysis based on the categories of the dream-work, especially since he regarded symbolism, the spring of creative imagination, as deriving not from the dream-work but from unconscious thinking. Still, his analyses of art, as of literature, centered on the psychic processes, with many of his insights grounded in the concepts he had worked out in the dream-work. Thus, in his discussion of the *Gradiva*, he emphasized those aspects of the story that turned on the hero's slips and fantasies and their accompanying mechanisms, such as condensation and displacement. In his analysis of the *Gradiva*, as of Michelangelo's *Moses* and Leonardo's *Virgin and St. Anne*, Freud explored the meaning of works partly in terms of mechanisms analogous to those of the dream-work, without ever equating the works to dreams, of course.

In a sense, Freud perceives all great works as unfolding dramas of the mind, as psychodramas, to use a term current in his time (Richard von Meerheimb, *Psychodramenwelt*, 1888), and later picked up by J. L. Moreno. We might term this approach a psychic realism: the landscape and details of the environment are reduced to a minimum, and the critic chooses to explore only the turning points in the emotional and intellectual life of the hero, a procedure very like that of the late-nineteenth-century critics, such as Leo Berg, and writers like Schnitzler and Proust. Adventurers in this mental landscape would be guided by laws and principles similar to the topographical ones of the dream-work (one thinks of the transforming of normal laws in the imaginative world of Flatland with its two-dimensional creatures, which the writer Abbot described, or, of course, in *Alice in Wonderland*). But the dream-work, on closer study, proves not quite up to the job of comprehending this buried or internal universe. In *The Interpretation of Dreams*,[19] Freud, commenting on the nature of the symbolism of dreams, much of which is shared "with psychoneuroses, legends and popular customs," noted that "the Dream-work is doing nothing original" in its use of symbolism, but merely following "paths which it finds already laid down in the unconscious." In "Creative Writers and

Daydreaming," Freud even more explicitly compared the "imaginative writer with 'one who dreams in broad daylight,' and his creations with day-dreams"; but he distinguishes the best writers from "the less pretentious writers of romances, novels and stories, who are read all the same by the widest circles of men and women." He was careful to point out that before the fantasy of daydream can become *art*, its egocentric quality must be eliminated. Still, in another work, "On the History of the Psycho-Analytic Movement" (1914c), Freud claimed for psychoanalysis that "the concept of unconscious psychic activity enabled us to get the first glimpse into the nature of poetic creativeness." It is especially to his ideas about symbolism that we must turn to understand what the nature of that glimpse might be, for Freud indicated[20] that dream symbolism, far from being merely one more device of the dream-work, actually "provides the Dream-work with the material for condensation, displacement and dramatization," and that it is not limited to dreams, but has a "dominating influence on representation in fairy-tales, myths and legends, in jokes and in folklore."

Symbolism has played a central role, not only in the applications of psychoanalysis to the arts, but in defining (especially with regard to sexual symbols) the image of psychoanalysis to the general public. Thus, Thass-Theinemann in 1968 could remark, "the often ridiculed 'Freudian symbol' held the key to the truth which since has become a trite axiom. This is the thesis that man is the symbolic animal [*animal symbolicum*], that the creation of symbols is a fundamental activity of the sound human mind." As employed by Freud, the symbol is characteristically sensorial and concrete, in some respects resembles what it symbolizes (for example, a long object for a phallus), and appears generally when a more primitive mode of thought prevails, as in fatigue, neurosis, or dream. The essence of the symbol, according to Rank and Sachs's book of 1916 (a work considered by Freud as saying "what is most to the point" on symbolism), lies in its having two or more meanings and in its representing ideas that are hidden or secret. While most symbols are sexual, their role extends to the deepest aspects of human experience, as Jones (1916) indicates: "All symbols represent ideas of the self and the immediate blood relations, or of the phenomena of birth, love and death." Jones explains the genesis of symbolism, its primitive tendency to throw together or identify different ideas, above all in terms of a pleasure-pain principle, exemplified by the savage mind, that only notices similarities, which are easier to see (less painful) than differences.

Freud offers numerous rich and suggestive examples (*Figs. 18 and 19*) of the symbolism of sexual and bodily functions drawn from his own and from other writers' experience (ideas of the kitchen or plant life as sexual images in Fuchs, 1908 and 1909–12; dream symbols in Stekel, 1911; and body symbols in Scherner, 1861, and Volkelt, 1875). He cites J. Marcinowski (1912), who "published a collection of dreams illustrated by their dreamers with drawings that ostensibly represent landscapes" but whose latent content peeps through: "Whereas to the innocent eye they appear as plans, maps, etc., closer inspection shows that they represent the human body, the genitals, etc., and only then do the dreams become intelligible. See in this connection O. Pfister (1911–12)." The many pages Freud devotes to dream symbols are among his most fascinating and suggestive, and some of the symbols Freud encountered among his patients have the quality of lyrical imagination: pillars and columns as legs, which Freud compared to the metaphors of the *Song of Solomon* and which we can now—though not quite so gloriously— compare in the visual arts to Dali's *Invisible Man* of 1929; gateways as one of the bodily orifices; and water pipes as suggestions of the urinary apparatus. Fairy-tale figures like the king and queen stand for the dreamer's parents, while the prince or princess represents the dreamer. The most simple and sweeping symbolism of male and female sexual organs has made the most impact on Freud's readers (*Fig. 20*): "All elongated objects such as sticks, tree-trunks and umbrellas (the opening of these last being comparable to an erection) may stand for the male organ." On the other hand, "boxes, cases, chests, cupboards and ovens represent the uterus, and also hollow objects, ships." Rooms (compare the German word *Frauenzimmer*, meaning woman), especially "if the various ways in and out of them are represented" signify women, while the key that enters the lock signifies the penis. Steps, ladders, staircases, or walking up and down them, represent sexual intercourse, and even clothing loses its apparent innocence when interpreted: a woman's hat or an overcoat represents a genital organ, just as a man's necktie in his dream means his penis.[21] The penis is

constantly represented by ploughs, weapons, snakes, even airships . . .
the list is evidently without end. Dreams of flying, falling, or floating
and those consisting in general of sensations of movement represent
an entirely distinct class of dream thoughts, susceptible to interpretations differing for each individual.

In the face of all this sexual symbolism, surely the most striking
part of his approach to the dream, Freud found it necessary to reply
to those critics who attacked this aspect of his book by adding the
caveat that, without forgetting the significance of sexual complexes
in interpreting dreams, "we should also, of course, avoid the exaggeration of attributing exclusive importance to them." Moreover, he
explicitly declares that "the assertion that all dreams require a sexual
interpretation . . . occurs nowhere in *The Interpretation of Dreams*."

Probably under the influence of Wilhelm Stekel, Freud intermittently abandoned his view that dream symbols are relative to the
dreamer producing them, and adopted the notion of fixed meanings of
symbols (as in old dream books). In 1910, addressing the Second International Psychoanalytic Congress ("The Future Prospects of Psychoanalytic Therapy"), he made the astonishing announcement that a
committee was at the time working out the fixed symbolic meanings of
dreams. The persistent trend within psychoanalysis (not only among
mystical Jungians) to deny the private and personal role of symbols
seems to point toward a rapprochement with the universal symbols of
some writers and critics. But the price for many of the psychoanalytic
critics has been the dilution of Freud's precisely clinical definitions. In
any case, this attempt to discover constant and universal symbols has so
far failed and perhaps never will succeed, for even such persistent and
obviously phallic symbols as the nose (in the late 1960's, the American
cartoonist R. Crumb invented a character with an erectile nose named
Dicknose) have been capable of an opposite re-interpretation: Friedman
(1951) remarks that the phallic significance of the nose "has been re-
peatedly dealt with in the psychoanalytic literature," but notes that
Leon J. Saul (1948) showed in a paper "that the nose has not only a
phallic but also a feminine vaginal significance."

Whether the symbol is "true" in a universal sense or conditioned
by the patient's own experience, and hence interpretable through the
analytic recovery of lost memories, it serves the analyst as a tool in

therapy. This employment of the symbol has been strongly criticized as trivializing and simplifying a rich and powerful source of human experience. An example would be the flying dreams, which seem to have resisted Freud's attempts to reduce them to a single meaning (although he favored a sexual interpretation of them, especially in men), but which he expected would yield a specific symbolism. A friendly critic of Freud, Ludwig Binswanger, the existential psychologist—who insisted that "the image is not a symbol [of something concealed behind it, as is the case in psychoanalysis] but an immediate expression"[22]—produced a highly suggestive phenomenological description of the vertical dimension of flying, and claimed to have demonstrated that the "who," or subject, of rising and falling dreams usually takes the image of a bird. Rudolf Allers (1961) states:

> The real concern of the analyst is not with a person but with his symptoms. By this term I mean not only symptoms in the sense of the clinic but also all that psychoanalysis designates as "symbol." The relation, viz., between the psychoanalytic symbol and the symbolized is that of effect and cause . . . The equation of the relation of causation with that of signification is open to serious objections.

Similarly, Ogden and Richards object to the psychoanalyst's symbol as a reduction of human experience to scientific language:

> The psychoanalyst often speaks of the meaning of dreams. When he discovers the "meaning" of some mental phenomenon, what he usually found is a conspicuous part of the cause . . . But by introducing theories of unconscious wishes, "meaning" in the sense of something unconsciously intended, and by introducing "universal symbols," Kings, Queens, etc., "meaning" in the sense of some intrinsic property of the symbol, may easily come to be what he believes himself to be discussing. In other words, for him as for all natural scientists the causal sign-relations are those which have the greatest interest.[23]

Just this property of Freudian symbolism induced Morris to welcome it into his behavioral theory of signs.[24]

The very strength of semantic precision of Freud's approach to the symbol that attracted Morris has, in the eyes of Jung and other former followers of Freud, proved to be an aesthetic weakness (Philipson, 1963), indicating a blindness to the rich variety of artistic experience. Certainly Freud, who in any case had a distaste for metaphysical speculation, would never have exalted art as the height of symbolism and the essence of what makes man most man, as Cassirer (1944) has done. From an opposite direction, some writers, regarding Freud's approach as uselessly vague, have denied that Freud uses "symbols" in any rigorous sense; thus, the scientist von Bertalanffy (1965), borrowing from S. K. Langer's *Philosophy in a New Key*, criticizes the Freudian "pre-symbol" as follows: "if there is a relation, not one-to-many, but one-to-anything (the tongue in Kubie's example means fighting the husband, coitus, Dr. Freud, etc., etc.) or anything-to-one (any 'elongated object,' according to Freud, is a penis 'symbol'), we should not speak of symbolism any more, but of free-playing 'association.'" This criticism (valid insofar as it objects to universal symbols) seems to miss the point that Freud does, in fact, consider that the objects employed symbolically share some common quality, whether an unconscious thought variously expressed, or an obvious attribute such as elongation, significant within a given context. A more relevant criticism to the interpretation of art in terms of Freudian symbolism was made by Roger Fry, in *The Artist and Psychoanalysis* (1924). Insisting that "nothing is more contrary to the essential esthetic faculty than the dream," he states that "in proportion as poetry becomes impure it accepts the Dream," concluding that "in a world of symbolists, only two kinds of people are entirely opposed to symbolism, and they are the man of science and the artist, since they alone are seeking to make constructions which are completely self-sufficient, self-supporting and self-contained—constructions which do not stand for something else, but appear to have ultimate value and in that sense to be real." In opposing formalist criteria to the conservative stand-point of the psychoanalyst, Fry touched on a crucial question of taste separating the older generation of Freud and his colleagues from modern movements in art. So crucial was Fry's formulation of the problem, that as late as 1967, in his survey of "The Problem of Form in the Psychoanalytic Theory of Art," Marshall Bush could come to the conclusion that "the basic problem which Fry posed for psycho-analysis, i.e., what is the nature of the emotional pleasure esthetically sensitive people derive from contemplation of formal relations, has come little closer to solution." Freud's hostility to modern art was characteristic, in varying degree, of his chief followers; for example, Jones,[25] who, unlike Freud, could probably abide Impressionism, felt that when the aesthetic element dominates, art becomes "arid," citing Cubism as a style whose increasing "aridity" was causing it to become "correspondingly limited" in its appeal. Clearly, the art that contains a secret buried in symbolic dress would be preferable to the average first-generation psychoanalyst's taste.

It is striking that the works of art chiefly chosen for analysis by Freud and his followers are those in which the sexual content, not being obvious, must be sought out and read into the work. Essays on obviously sexual or pornographic art belong among the least significant treatments of art by Freudians. Freud himself sparingly sought out sexual symbolism in works he studied: he needed to add nothing to the explicit sexuality of *Oedipus Rex*, he found the archaeopteryx an apt symbol for an old bird like Hanold the archaeologist, but made little use of the phallic nature of the lizards passing through cracks in the wall; and he treated the drives and motivations of Moses as seen in Michelangelo's statue without the slightest allusion to sexual matters. Of course, he based his analysis of Leonardo's art on what he thought to be a sexual fantasy about the artist's childhood, but he did not link the sexual component to works outside the restricted group in which the "smile" appeared. While Freud hesitated, his followers have often plunged into the stew of sexual symbolism, with curious results, implicitly defended by the astounding remark of Sandor Ferenczi: "The derisive remark was once made against psychoanalysis that the unconscious sees a penis in every convex object and a vagina or anus in every concave one. I find this sentence well characterizes the facts."[26] Otto Rank (1924) imaginatively developed out of the sexual symbolism of dreams a theory of the origin of cultural and artistic techniques, and the aberrant but at times stimulating psychoanalyst Georg Groddeck went much further. Thus, in his essay "Unconscious Symbolism in Language and Art," Groddeck (1926) did not hesitate before Raphael's *Sistine Madonna* in Dresden, to discover mysteries of the unconscious and indications not only of "*Das ewig Weibliche*," but of sexual symbolism even in Saints Barbara and Sixtus, whom he fails to identify except as a woman and a man. He notes the crown lying near the man, which he calls the symbol of the female, and "near the woman, not touching her, stands a tower, the symbol of the male." How innocent Freud's comments on the same painting about forty-three years earlier seem in comparison: he merely discussed the too-youthful quality of the Madonna, finding less of the "divine" in it than in what he took to be Holbein's *Madonna* (a copy then in the Dresden Museum).

Sex as a factor in the creation and appreciation of art is a key idea in Freud's aesthetics, despite his restrained application of sexual symbolism to art; thus, he pointed out in 1915 that the "concept of 'beautiful' has its roots in sexual excitation."[27] By 1930, in *Civilization and Its Discontents*, he challenged the "resounding and empty words" of aestheticians attempting to explain the nature and origin of beauty, with his own formulation: "All that seems certain is its derivation from the field of sexual feeling."[28]

Freud, both as a Viennese and a contemporary of Schnitzler, was surely aware of nineteenth-century materialist reductions of art to sexuality;[29] and many of his contemporaries, echoing these notions, wrote books developing the thesis that beauty derives from sexuality.[30] In spite of Freud's blanket rejection of aestheticians, there were some who, in the early years of the twentieth century, made sexuality fundamental to their explanations of beauty.[31] While doubtless aware of this position, Freud was by no means satisfied with the simple reduction of art to sexuality, and so he not only broadened his concept of sexuality to a "libido," which included cultural activity and not merely sexual biology, but he added to the idea that beauty derives from "sexual feeling" a second, qualifying sentence: "The love of beauty seems a perfect example of an impulse inhibited in its aim." This is the very important idea of sublimation, first published in the *Three Essays* of 1905, in a discussion of sexual curiosity, which he notes, can be "diverted (sublimated) in the direction of art, if its interest can be shifted away from the genitals onto the shape of the body as a whole." Here, symbolism functions as a channel conducting unconscious impulses upward to artistic expression. In the words of Jones, "All symbolism betokens a relative incapacity for either apprehension (affective or intellectual), or presentation, primarily the former," [32] which causes the mind to revert to more primitive mental processes, especially those costing the least effort, such as the concrete and sensorial—usually visual, because "most perceptual memories become converted into visual forms." In order to reach expression, repressed ideas make use of symbols that are noninhibited, conscious, and socially useful, so that the repressed sexual motives are, essentially, sublimated. This cultural transformation of libidinal impulses into symbols, replacing actual gratification by sublimating the instinctual energies into language, art, and ritual was discussed rather pessimistically by Freud in *Civilization and Its Discontents*; but others seeking to liberate instinct from the repression of culture, were to build utopian superstructures on this Freudian base. Such theorists usually override Freud's own skeptical and conservative bias, and his insistence that "sexual need does not unite men; it separates them" (*Totem and Taboo*).

What motivates the artist constantly to produce these "sublimations"? Freud's answer would be that the artist has unusually powerful instinctual demands that his introverted disposition prevents him from satisfying, so that he must live in a fantasy world, on the border line of neurosis.[33] For Freud, the next question naturally arises: given his problems, how does the artist succeed and *not* succumb to neurosis? Freud could essentially offer two answers to this question: first, the artist, whose ego is overloaded with energy charges from his strong instincts, can partly discharge them in the fantastic world of his art, by techniques Freud never presumes to explain; secondly—and this point Freud does develop—the artist, though involved in illusions and failing to cope with reality like others, has, in fact, a means to coin real success out of the vaporous world of his fantasy. In a famous remark published in 1913,[34] Freud explains that the artist represents his most personal wishes and fantasies as fulfilled, but turns them into art through a transformation, which "softens the offensive aspects of these wishes, conceals the origin in the artist, and by observing aesthetic rules, offers to other men an incentive bonus [*bestechende Lustprämien*]." This conception of form as the sugar-coating of content is foreshadowed already in the book on jokes of 1905, in which Freud describes the function of the joke form or wrapping, which "bribes our powers of criticism." Freud's proper

Victorian distaste for the genital side of sex contributed to his view of art as a refinement upon its sexual origins, and his definition (1924) of sexuality itself as "by no means identical with the impulsion towards a union of the two sexes or towards producing a pleasurable sensation in the genital," but rather as "the all-inclusive and all-preserving Eros of Plato's *Symposium*."

Freud's later concept of sublimation as a turn from orgastic sexuality was foreshadowed in his views on catharsis. Already in the first and most decisive act in his development of psychoanalysis, Freud turned from the limited and physically direct approach that Breuer and he had evolved in their cathartic method, rooted in hypnosis, toward the less direct and more "sublimated" approach of psychoanalysis.[35] Ultimately, of course, Freud was to try to achieve for his patients self-knowledge, hopefully leading to self-control, rather than momentary relief;[36] and he disapproved of Ferenczi's "Principle of Neo-Catharsis," with its indulgence of a cathartic experience as a termination of therapy, even though Ferenczi claimed to distinguish it from the older technique as a "neo-catharsis," which would remain as a "recollection" and "provide a yet firmer basis for the subject's future existence." Freud's attitude toward the role of catharsis for the writer is summed up in the words of Clarence P. Oberndorf (1947):

> In most cases . . . the attempt of the author to free himself of the neurosis by writing it out is unsuccessful . . . Writing out or writing off by an author may equate itself with the confessional or cathartic elements of the clinical analytic procedure, but such self-revelation as a rule does not suffice to relieve permanently the essential conflicts of the writer any more than it does the troubled mind of the neurotic patient.

Cathartic therapy, with its reliance on hypnosis for the recovery and discharge of stored-up traumatic memories repressed from consciousness, might have suggested to Freud a theory of art as therapeutically expressive behavior, not unlike the psychological purgation of Aristotle. Ellenberger (1970) has shown a link between Breuer's therapy and the widespread interest in catharsis—especially in Vienna —following the publication of the second edition (1880) of Jacob Bernays's book on Aristotle's theory of catharsis. Bernard Bosanquet

(1904) has emphasized the importance of Bernays, who replaced the older view of Aristotle's catharsis as leading to a virtuous "purification" of emotions, by the version of it as purgation, which certainly was the one that reached Breuer and Freud. In his paper "Psychopathic Characters on the Stage" (1905), Freud assumed the truth of Aristotle's theory that the object of drama is "to awaken 'fear and pity' and to bring about their purgation [*Reinigung der Affekte*]"; but he reinterpreted the theory by showing that the real object of drama is to open to us sources of pleasure otherwise denied, not only through the release of tension but through the accompanying gain of sexual excitement. Furthermore, Freud did not treat catharsis systematically, and used the term in a very different sense from the Aristotelian, in his Goethe address of 1930, as the equivalent of the unburdening by a sufferer of the guilt weighing down on him. In Bernays's version, the contemplation of our unwanted feelings projected into a work of art can serve innocuously to relieve us of unwanted feelings, to provide us with an outlet (especially in the form of rites and dances) of dammed-up feelings. Although as early as his *Project for a scientific Psychology* of 1895, Freud had equated pleasure with "the sensation of discharge,"[37] he seems consistently to have shied away from the potential for mere motor release in catharsis. Still, he apparently favored a mild version of catharsis, judging from his approving preface to his friend and follower Marie Bonaparte's book on Poe (1933), where the idea is stated that fiction functions as a safety valve for humanity's over-repressed instincts.

Freud valued, if not the repression of instinctual energies for use in cultural productions, then at least the achievement of a balanced use of human energies. Like an economist, he set up a system for calculating the gains and losses of energy.[38] As Freud put it in his *Three Essays*, the process of sublimation enables excessively strong sexual excitations "to find an outlet and use in other fields," and leads to a considerable "increase in psychical efficiency." "Here," Freud continues, "we have one of the origins of artistic activity." This view of sublimation has been sharply criticized by the novelist Hermann Hesse, whose early sympathy for psychoanalysis ("Künstler und Psychoanalyse," 1918) turned gradually into criticism, leveled particularly against the psychoanalytic concept of sublimation. In an essay of 1930 ("Über gute und schlechte Kritiker: Notizen zum Thema Dichtung und Kritik"), he noted that psychoanalysis is silent on the crucial question concerning sublimation: why an artist produces a masterpiece out of the identical bellyache experienced by the neurotic mediocrity (*der neurotiker Meier*), and, in a letter to Jung of 1934,[39] Hesse rejected both Freud's and Jung's versions of sublimation, asserting that he would prefer the false sublimation (*Scheinsublimieren*) of a pathologic but productive genius to the psychoanalytically successful sublimation of a mediocrity. Arthur Koestler[40] has claimed that since, to Freud, "all cultural achievements appear as ersatz formations for goal-inhibited sexuality," Freudian sublimation really amounts to substitution (cultural achievements being reduced to coitus substitutes). Other critics, such as Lawrence Kubie (1958), consider sublimation an unnecessary assumption for explaining creativity. On the other hand, Melanie Klein (1930) accepts the importance of sublimation, but makes it dependent on symbolism.

Freud's tracing of art to sublimation, and his indifference to the cathartic aspects of its expression, correspond to his description of the role of beauty as a lure and incentive bonus. Here Freud approaches the theories developed by Darwin concerning the origin of the sense of beauty in the "artistic" display of decorative finery in order to attract a mate.[41] However, an important difference separates this sexual theory from Freud's view that the fantasy of the artist leads the spectator not to orgasm but to the satisfaction, also through fantasy, of the "same unconscious wishful impulses."[42] Freud's sexual model for artistic pleasure is the forepleasure of sexual play, as in looking (scopophilia) which he regards as becoming a perversion, when "instead of being *preparatory* to the normal sexual aim, it supplants it. This last is markedly true of exhibitionists." Here, it seems, Freud is unclear about the relation of perversion and sublimation; at which point does the artist's love of exhibiting (art, or rather himself through art) become a perverse substitute for sex? And given Freud's disgust over the genital encounter, why is the artist's behavior not a triumph of sublimation? The same unclearness stamps his discussion of the "unique" kind of sublimated homosexuality Freud found in Leonardo. One is left with the feeling, once more, of the intrusion of his own problems into his discussion of art.

The "forepleasure principle"[43] used by Freud to explain aesthetic experience implies for him, as Richard Sterba (1940) put it, that "the effect of the aesthetic side of the work of art is considerably over-estimated," since the "pleasure radiating from . . . unconscious sources is automatically ascribed to the . . . aesthetic features of the work of art." The thesis that the pleasure of art is only preliminary (*Vorlust*) to the final pleasure (*Endlust*) of complete gratification, and that art is essentially a superficial incentive bonus "to lure the observer into further depths,"[44] has been hotly contested by art critics such as Roger Fry, who rejected the psychoanalytic use of the dream and its symbolism as a model for appreciating art. Fry, in a famous lecture, "The Artist and Psychoanalysis" (1924), questions psychoanalysis for its attempt to explain art in terms of wish fulfillment, its theory that symbolism can lead to the highest art, and its suggestion that studying the origins of art can elucidate art itself. Clive Bell (1925), who knew Fry's lecture, added the militant declaration that the artist is "not concerned with 'sublimation' of his lusts, because he is concerned with a problem which is quite outside normal experience. His object is to create a form which shall match an aesthetic conception, not to create a form which shall satisfy Dr. Freud's unappeased longings." He cites Cézanne's interest in apples rather than flowers as a subject for his still-lifes as involving nothing more complicated than the artist's requirement to have objects for study that would be permanent and not wilt or change too quickly.

Of course, a whole series of writers on art, beginning with the last half of the nineteenth century, have made imposing claims for the independence and emotional significance of form: Konrad Fiedler, Wilhelm Worringer, Henri Foçillon (for whom "life is form"), Herbert Read, and more recently, Clement Greenberg (1961), who looked back in alarm on a time when the arts "looked as though they were going to be assimilated to entertainment pure and simple, and entertainment looked as though it were going to be assimilated, like religion, to therapy." Like Fry, all of these writers in some degree hoped that art would elude the nonartistic systems attempting to embrace, categorize, and "explain" them. In a letter to Ernest Jones of February 8, 1914,[45] Freud seems to have come close to comprehending Fry's view, albeit from an opposite standpoint, and with disapproval. In the letter,

Freud described an evening spent with an artist, remarking: "Meaning is but little to these men; all they care for is line, shape, agreement of contours. They are given up to the *Lustprinzip*." Freud generally emphasized the motivational relevance of subject matter in art, finding it ultimately rooted in unconscious drives and not in the superficial and "coquettish" aspects of form.

Complementing Freud's theory of sublimation as the transformation of sexual energies into "higher" ones of art or culture, has been his speculation, derived from his theory of dreams, about the degree of freedom available to the artist through relaxation of the controls of reason. As in the moment before falling asleep, when "involuntary ideas" emerge, the patient allows his thoughts to move freely, but—unlike dreams—he does *not* transform his thoughts into visual and acoustic images; instead, he uses the energy saved from the normal dream-work to retain the character of ideas. This method, free association, which Freud called "the most important innovation of psycho-analysis,"[46] in part resembles the creative process as outlined by Schiller, who in a passage Freud quotes at some length, explained to a sterile friend that "where there is a creative mind, Reason . . . relaxes its watch upon the gates, and the ideas rush in pell-mell." An important discussion of the artist's creativity occurs in the *General Introduction* (1917a), particularly in the sentence that Jones[47] claimed contained "the essence of what he had to say" concerning the psychology of the artist: "Artists are endowed with a powerful capacity for sublimation and with a certain flexibility (looseness, *Lockerheit*) of repression." This sentence occurs in the context of a discussion of the fantasy life, in which Freud represents the artist as a being who has "an introverted disposition and has not far to go to become a neurotic." His clamorous instinctual needs can be gratified only in fantasy. Here, Freud finds a paradoxical ability of the artist to find his way back to reality; for when he can successfully embody his fantasy in his art, and provide non-artists with "the comfort and consolation of their own unconscious sources of pleasure," then he will be admired for his fantasy, and he "has won—through his fantasy—what before he could only win in fantasy: honor, power, and the love of women."

Freud's approach to the artist in terms of his unconscious fantasy life and his access to repressed materials unavailable to others, has been adapted by a number of writers to the field of artistic and literary creativity. In contrast to psychoanalysts like Otto Rank, who considered art a triumph over biological dependencies and who attributed to the artist a stronger mastery of his ego than to the average man, or to Ella Sharpe (1930), who declared that "during creative periods omnipotence is vested in the ego, not the super-ego," these writers feel that all creative experience demands at one point a giving up of adult, culture-derived inhibitions in order to release the flow of images and ideas. Influenced by both Rank and Sharpe, Ernst Kris, an analyst first trained as an art historian, has dominated the aesthetic training of many psychoanalysts through his book *Psychoanalytic Explorations in Art* (1952), with its well-known and influential designation of the artist's ability to tap unconscious sources without losing control, "regression in the service of the ego." An earlier treatment of regression as necessary according to the principles of mental life appears in Oskar Pfister's study of Expressionism (1923), which notes that "every advance (Jesus, the Reformation, Rousseau, Tolstoy) is possible only through the detour of such a regression." The chief thing, he adds, is not to remain stuck at the infantile level, but to make a "healthful progression" out of that regressed state.

Kris, perhaps building his ideas implicitly on the model of Freud's therapy session, in which the patient free associates in a controlled situation, speculated that the relaxation or regression in all artistic creation—in contrast to fantasy or dream—is purposive and controlled. There is a continual interplay between creation and criticism, "a shift in psychic level, consisting in the fluctuation of functional regression and control. When regression goes too far, the symbols become private," whereas when there is too much control, the result will be "cold, mechanical and uninspired." Kris approaches an old aesthetic formula for artistic success in his effort to balance the critical and controlled activity of consciousness against the uncontrolled primary process, with its overdetermined and ambiguous symbols; however, being allied to the school of ego psychology led by Heinz Hartmann, Kris liked to emphasize the dynamic role of the ego in creativity—a departure from the less optimistic emphasis of Freud on the involuntary unconscious. Still, Kris shared with Freud a penchant for prying out the secrets of apparently playful productions. Thus, working out of

Freud's brilliant surmise that jokes are allied to dreams and the unconscious, and perhaps Ferenczi's (1916) notion of the "magic gesture" of drawing, Kris and Gombrich sought out the hidden and dark side in the visual fun of caricature, finding in it that the childish joys of regression are converted into the nasty pleasures of aggression. Kris, in his essay "The Psychology of Caricature," noted the "aggressive nature of all caricature";[48] and, in their collaborative essay "The Principles of Caricature,"[49] Kris and Gombrich discovered "under the surface of fun and play" of a successful caricature the working of a hidden "image magic. How otherwise could we account for it that the victim of such a caricature feels 'hurt.'" Although they quote Baldinucci's description of caricature as "for the purpose of fun, and sometimes of mockery," the writers do not do justice to the playful and not at all aggressive exchange often enjoyed by the artist and his "victim"; for example, as noted by Irving Lavin,[50] Baldinucci (in a passage ignored by Kris), in his *Life of Bernini*, mentioned that "Bernini's caricatures of great personages were avidly appreciated by them, and they themselves joined in the fun."

Jungian critics (for example, Philipson)[51] have lumped the views of Kris on the relation of psychoanalysis and art with those of Freud, as "a form of imaginative archaeology in which the diggers are looking for the elements of the 'foundation' in the individual artist's unconscious conflicts." Philipson notes that Kris treats symbolism in art (in contrast to its appearance in children's play and in fairy tales) inadequately and that he admits his lack of concern "with the formative process by which the unconscious content is actually transformed into a work of art"; however, with regard to this last question, Philipson sees both Freud and Jung equally remiss.

Orthodox Freudians such as Bronson Feldman (1968) dismiss not only Kris but the ego-psychologists generally. Feldman notes that Hartmann's discourse on "Ego Psychology and the Adaptation Problem," published in 1939, "took a proposition of Freud's in *The Ego and the Id*, that there might be a third power in the psyche between libido and the mortal current, a neutralizing power, and expanded it into a doctrine of a 'conflict-free sphere.' From this comforting assertion, Hartmann advanced to the claim that the ego was not an outgrowth of the id but a sovereign domain springing up at the same time as the id.

This teaching became quite fashionable in United States medical psychology, receiving flank support from the argument of Ernst Kris that art was not, as Freud had insisted, a sublimation of brute impulses, but rather a 'regression in the service of the ego.' "

Ernest G. Schachtel (1959) has been sharply critical of the views advanced by Freud, and of Kris's version of them, especially the attempt to show artistic creativity as a product of repressed libidinal and aggressive impulses, and of a regression to infantile modes of thought or experience (primary process), even though in the service of the ego. More than the temporary removal, or "flexibility," of repression is needed to explain why the artist's ego can hold on to an unconscious impulse, and Schachtel finds his explanation in the "conviction of the truth of artistic or scientific creation in the face of the opposition by "those who share conventional perception and thought." The artist's "childishness" is really his openness toward the world, and the adult's amnesia for early childhood results not from the repression of forbidden sexual impulses but from the transformation of the whole way of perceiving and thinking, leading to "the encroachment of an already labeled world upon our spontaneous sensory and intellectual capacities." The values of honor, wealth, and so forth that Freud claimed for the artist seem irrelevant to the candid, honest, and open personality attributed to the artist by Schachtel. Turning to Kris's point about the artist's regression, Schachtel denies that creative thinking—like the primary process thought of revery and daydream—aims at discharging tensions and arriving at a tensionless state:

> What the early stages of the creative process have in common with such reveries is mainly the fact that they, too, wander freely without being bound by the rules and properties of the accepted, conventionalized, familiar everyday world. In this free wandering they center, however, on the object, idea, problem, which is the focus of the creative endeavor. What distinguishes the creative process from regression to primary-process thought is that the freedom of the approach is due not to a drive discharge function but to the openness in the encounter with the object of the creative labor.

In line with Schachtel's argument, we may note that psychoanalytic criticism has almost exclusively considered problems of an emotional and personal kind, and rarely tried to elucidate what Freud called the "technical" side of art.

While Freud speculated little about the technical side of art, he nevertheless granted (without ironing out the inconsistencies) that the artist's mastery of his subject was a major criterion for distinguishing childish play from adult work, and so art was not merely illusion or a sublimation of sex, but a means for coping with the real world. Although the writer, in creating a world of fantasy, "does the same as the child at play" ("Creative Writers and Daydreaming," 1908), his intentions and values are more closely attuned to "reality." Thus, concluding chapter 23 of the *General Introduction* (1917a), "The Paths of Symptom-Formation," Freud asserted that art had a special role for the neurotically inclined artist as a road leading the fantasy-bound man back to reality. Here, Freud seems to regard art as a useful tool, as a means for other ends, just as he regards the child at play as longing for and aiming toward adulthood, for which his play is preparatory exercise. The child matures out of his childhood as the neurotic is cured of his neurosis, for both must "make that advance from the pleasure-principle to the reality-principle, through which the mature adult may be distinguished from the child" (1916a). It is remarkable that Freud, who had six children, never studied their drawings or poems with any seriousness, though he made scattered amused observations on their productions in his letters. That Freud—considering the whole of childhood as a transition to adulthood—never so much as alludes to the character of child art, is all the more surprising in view of the late-nineteenth-century surge of interest in such art, particularly by the outstanding psychologist James Sully, whose writings on dreams Freud praised so highly in *The Interpretation of Dreams*. The question of the seriousness of the artist, who in a real sense retains links to his own childhood, seems to have given Freud trouble, though he rarely struggled with it. In an ambiguous statement of 1911 ("Formulations on the Two Principles of Mental Functioning"), Freud, going a shade beyond his earlier idea that the artist succeeds by seducing the approval of his audience, allowed that the artist, a man who cannot really change the outer world, can at least mold his fantasies into a new kind of reality, a valuable reflection of actual life that other men would find attractive and therefore reward. Reality for Freud, in the stance of the hard-headed materialist and scientist, meant the opposite of the fuzzy-headed dream worlds conjured up by the Symbolist poets, brothers of Freud's neurotics and dreamers: it meant pain and hunger and the demands of survival. As in the egoistic world of Hobbes's *Leviathan*, one defines the good as what leads the individual to self-preservation, and the bad as what threatens him with the loss of love or life. Art, in such a world, ultimately means a precariously suspended moment in the on-rush of reality toward death, an illusion like religion, bound to dissipate under the cold light of reason.

Perhaps Freud's use of the concept of the ego or the self, concerned above all with its own preservation, can help us to understand his notion of the instability of art. Freud distinguished the conscious portion of the personality, which wills, reasons, and shapes, from the dark lower region of instinct and drives—called the id—and the censoring and judging region of ideals and counter-ideals—called the super-ego. The ego, touted for so long by philosophers of reason and morality, is quite weak and helpless in Freud's system. Originating in the id, from which it always must receive its energies, and giving rise to the super-ego, which becomes a second governing and restricting force, the ego must also confront the demands imposed by the external world. Yet, it is this same frail element of the mind that wrestles to gain mastery of its economic task of establishing harmony among the forces and influences acting in and on it. Anna Freud [52] has noted that the ego achieves a "victory" when its defensive measures are effective in minimizing anxiety and pain. "Life is not easy," Freud observed, a view only one step removed from the pessimist Schopenhauer's, although Freud would probably not have agreed with the philosopher that in such a world art could—though only for a moment—deliver men from the painful oppression of the will. The new topography of ego, super-ego, and id provided a means for Freud to extend his theory of the unconscious, which had applied mainly to the dream and neurosis, to larger aspects of personality. Moreover, by incorporating his broadened ideas about libido and aggression into the system, he could account for questions unsatisfactorily solved in his older theories, such as the nature of sadism and narcissism.

When we try to locate art within this scheme, we conclude that the seat of aesthetic activity must be in the ego, judging from Freud's remark that although the ego draws its energies from the id, what distinguishes the ego from the id is "a disposition for synthesizing its contents, for concentrating and unifying the emotions, completely missing in the id." But, lacking a source of energy within itself, this disposition has no more value than a network of wires without an electrical input; and, as he pointed out in 1923 ("The Ego and the Id"), the id is the source of life-energy (Eros) guided by the pleasure principle; for example, by erotic tensions which it seeks to discharge in copulation. Ejection of sexual substances for Freud corresponds to "the separation of soma and germ-plasm," and the condition that follows complete sexual satisfaction corresponds to dying (a desperate intensification of the old "post coitum tristem" formula). Freud's ideas about the energy source of the ego and the id, and of the possibility of a neurotic regression of the ego (*New Lectures*, chapter 22), doubtless helped stimulate those post-Freudians who, feeling less pessimistic than Freud about the ego's ability to survive the interminable conflicts of the life and death instincts, claimed that it could rise above the bleak determinism sketched by Freud, making use, in Kris's words, of a "regression in the service of the ego" to produce art and other culturally valuable products.[53] It is not necessary to discuss in detail this new and not always coherent topography of the mind, since Freud himself did not substantially modify his own views on art to accommodate his altered system and nomenclature. Even in his rare applications of the new language to literature, as in his essay "Dostoievsky and Parricide" (1928), he adds little to his earlier formulations. Freud describes the passivity of Dostoievsky's ego, before the aggressive super-ego (derived from an identification with his sadistic father), in attempting to explain the novelist's complex personality; but the main lines of his analysis, especially insofar as it concerns the writer's art, still depend on the old concept of the Oedipus complex.

Freud's later innovations in his psychological theories did not, as we have seen, substantially affect his formulations about the psychology of art. So true is this point that those students of Freud who wish to locate his most important ideas about art, point to his work of 1905, the book on jokes. Sterba (1940) and Kris (1952) both indicated its importance, and Gombrich (1966) claimed that Kris was the one who pointed to the *Jokes* as the model for any account of "artistic creation on Freudian lines." But Freud, in his essay "The Claims of Psycho-Analysis to Scientific Interest" (1913b), had already recommended his book on jokes for its "application to aesthetic problems," and stated clearly in his "History of the Psycho-Analytic Movement" (1914c) that "my book on jokes gave the first examples of the application of psycho-analytic thinking to aesthetic themes." These estimates of the import-ance of the book for understanding Freud's aesthetics I believe to be entirely justified, and I will try to show that portions of it bear on such questions as the relation of play to sex in art, of play to reality, and of the spectator to the artist.

At the beginning of his book, Freud quotes Kuno Fischer's (1889) view characterizing our aesthetic attitude toward an object in terms of a contrast between play and work, and as one in which we make no demands or attempts to satisfy our "serious needs," but "content ourselves with the enjoyment of contemplating it." In spite of these remarks, Freud did not remain content with notions of "mere play-ing," and pursued the question on deeper levels, ultimately finding a purpose for jokes as sexual expressions, and a mechanism for linking them to the unconscious and to the dream. The discussion of art in the context of jokes doubtless minimizes the importance of the sexual element, but in other writings on art, sex appears to be the major element. Roland Dalbiez (1947) has noted an "incoherence" in Freud's attitude to art, since he "wavers between the sexualist and play theories," alternately ascribing a causal role to sexuality in the genesis of art, and admitting that man can experience satisfaction "in allowing his psychic apparatus to work without constraining it to conform to reality. This gratuitous exercise is play." After quoting Freud's view, expressed in *Civilization and Its Discontents* (1930a), that beauty is essentially sexual, Dalbiez cites a passage from the book on jokes contradicting the first viewpoint, by showing that "Freud's orientation happened to be towards an aesthetic theory very far removed from sexualism, a theory which seeks the essential condition of the beautiful in the gratuitous exercise of the activity of the imagination." The contrast between the elements of play and sex in Freudian aesthe-tics noted by Dalbiez points directly to Freud's attempts to advance beyond the more confining views of *The Interpretation of Dreams* to those of the *Jokes*.

That the book on jokes grew directly out of *The Interpretation of Dreams* is well known from Freud's letters. The later book extends the thesis of *The Interpretation of Dreams*, in attempting to show the relation of jokes to the unconscious, and maintains the link to Freud's father exhibited in the book on dreams. Freud, who "inherited his sense of humour from his father," [54] an inveterate raconteur of Jewish anecdotes, started a collection of Jewish jokes long before writing his book. While *The Interpretation of Dreams* represented a memorial to his father, possibly the *Jokes* shows the liberated and self-analyzed Freud assimilating at least one traditional element in his father's personality; for, as Rieff [55] has perceptively observed, the "Jewish jokes are the nonsexual ones." Although the book fails to give answers to the important aesthetic questions it raises, the very ability to wrestle with these problems may be inseparable from this moment of calm poise, when he could identify with his father and shrug off his guilt through the sense of humor he shared with him.

Freud's book proceeds as follows: first, in his "analytic" section he presents a review of inadequate but suggestive earlier theories, as he did in *The Interpretation of Dreams*, followed by an extensive catalogue of the techniques of jokes and their purposes, which reduces the aim of all joking to that of "evoking pleasure in its hearers"; next, in the "synthetic" part, Freud defines the source of our pleasure in jokes in terms of a general mechanism of pleasure, then turns to a discussion of the motives of jokes as a social process involving the joker and his audience; finally, in a theoretical discussion, Freud shows first the relation of the asocial process of dreams (which "serve predominantly for the avoidance of unpleasure") to the social one of jokes (which serve "for the attainment of pleasure"), and the relation of the dreamwork to the joke-work, both of which are unconscious. The thesis of the book is summed up in a formula at the very end, which describes the pleasure in jokes as arising from "an economy in expenditure upon inhibition," that of the comic from "an economy in expenditure upon ideation (upon cathexis)," and that of humor from "an economy in expenditure upon feeling." The pleasure in all three "modes of working of our mental apparatus," Freud asserts, "is derived from an economy." Through this economy of "humorous pleasure," energies are gained that would have been used for various purposes linked to the unconscious, thinking, or feeling, and can be discharged suddenly in laughter.

This theory of discharge Freud found in Herbert Spencer, whom he quotes as follows: "Laughter naturally results only when consciousness is unawares transferred from great things to small" (*The Physiology of Laughter*, 1860); but he criticized Spencer for not explaining why the energy that had been used "for the cathexis [i.e., the filling up or occupying] of particular psychical paths has become unusable, so that it can find free discharge." In all fairness to Spencer, it should be added that Freud himself never explains the crucial question of just how the energy becomes freed from its practical purposes for the discharge in laughter. Other psychologists were to develop the nonutilitarian side of play into a theory of beneficial discharge (in some respects linked to Aristotle's theory of catharsis). Karl Groos (1912) elaborated a theory of "play as catharsis," and Otto Rank (1924) followed him, noting the "therapeutic" character of life-activities, and adding: "We should like here to point out the high 'cathartic' value possessed by just those manifestations possessing least obvious utility, viz., the activities expressing unconscious tendencies, from childish games to grown-up people's play, which in tragedy reaches its highest cathartic development." Instead of accepting, as these two writers had done, the equal validity of the child's and adult's experiences, Freud explained that the adult gains pleasure from jokes because of their ability to restore momentarily the euphoria of childhood, a period in which the comic, jokes, and humor played no role and were unnecessary.[56]

David Riesman, commenting on Freud's attitude to play, observed (1950): "It is . . . the more pessimistic, middle-class, nineteenth century attitudes to work and play that are reflected and elaborated in Freud's thought." The hypothesis of the child's humorlessness especially piqued Max Eastman, who in his well-known book, *The Enjoyment of Laughter*,[57] contested Freud's belief that

> there is no humour in the playful nonsense of children, and that humour arises only when grown-up people elude their ideals of rationality and other inhibitions, and escape back into that non-humorous childish fun . . . He does not explain why this nonsense

which is not comic to a child, should be comic when it is furtively returned to by an adult.

Eastman ignores, of course, Freud's various theories of release, memory, and so forth, advanced as explanations of just this phenomenon. In general, the down-to-earth Eastman ridiculed all attempts to "solve the problem" of how a feeling-shift from painful to comic-pleasurable occurs in the brain and nerves, for example, through

> theories like that of Herbert Spencer with his idea that laughter occurs only when our nervous energy is prepared to perceive a big thing, and a little one follows; the "psychic damming" theory which the Austrian psychologist Lipps built upon Spencer's foundations; and Freud's idea, derived from Lipps, that comic pleasure is due to an "economy of psychic expenditure."

Some psychoanalysts have been stimulated by Freud's book enough to base their own theories of art on it. J. Weiss (1947), for one, extends the analysis of condensation and economy of psychic energy as leading to pleasure, to describe a "perceptual economy" which is quantitative, in that our ease of perception of an art work leads to pleasure, and qualitative in that, in appreciation, we share the childish and primitive visualization of the artist. Needless to say, these formulas hardly bring us closer than Freud's to understanding the dense and highly complex acts of creation and appreciation.

The criticism, advanced by Eastman and others, that Freud ignores play in his theories of art is not entirely just. Freud takes this factor into account, regarding it, in fact, as essential, but he adds qualifications in order to find a place for it within his general deterministic view of human behavior. Thus, he cites from Kuno Fischer's book on jokes (second edition, 1889) the remark, "This enjoyment, this kind of ideation, is the purely aesthetic one, which lies only in itself, which has its aim only in itself and which fulfils none of the other aims of life." Freud comments that he doubts "if we are in a position to undertake *anything* without having an intention in view." And a joke has the "aim of evoking pleasure in its hearers." But, Freud continues, this aim is not concrete and functional in the same sense as at other moments when our mental apparatus aims to supply "our indispensable satisfactions." And here Freud trembles at the edge of a (for him) wholly new idea, which some students have magnified out of all proportion as a new Freudian aesthetic: translating Fischer's aimless condition into his own terms, Freud sees art emerging when we allow our "mental apparatus" to "work in the direction of pleasure," but he disclaims having sufficient understanding of aesthetics "to try to enlarge on this statement." Given Freud's restless and interminable search for explanations within the dynamics of mental activities and his hunt for the motivations of human behavior, it was inevitable that he would not tie himself to a view that allowed the activity itself to be self-sufficient or "unexplained." The apparent senselessness of dreams spurred him to find their purpose in satisfying the wish to sleep, and he linked jokes (those called "tendentious") as well as art to the field of the unconscious, with its sexual and aggressive urges. In order to establish this link, Freud distinguished technique from purpose in both jokes and art (only jests have no content and depend solely on the pleasure of technique coupled with a certain amount of licence). But this solution did not satisfy some critics who saw the two aspects as unreconciled. We have already seen that Dalbiez found precisely here an incoherence in Freud's thinking.[58]

Freud realized that if aesthetic ideation functioned as a narcissistic product solely for the satisfaction of its maker, like bad jokes, daydreams and dreams, it would certainly not lead to genuine art nor even to a communication to others. Although Freud avoided most aesthetic questions, he felt here an issue he had at least to touch; namely, by what means, by what vehicle, was the artist able to reach the spectator with his ideas? Gombrich (1966) thinks he can find an answer in the book on jokes, both to this question and to a key criticism of Freud's views—that he regarded form as "little more than a wrapping for the unconscious content." Gombrich summarizes Freud's definition of jokes as the momentary exposure of a preconscious idea to the workings of the unconscious, and notes that in this formula the joke derives from the unconscious "not so much its content as its form, the dream-like condensation of meaning characteristic of . . . the primary process." He then expands this point to art: "Far from looking in the world of art only for its unconscious content of biological drives and childhood memories," he maintains, Freud insisted that the dream had to adjust to reality before becoming a work of art. According to Gombrich,

Freud's view is that the "wrapping" determines the content, so that "only those unconscious ideas that can be adjusted to the reality of formal structure become communicable, and their value to others rests at least as much in their formal structure as in the idea."

In his enthusiastic efforts to evolve a Freudian theory of form applicable even to modern art, Gombrich seems to exaggerate isolated comments by Freud, which are ill adapted to the axiom that the unconscious content determines the form. By interpreting Freud's position in a converse sense—that form can determine content—Gombrich, in fact, points toward the trouble spot of a psychoanalytic aesthetics, but neither Freud nor his followers (including Gombrich) have ever shown concretely how specific formal techniques correspond to the processes of the unconscious as described by Freud. This is not to deny the possibility, only the prematurely affirmative conclusion. Moreover, Freud's concept of "form" in dreams had a very specific meaning, difficult to translate into the field of aesthetics, and when he considered (in Section C, "The Means of Representation," of chapter 6, "The Dream-Work," of *The Interpretation of Dreams*) what the "*formal* characteristics of the method of representation in dreams signify in relation to the thoughts underlying them," he found that "the most prominent among these formal characteristics . . . are the differences in sensory intensity between particular dream-images and in the distinctness of particular parts of dreams or of whole dreams as compared with one another." The basic formal principle of clarity vs. lack of clarity, which Freud here touches on, he instances by the dream of a promiscuous woman who had become pregnant. The confusion of her dream as to "whether her husband was her father, or who her father was" revealed her own doubts about who the baby's father really was. Here, the lack of clarity represents the *formal* element of the dream, and the form of the dream represents concealed subject matter. This emphasis on the clear vs. the obscure as the essence of form is by no means a Freudian innovation but has roots in the intellectualist aesthetic of Baumgarten (in the line of Descartes, Spinoza, and Leibnitz), for whom clear and confused "may be illustrated by the possibility of adequately expressing this or that matter in words." [59] In itself, the "formal" element may bear on any number of fields, such as epistemology and semantics, without thereby being linked to art.

Not until thinkers in the fields of art history and criticism turned their attention to the distinction between clear and confused imagery was it finally drawn into a genuinely aesthetic context, as in Heinrich Wölfflin's *Principles of Art History* (first edition, Munich, 1915). The gap between the aesthetic and the psychoanalytic contexts has yet to be bridged.

Another claim made by Gombrich for the *Jokes* concerns its treatment of medium. Usually, when he discussed art, Freud saw the work not as an object, but psychologically, and paid little attention to the medium involved, so that questions of the specific qualities of painting and sculpture—or of the novel, poem, and drama—tended in his writings to be minimized. Exceptionally, in his book on *Jokes*, Freud gave considerable attention to the medium of language and to such formal aspects of sound as rhyme, assonance, and rhythm. It is possible that this emphasis on medium was a first step toward a more penetrating and satisfactory psychoanalytic aesthetics. However, I cannot agree with Gombrich or with N. N. Holland (1968), following him, that this is already a significant contribution to the larger field of aesthetics; for Freud in this respect does not go beyond many earlier studies. Moreover, he ignored the aesthetic and sensuous aspects of medium whenever possible, and did not attempt to extend his interest in media beyond the language of jokes. His interest in the medium of language arose because the fusing of sense and sound in jokes made such treatment practically unavoidable. In fact, since at its lower limits the "bad jokes" degenerate into pure "medium," that is, into nonsense sounds, one is surprised to find that Freud, aside from slight allusions to the pathology of nonsense jokes, nowhere undertakes a study of psychotic joking in the book.

Another solution to the question of the means used by the artist to reach the spectator was developed by Freud in his generally neglected theory of "ideational mimetics," which I regard as potentially his most valuable contribution to aesthetics, and the best bridge leading from his psychoanalytic views on art to the general field of aesthetic appreciation. This theory emerges from Freud's discussion of the comic and its associated techniques of mimicry, disguise, unmasking, caricature, parody, travesty, and, in its most primitive form, the comic of movement—pantomime. The comic is especially important since it operates within the same domain as art—the preconscious—and not that of jokes—the unconscious. Freud asks why we laugh when we have recognized that some other person's movements are exaggerated or superfluous (the convulsions of St. Vitus's dance or the sticking out of his tongue by a child mimicking the movements of his pen as he learns to write), and answers that the comic here results from our making a comparison between the movement observed in the other person and the one we would have performed in the place of the other person. The standard of comparison is our "expenditure of innervation," our "psychical expenditure," which is not independent of the content of the idea; thus, "the idea of something large demands more expenditure than the idea of something small." We acquire an idea of a movement, and thereby a standard for comparison, by carrying it out at some moment and thereby forming a memory of the "innervatory expenditure." When we perceive a similar movement of different size and wish to compare it to our own, we need not actually imitate it in our muscles, but may do so "through the medium of [our] memory-traces of expenditures on similar movements." Such "ideation or 'thinking,'" in comparison to acting or performing, displaces far smaller energy charges and "holds back the main expenditure from discharge."

At this juncture, Freud asks how this *quantitative* factor of greater or lesser size of the movement perceived can be given expression in the qualitative idea. In his answer, Freud draws on physiology, which affirms that "even during the process of ideation innervations run out to the muscles," though with very slight expenditures of energy. This allows Freud to suppose that the energy accompanying ideation can represent the quantitative factor of the idea, and that "it is larger when there is an idea of a large movement than when it is a question of a small one." Here, Freud calls upon his direct observation of how people express "largeness and smallness in the contents of their ideas by means of a varying expenditure in a kind of *ideational mimetics*." This is especially obvious in an uninhibited person—a child, an uneducated or a primitive man who, in narrating something, will tend to combine mimetic and verbal forms of representation. Even when he gives up this habit of "painting with his hands," he will do so with his voice, or through opening his eyes wide when describing something large and squeezing them shut when he comes to something small.

"What he is thus expressing is not his affects but actually the content of what he is having an idea of." (To the widely accepted view that an "expression of the emotions" serves as a concomitant of mental processes, Freud here adds his "expression of ideational content.") Freud speculates that there is a "need for mimetics" not only independent of communication, but involving processes that may have given rise to "mimetics for the purposes of communication." Several years after Freud published these ideas, his follower Herbert Silberer (1909, 1912) described a method for directly observing in himself the transformation of thoughts into images in dreams (the shortest of several interesting examples: while sleepy, he remembered he had to correct a halting passage in an essay, and then produced the symbol of himself planing a piece of wood, to smooth out the rough edges). Moreover, and of great potential interest in the context of Freud's ideational mimetics, Silberer defined a category of "functional symbolism" that Rank and Sachs describe as an "introjecting [as contrasted to a projecting] symbol-formation representing plastically, conditions and processes of the individual mental life perceived endopsychically [the constant functioning of the mind], such as a sad mood by the picture of a dismal landscape, the following of difficult trains of thought, by the difficult mounting of a horse which is all the time getting farther away, etc."[60] Unfortunately, while Freud appreciated Silberer's contribution and discussed it in passages added to *The Interpretation of Dreams*, he failed to follow up systematically the hints that might have helped link this aspect of dream symbolism to the analogous perceptual theory of empathy and his own ideational mimetics. This is all the more regrettable since he felt his theory of ideational mimetics to be so important that he concludes the discussion by suggesting, if it were followed up, it "might prove as useful in other branches of aesthetics" as it had been for understanding the comic.

In order to extend the more obvious example of the comic of movement to those cases of the comic found in "someone else's intellectual and mental characteristics," where no visible movements can be compared, Freud turns to the mechanism of "empathy." Although he never clearly defined the meaning or significance for his theories of this mechanism, Freud made use of it more than once; for example, in "Group Psychology and the Analysis of the Ego" (1921). Here Freud, in his effort to explain how people are able to interpret the reactions of others, assumed an apparatus found in each person's unconscious psychic activity, which very closely resembles empathy, but which is not so named. At the several places in his book where this notion appears, it is defined chiefly by its context; here, it helps explain the origin of comic pleasure when we compare our own expenditure of energy to that of others. Freud observes that, whereas in the comic of movement we laugh because someone has used too much energy, in the case of a mental function we laugh at just the opposite. If, however, a reversal occurs in the two cases, and the other person's expenditure on physical energy is found to be less than ours, or his mental expenditure greater, "then we no longer laugh, we are filled with astonishment and admiration." Freud admits that the entire business of greater and less energy is rather confused, but nevertheless finds the tendency to admire intellectual as opposed to physical output as a good basis for some general reflections on cultural success: "A restriction of our muscular work and an increase of our intellectual work fit in with the course of our personal development towards a higher level of civilization." It is interesting that Freud's idea of progress toward increasing intellectual, as opposed to physical, effort seems to transcend those earlier distinctions in *The Interpretation of Dreams*, previously discussed, between a "progressive" direction from perception to motor responses and a "regressive" one from memory traces (including those of movement) toward perception, and to point toward a mysterious state where intellectual forces dominate, a Platonic realm of mind to which he never admitted art (as already pointed out, his opinion of creativity and aesthetic appreciation seems never to have risen beyond a vague compliment or concession that they are beyond the reach of psychoanalytic explanation). Ultimately, in *Beyond the Pleasure Principle* (1920), Freud would explain the impulse of the few to perfect themselves, in terms of the effort to repress the persisting tension of the instincts.

The basic comparison in the comic between large and small attracted Freud's attention to a comparison of adult and child, since this is "the essential relation" between them. While Freud asserts (as Eastman complained) that the child is without a feeling for the comic, he finds the child's feeling of superiority or even sadistic delight a pure pleasure that adults wish to return to. When one regains the "lost laughter of childhood," one can then say, " 'I laugh at a difference in expenditure between another person and myself, every time I rediscover the child in him.' " Freud reduces the several varieties of the comic he treats to comparisons in which the other person either appears as a child or is reduced to a child, or, when the comparison is entirely within oneself, one discovers the child in oneself. A final theory that Freud hesitates to take seriously suggests itself to him; namely, that "those things are comic which are not proper for an adult." The last principle would explain the comic as the degradation of the adult to a child.

This hunting for origins in childhood experience seems to me a digression on Freud's part from the main theme that his ideational mimetics led to: the relation of the performer (actor, artist) to the spectator, and the mediating role served by the process of empathy along with a related problem of the utmost importance, the role of the object in the acts of creation and appreciation. I should like to close this chapter first with a discussion of these and related issues, and then with a suggestion of how some of Freud's psychoanalytic ideas can be construed in terms of an aesthetic.

Freud's "aesthetics," failing to work out the connections among artist, spectator, and work of art, has little to say about the key areas of perception and emotion in art. In his theory of ideational mimetics and the associated theory of *Einfühlung*, Freud made hesitant steps that might have filled in the gaps of his perception theory. The notion of *Einfühlung* first conceived by Robert Vischer was of great importance at the end of the nineteenth century, in wrestling with aesthetic questions that the opposed camps of the Gestalt psychologists and the associational psychologists were to continue later.[61] Freud's guide in these matters, Lipps (1897), well illustrates the new viewpoint available to Freud. Discussing the aesthetic impression produced by a Doric column, Lipps remarks: "The vigorous curves and spring of such a pillar afford me joy by reminding me of those qualities in myself and of the pleasure I derive from seeing them in another. I sympathize with the column's manner of holding itself and attribute to it qualities of life because I recognize in it proportions and other relations agreeable to me." In a slightly later work (1903), Lipps tried to explain "aesthetic empathy" on the basis of an "inner imitation," which "takes place, for my consciousness, solely in the observed object . . . In a word, I am now with my feeling of activity entirely and wholly in the moving figure . . . This is esthetic imitation . . . Here, the whole emphasis must be laid on the 'identity' which exists for my consciousness." Esthetic imitation or contemplation does not lead to kinesthetic activity, but on the contrary "the feelings of my bodily states must disappear from consciousness." In his analysis of Michelangelo's *Moses* in terms of its imagined preliminary states, Freud (who knew both Lipps and Johannes Volkelt, both exponents of *Einfühlung*) ignored their emphasis on esthetic contemplation, precisely in relation to sculpture like the *Moses*; for example, Lipps (1903) writes: "When I see the sculptured image of a man in the act of rising, the sense-feelings which a real man would have who thus arises, do not exist for my esthetic contemplation, any more than my own sense-feelings so exist. What I immediately intuit in the plastic form is its willing, the power, the pride." And Volkelt[62] stated, "When we contemplate Michelangelo's *Moses*, the posture of his mighty figure and the turning of his head, the wrath of the prophet is actually seen with [*mitgesehen*] a gesture which otherwise would be unintelligible."

Following Lipps (1897), Karl Groos (1898) attacks strongly the "inadequacy of the whole associative method," which is too much concerned with past events in its attempts to explain aesthetic feelings:

> The sympathy of an aesthetic nature possesses such warmth and intimacy, and such progressive force, that the effects of former experience, however indispensable, are not sufficient, as Volkelt, Dilthey, Theodor Ziegler, and A. Biese have justly remarked. Mere echoes of the past can not bring about what I understand as the play of inner imitation (*Einfühlung*). On the strength of my experience I hold fast to inner imitation as an actuality, and one connected with motor processes, which bring it into much closer touch with external imitation than the foregoing dissertation would indicate.

In an interesting development of *Einfühlung* theory, Herbert S. Langfeld (1920) notes that classical Greek figures produce an empathetic response in us without painful facial expression, instancing that ever-popular example for empathy, Michelangelo's *Moses*: "It is not necessary to know the history of the man. Every line of the figure, as one experiences it, gives an indication of his character, and of the idea of which he is a symbol." More commonly in the twentieth century, the sculpture and its empathetic interpretation have shared a similar and unhappy fate: empathy has been repudiated by those involved with a more objective aesthetics, and the very concept of the unique genius associated to the work has yielded to the notion that all men are artists (or potentially so); thus, the Dadaist Jean Arp could impishly compare Michelangelo's *Moses* to an "inspired snowman," both being in his opinion equally valid art.

When Freud analyzes works of art, he seeks out hidden, symbolic allusions to the unconscious in the picture or sculpture, beyond the immediately empathetic response and the obvious aesthetic details of color, form, line, and iconography. Here he follows a method clearly prefigured by his master Charcot, who interpreted (1887, 1889) various states such as the demoniacal possession depicted in older art as hysteria. Charcot's methods were appreciated in Vienna among Freud's colleagues; and his own teacher, Sigmund R. von Exner, Brücke's assistant, cited (1889) the French psychologist's use of photographs to diagnose certain cases of neurosis. This modern neurological diagnosis of older art and literature directly affected Freud, who acknowledged his debt to Charcot (1923b). In his discussion of Leonardo's *Virgin and St. Anne* in the Louvre, Freud asserts that the figures of Anne and Mary are "fused with each other like badly condensed dream-images," a defect in composition to a critic's eye that "is vindicated in the eyes of analysis by reference to its secret meaning." Freud suggests that for Leonardo "the two mothers of his childhood were melted into a single form." Although Freud's criticism may not be acceptable to most students of Leonardo, it introduces the stimulating idea that precisely where a master might falter, a problem of his personality might lie, and just at that point would a rapprochement between psychoanalysis and aesthetic criticism most profitably occur.[63]

Freud's critique of Leonardo's art goes only as far as his own psychography required, and served to support and illustrate the thesis that links Leonardo's adult personality to decisive occurrences of his childhood; however, the heady stimulus of Freud's insights inspired his follower Oskar Pfister to the imaginative claim, which Freud quotes at length without entirely subscribing to it, that "in the picture that represents the artist's mother [Pfister fully accepts Freud's analysis of the Louvre painting] the vulture, the symbol of motherhood, is perfectly clearly visible." Pfister's interest in reading farfetched meanings into the shapes of the painting remind one of the famous ink-blot test of his colleague Hermann Rorschach. Viewing the painting almost in terms of a Rorschach ink blot (in its turn analogous to the Swiss children's game of ink blots, *Kleksographie*), Pfister sees a vulture's head, neck, and body in the cloth "around the hip of the woman in front and which extends in the direction of her lap and her right knee." In light of the certainty that the bird of Leonardo's fantasy was *not* a vulture, one can only wonder at the Polonius-like gullibility of Pfister's audience, of whom he said: "Hardly any observer whom I have confronted with my little find has been able to resist the evidence of this picture-puzzle."[64]

In working out the fusions and condensations of images, Freud often makes use of his idea of the composite figure, which he explains by comparing it to the "composite photographs" of Francis Galton (*Fig. 21*). Galton, a follower of Darwin and one of the most gifted and wide-ranging of nineteenth-century English scientists,[65] developed a method of combining multiple photographs through overlaying one upon the other, so that features thus filtered became clear or blurred depending on the frequency of their recurrence. (One might compare this to Freud's "architectonic principle of the mental apparatus," which consists of "stratification—a building up of superimposed agencies." See Freud, 1901.) In speaking of "Composite Portraits" (1878), Galton wrote: "Those of its outlines are sharpest and darkest that are common to the largest number of the components; the purely individual peculiarities leave little or no visible trace. The latter being necessarily disposed on both sides of the average, the outline of the composite is the average of all the components."[66]

Freud applied Galton's method to his dream "My Uncle with the Yellow Beard" in which the features of a face appeared blurred, while the beard stood out clearly: the dream "composed" two faces, both bearded, a common feature that was strengthened whereas the differences weakened one another. In explaining complex visual images,

Freud seems not to have relied only on Galton's purely visual analysis, and to have found it indispensable also to interpret the images as linguistic phenomena, as hieroglyphs; here, his archaeological interest turned into a pursuit of etymological origins, in the manner of Karl Abel, whose essay "The Antithetical Sense of Primal Words" (1884) Freud reviewed in 1910. Thus, in his discussion of "A Mythological Parallel to a Visual Obsession" (1916b), he was confronted with a patient who was obsessed by the word *Vater-Arsch* (father-arse), as we have seen; the patient also produced an accompanying picture that represented "the lower part of a trunk, nude and provided with arms and legs, but without head or chest, and this was the father." There were no genitals visible, but "the facial features were represented on the abdomen." Freud explained the odd word as an expression of the patient's conflicting love and fear of his father (whose title to respect as a "patriarch" is humorously distorted); he then compares the bizarre image to a caricature that "recalls other representations that derogatorily replace the whole person by one of his organs, e.g., the genitals." These representations include a caricature of "England" (*Fig. 22*) and a Greek terra cotta illustrated in Reinach (*Fig. 23*), representing a woman named Baubo who made the unhappy goddess Demeter laugh by lifting her clothes and exposing her body. In an essay on "The Medusa's Head" (1922), Freud cited a similar occurrence—the display of the genitals—as an apotropaic act, to ward off evil. "We read in Rabelais of how the Devil took to flight when the woman showed him her vulva." The terra cotta of Baubo "shows the body of a woman without head or bosom, and with a face drawn on her abdomen: the lifted clothing frames this face like a crown of hair." This bizarre compounding of face and genitals occurred earlier in Freud's own dream of the three fates. It will be recalled that in this dream there appeared a "stranger with a long face and pointed beard," a businessman like his father, whose name Popović in German links the respectful word Papa to the colloquial term for behind, "Popo." In a letter to Fliess of January 16, 1899, Freud had already explained hysterical headaches as "due to a fantastic parallel which equates the head with the other end of the body," with hair in both places, cheeks compared to buttocks, lips to labiae and mouth to vagina.[67]

Freud "read" some works of art, such as the Mona Lisa, as he "deciphered" neurotic and dream images, in order to find hidden meanings, in a manner suggestively parallel to that of Biblical exegetes, or to the hermeneutic efforts of some modern students of medieval poetics such as H. Flanders Dunbar (1929), who feels that every poem should be read as a "cryptographic code." However, usually Freud's aim was not to arrive at some fixed allegorical or tropological meaning, but to unfold interpretations that could lead to a deeper understanding of the artist's intentions. In some instances, though, Freud analyzed works as self-sufficient entities and without reference to the artist's personality. The major example of this approach is his essay on Michelangelo's *Moses*, which has already been considered as a biographical expression of Freud, but which we will now treat as art criticism. In this essay, Freud bypassed completely the artist's legendary and complex personality, and became simply and totally absorbed in a dialogue with the figure before his eyes, and with certain of its commentators. Parenthetically, even the apparently un-Freudian art historian Erwin Panofsky saw value in approaching Michelangelo's work psychoanalytically.[68] Freud tended generally to become deeply engaged with one major work of an artist to the exclusion of other, equally relevant and important ones (witness his focus on *Hamlet*, while ignoring the psychologically significant and much-discussed *Sonnets*). Freud started essentially with his own impressions of the work, which he then proceeded to analyze. This analysis might be compared to "decomposition," the reverse of the dream-work process of composition, and a working-backward from an initial act of perception and appreciation. Freud tried to avoid subjectivity by reviewing the earlier criticisms of the work and by grounding his speculations in his principles of psychology as well as on his direct observations.

On matching his own response to the *Moses* against those of earlier critics, Freud found much left unexplained, above all, certain seemingly unimportant details, such as the unstable position of the tablets pressed against the body and the way in which the beard falls. Freud sees a problem in the position of the right hand, a finger of which presses the beard growing from the *left* side of the face, and remarks that even if merely formal considerations induced Michelangelo to draw the downward-flowing hair of Moses "to the right of the figure which is looking to its left, how strangely unsuitable as a means appears the pressure of a single finger!" Another problem concerns the tablets, which have straight edges on top and a "protruberance like a horn" on the bottom. From this detail Freud concludes that they are upside down, for "it can hardly be doubted that this projection is meant to mark the actual upper side of the Tables." Freud insists that Michelangelo can hardly have been guided by formal considerations to have treated such sacred objects so singularly. Freud's solution sweeps all these details together and explains at once the problem of arm and tablets: Michelangelo wanted to show "the remains of a movement that has already taken place"; thus, Moses upon seeing the faithless people around the golden calf, felt such wrath that he clutched his beard with his right hand, forgetting the tablets, which slipped from his hand. In an impulsive effort to save the already-inverted tables, Moses' right arm lunged back, drawing the beard with it, while his left hand also reached over the beard toward them, movements explaining the odd torsion bet- ween left and right sides of the body. So impressed have some of Freud's followers remained with this analysis, that Hanna Segal (1952), for example, claimed that not only did Freud clearly show in this essay "that the latent meaning of the work is the overcoming of wrath," but that the artist's achievement in general is in "giving the fullest expression to the conflict and union between the life- and death- instinct."

Freud had several drawings made illustrating the three phases of quiet, wrath, and recovery (*Figs. 24 and 25*). The partiality of his interest in the gestural details at the expense of the whole form in its intended architectural setting is betrayed by these drawings, which illustrate the body of Moses only to a point below the knees, but especially by the photograph of the statue used to illustrate the original article in *Imago* (1914a), which shows only the torso of the *Moses*, down to the left arm. He believed so strongly in the validity of this emotional sequence, that when he was shown years later an illustration of a twelfth-century statuette (in the Ashmolean Museum, Oxford) of Moses clutching his beard with one hand and the tables with the other (*Fig. 26*), he claimed it—in a postscript to his 1914 essay, written in 1927—as support of his thesis, assuming that he had found an example of the phase immediately preceding the one represented by Michelangelo. Freud acknowledged striking differences between the twelfth-century statue and Michelangelo's, but hoped that one day a connoisseur would be able to close the gap in time by finding examples of the Moses from the intermediate period. By reifying his imagined sequence of the emotions and postures of Michelangelo's statue, and regarding them as "real," Freud could believe that other artists treating the same theme—even in unrelated times and places—would likewise choose one of the moments available to them; in sum, he wished to psychologize the iconography of his subject.

In an article on "The Right Arm of Michelangelo's Moses" (1968), the art historian H. W. Janson, who had not read the 1927 postscript before writing his article (according to a note to me), apparently fulfills Freud's hope that some future critic would search out intermediate examples between the twelfth and sixteenth century; but Janson seeks works revealing stylistic influences, rather than ones illustrating Freud's imagined sequence. Janson's candidate as an influence on Michelangelo's statue is a northern Gothic medal dating from about 1400 and showing, not Moses, but the inspired Byzantine emperor Heraclius. Despite the difference in subject, Janson finds similarities that convince him this must be the source of Michelangelo's rare figure: "it has the same long, stringy beard of the statue, unique in Michelangelo's *œuvre*," the beard is engaged with *both* hands, it looks up showing not anger but "awe in the presence of the divine,"[69] and the horns correspond to the rays of light issuing from the head of Heraclius. Whereas Freud thought that the Ashmolean *Moses* represented the stage of the prophet just before that of Michelangelo's figure, Janson asserts that "we may substitute the Heraclius bust for Freud's drawing as representing Moses' condition just before Michelangelo portrayed him."

In these parallel projects—a parallel all the more impressive because unwitting—it is important to note that both the psychoanalyst and the art historian have overlooked the all-important changes Michelangelo made in his designs for the Julius tomb, in the versions of 1513. In the earlier version three other figures on a level with Moses were set diagonally to each other at the corners of the square platform, and Moses sits solidly with one tablet in each hand, horns on his head, and with a long beard that falls straight down (*Fig. 27*). If this sketch offers us any clue to Michelangelo's conception of Moses, we must conclude that—as in the other tomb figures ignored by Freud—he intended none of the kinds of subtleties Freud speculated about, and wished mainly to display the tables as an attribute of the law-giver. Nor can this version have anything at all to do with the Ashmolean statuette, although in contradiction of Janson's thesis that Michelangelo derived the horns and long beard from the Heraclius medal, both these details are *already* present. How, then, can one explain the remarkable change from this first version to the second one of 1513? The solution, I believe, relates to major changes in the over-all design, including placing the figures on the platform (six now instead of four) at right angles to each other instead of diagonally. In this final version of 1513 (reconstructed by Panofsky), Michelangelo solved the problem—analogous to one faced in the Sistine ceiling, the immediately preceding project—of linking the front and side figures.[70] It was to this end that he broke the symmetry of the form, placed the tables in one hand, rotated the head and arms, and used the beard as a "streaming" motif to unite the head to the right hand holding the tables. Contrary to Freud (and to Janson, who does not distinguish between touching and grasping), Moses does not grasp his beard, but touches it exactly as the figure of the Louvre *Slave*, carved along with the *Moses* for the same façade of the Julius tomb, touches the line of drapery on his chest, which serves to link the right hand to the uplifted left arm.

Freud chose to minimize the formal consequences of the changes in the two projects (he was evidently aware of the two versions, for he speaks of the Moses "together with three or five more seated figures"), clearly preferring his more dramatic interpretation, with its series of imagined stages, and with its potential for his own identification. Freud's zealous interpretation has been well characterized in an article by Earl Rosenthal (1964) as "cinematographic," an epithet also applicable to Freud's use both of serial images to represent dream symbolism and of the condensed images of Galton's photographs. The whole problem of the perception of movement through its static plastic representation already troubled the generation of Freud's teachers, such as Brücke, who wrote an essay on the subject (1881). Brücke incorporated Muybridge's photographic proof that artists had always represented the position of the legs of running horses incorrectly; but he was wise enough to realize that the inaccuracies of good artists had a poetic truth to motion lacking in the photographic frames taken one at a time. Thus, art, by combining elements of more than one position, could imply succession and motion. We must not forget that the broad question of how direct perception and memory are related preoccupied the collaborator and inspirer of Brücke, Hermann Helmholtz, a genius much admired and studied by Freud.[71]

Certainly Freud's study exaggerates the psychological dimension, and, as Janson points out, it ignores the plastic tradition from which Michelangelo could have drawn conventional expressive gestures for his *Moses*. As we have seen, Freud combined the cinematographic with the psychological in considering the statue's form as the epitome of preliminary postures and emotional attitudes; however, this approach of the conservative Freud may perhaps be understood in the more conventional terms of the eighteenth-century ideal of the "pregnant moment." This idea of academic criticism, stemming from Shaftesbury and passing to Lessing, raised problems about the "history" of a static form and its potential for representing motion analogous to those that Freud considers. In Shaftesbury's words:

> How is it therefore possible . . . to express a change of passion in any subject, since this change is made by succession; and . . . the passion which is understood as present, will require a disposition of body and feature wholly different from the passion which is over and past? To this we answer, that notwithstanding the ascendency or reign of the principal and immediate passion, the artist had power to leave still in his subject the tracks or footsteps of its predecessor: so as to let us behold not only a rising passion together with a declining one, but, what is more, a strong and determinate passion, with its contrary already discharged and banished.[72]

Freud approaches art from two points of view: in Shaftesbury's sense, as a "pregnant moment," when he describes how Michelangelo compressed into a static work the series of emotions preceding and following the moment depicted; and in a romantic sense, when he reads into Leonardo's painting the artist's intentions and associations. Actually, Michelangelo's sculpture and Leonardo's painting were not as well adapted to his projects as other, often lesser works. While Freud by virtuoso maneuvers could interpret the moment represented in Michelangelo's *Moses* as a "serial event" stretched out in time, he found of course those works which laid bare such series especially fascinating and useful. The sequence from frame to frame of comic strips sometimes exposed a hidden motivation with vivid and humorous clarity—one thinks of Wilhelm Busch's work in general, and specifically of "A French Nurse's Dream,"[73] which reveals the correspondence between the expanding water images of the nurse struggling to remain asleep, and the growing urgency of the child's need registered in the loudness of its crying—a droll analogy to the "stream" of consciousness. Even more striking is his choice of the painting *The Dream of a Prisoner* (*Fig. 28*) by Moritz von Schwind, a Viennese artist (1804–71). The painting, with its prisoner longing to escape, illustrates Freud's concept of wish fulfillment in dreaming or, as in this instance, in daydreaming, through the implied series of steps from captivity to escape represented by the group of dwarfs in different positions. Freud remarks: "It is a happy thought that the prisoner is to escape by the window, for it is through the window that the ray of light has entered and roused him from sleep. The gnomes standing one above the other no doubt represent the successive positions he would have to assume in climbing up to the window." An amusingly exaggerated extension of Freud's analysis of the picture occurs in Alexander Grinstein (1951), who notes a difference between the pitcher next to the prisoner and the one held by the woman, and who conjectures that the one beside the prisoner refers to a moment of his past history "perhaps from his childhood, when he was asleep," and may be associated to his mother's milk, and so forth. Grinstein illustrates a sketch for the painting in which he overlooks a difference between the form of the dreamer's pitcher there and the final version, a change suggesting a question rather than the brashly simplistic "solution" of Grinstein: *which* pitcher (sketch or final version) belongs to the dreamer's (or the artist's) childhood? Perhaps neither, if the change was motivated by aesthetic considerations rather than by urgently subjective drives. But we have so little at hand to work with, and would need more sketches and paintings, along with a mass of biographical materials, to *begin* to make solid psychological interpretations of the painting.

A psychoanalytic theory of art must take into account the fact that whereas perception may turn art into fantasies of wish fulfillment for the neurotic and the dreamer, this faculty in most waking persons serves not merely as an instrument of the "reality-principle," but as a vehicle for the pleasures of aesthetic contemplation or for the joys of imaginative "in-sight." While Freud did not make full use of empathy as a process to explain the linking of the mental image to the non-verbal, aesthetic object perceived, he did confront the analogous problem of explaining how the individual comes to share the values and conventions of his group; accordingly, Freud proposed (1921) a process of identification very close to empathy as a means of interrelating persons, together with an allied process of "projection." This process had already been linked to *Einfühlung*—one *fühlt sich hinein*, or projects oneself into, nature through symbols—as a universal and normal process by distinguished writers known to Freud, such as F. T. Vischer (1873); but Freud himself first used the term to explain cases of hallucinatory paranoia in 1896 ("Further Remarks on the Neuro-Psychoses of Defence") and again in the famous Schreber case of 1911. Freud describes in *Totem and Taboo* how this "defense mechanism" works for the primitive who has just suffered the painful loss of a loved one; the savage was unconsciously ambivalent toward the departed, at once hating and loving him. Unable to accept the unconscious hatred, he defends himself against the feeling by attributing it to (projecting it onto) the departed soul, whom he considers now a demon against whom one must protect oneself. According to Freud, like the projections of the primitive, the personifications of the poet project his warring impulses out of himself as separated individuals. Freud applied his concept chiefly to neurotics or primitives who really believe something (though untrue) about another person, which is in fact a significant but unacceptable (hence repressed) part of the person's own personality. An artist who worked by this kind of projection would be too tied to a "participation magique" to produce art as communicating to or even of interest to others. Henry A. Murray, in his foreword to a standard book on projective techniques by Anderson and Anderson (1951), has signalled this problem by showing that Freud uses the term in a very different sense from that of the contributors to the volume, whose subjects were not confronted with "reality," but with ink blots, etc., and who were playing a game of "make-believe," encouraged to imagine something, or to speak out or act out responses. This approach values the activity of the imagination as such far more than Freud's, in which the projection has value, above all, as a clue to the state of mind (and neurosis) of the person projecting, rather than as a mode of communicative or productive behavior.

Freud needed a device for explaining the fact that we do understand one another and get out of our own skins and that we do respond strongly to another's art; and, *Einfühlung* seemed to advance toward such an explanation. The question of the spectator's "feeling-into" an object or person by *Einfühlung* may have stimulated his exploration (1905b) of the primitive connection between the senses of sight and touch, both of which originate in a sexual impulse "to feel into"; but, if this was intended as a first step toward an aesthetic theory, it was perhaps bound to fail, since the voyeur is only a feeble counterpart to the aesthetically motivated contemplator of beauty. At this juncture, a psychoanalytic aesthetics, saddled with Freud's limited perspectives in art, would confront a dilemma: it must explain why we are not merely narcissistic in our enjoyment of art, but it does not properly appreciate the significance and value of the aesthetic experience as an "objective" condition like mature love; for Freud, with his biological reductionism, regarded aesthetic experience not as valuable in itself, but as a means, an illusion whose pleasure was a come-on through its attractive surface to the "true" and "real" experiences of the unconscious. Freud consistently chose to ignore the voluntary aspect of artistic "illusion," which is begun, enjoyed, and terminated by our will, and not induced by or subservient to biological demands of our nature.[74]

Psychoanalysis might have found a more adequate model for artistic response in the earliest years of infancy, when the suckling child experiences a sensuous fusion with the object of the mother's breast, a favorite, even idyllic, moment for Freud. Otto Rank[75] took a slightly different tack, in trying to resolve "the very root of the problem of art, which is finally a *problem of form*." He speculated that "all 'form' goes back to the primal form of the maternal vessel, which has become to a large extent the content of art; and indeed in an idealized and sublimated way, viz., as form, which makes the primal form, fallen under repression, again acceptable, in that it can be represented and felt as 'beautiful.'" Freud himself regarded the mother's breast as the first and most important object of man (in chapter 20 of the

General Introduction), a point ballooned into a whole theory of art by Adrian Stokes (1959). Stokes (whose ideas in several points resemble Rank's), like his colleague Herbert Read, answered Freud's pessimism and disillusion with the theory that art was fundamentally healthful and that artistic activity is the most successful outcome of psychoanalytic therapy. He maintained that the basic drive in artistic creation is for coherence or clarity of form and to restore the harmonious unity of the primary mother-child relationship. Theorizing about the obscure earliest years of infancy, Stokes shared the views of the English school of psychoanalysis, with its emphasis on projection and "introjection," as in the writings of Klein (1930) and Milner (1952). The whole object that is restored or reconstituted, according to Stokes and his mentors Melanie Klein and Hanna Segal, is "an unconscious memory of the mother's breast." This extension of Freud parallels Jungian archetypes, best applied perhaps to artists like Henry Moore, whose work was described by Erich Neumann[76] as revolving around "the Primordial Feminine." One can see value in specific studies made of sculptors obsessed with the rotund, such as Moore and Gaston Lachaise, but how plausible would the application of Stokes's theory of the breast be to artists whose works were dominated by long "phallic" or flat forms? Perhaps one could reduce all variants to an ultimate roundness, rather like attempts from before the Greeks to after Descartes to reduce the universe to a small number of ultimate elements, at the price of the object's sensuous concreteness, but once the theoretician came back to the object itself, all the complicated language would be beside the point, and we would be left where we started, requiring words to describe the object's valued and tangible qualities.

For Freud, the happiest time of one's life is spent during the "golden years" of early infancy. Rarely did Freud in his writings characterize moments after this period as beautiful and valuable in themselves; rather, like Faust or Peer Gynt, Freud's human being, expelled from the paradise of mother's home, to which he is bound by memories of lost pleasures, is obsessed with the need to return, which he finally achieves in death. Freud sees earliest infancy governed by purely physiological needs like hunger; and, until he comes to sense his own lips and bowels as his own, the child attempts to engulf the mother's breast, but failing this ingestion, he is cast out into a world where hard and cold things surround him. Driven from his nest, where his identity is fused with his mother's, the child must let sight and hearing, senses operating at a distance, replace the warm touch of the breast, and feeling that the provident parents (the father being more and more included) are the most satisfying beings in the world, he seeks to "ingest" not their bodies but their qualities of power and love—in a word, to identify with them. Now, when the child starts imitating his parents, ideational mimetics is introduced as a mechanism directly linking the perceiver to the object perceived. Ideational mimetics, even more than empathy, which it resembles, might offer a starting point for the development of a sound Freudian aesthetics, for it reveals the interdependence of perceiver and object rather than making the object a blank screen on which the person projects his ideas and feelings. Possibly the first instance of this mechanism occurs when the child, who has responded physiologically to its satisfaction at the breast by smiling, later reacts to the mother's smiling tenderness with its own smiling response.

Throughout this discussion of Freud's aesthetics, we have seen how essential the role of pleasure is: starting from biological drives and sexual needs, it is the pleasure principle that draws men to other persons and to objects, and is at the base of all aesthetic pleasures. The evolution of human sexual feeling from narcissism to the choice of an object (*Objektwahl*) depends upon the individual's ability to grow beyond his self-centered egocentricity and to direct his feelings to others such as, first his mother, then to someone further removed from the immediate family circle, and eventually to a mate. Freud would derive this ability from the power of Eros to attach to objects "out there"—a situation parallel to the loving contemplation of art. But, as Norman O. Brown[77] has observed, Freud never felt that his psychoanalysis comprehended the attachment of libido to objects, and his thought was "inhibited by a conception of Self and Other as mutually exclusive alternatives"; furthermore, as H. J. Home (1966) notes, "psychoanalysis has not been successful in finding a framework for describing what actually happens between two persons." Presumably, Eros or libido would have a central role in the process of finding oneself through identification: we imitate prototypes we love and who provide us with pleasure, and memory or recognition, the key process for identification, is in itself, Freud points out, a pleasurable act. Thus, we would expect Freud to conclude that the unfortunate human being, lost within himself and his own (generally repressed) childhood memories (sexual and nonsexual), and caught up with the problem of finding his own identity, could finally displace his energies out toward "the other," whether a person or an object. Here, aesthetic contemplation would be equivalent to fulfillment and completion through losing oneself in the work, and sexuality could be situated not merely in either of the opposed limbos of teasing forepleasures or sad postcoital exhaustions, but in the fulfilling condition of a shared orgasm. Yet Freud, in his numerous allusions to art, never arrived at a theory grounded in sexual or aesthetic fulfillment.

We have already seen how Freud eschewed a simplistically healthful view of all culture, art included, and felt the burden of painful realities within and without weighing on the minds of all those destined to attain cultural distinction. Even the culturally indispensable mechanism of identification was fraught with treacherous difficulties, such that Freud's own development led him on an endless quest for heroes with whom he felt deep fascination followed by alienation and rejection, with the sole exception of Goethe, a genius who remained to the end inscrutable (distanced from Freud in time, in religion, as a German and as an artist-scientist, whose many works Freud felt concealed as much as they revealed him). And except for a minor episode of Goethe's childhood, Freud never tried to psychoanalyze his model. This difficulty in finding a suitable model is only one of many that corroborated Freud's broader pessimism about man's nature, with its instinctual aggressions. Probably, Freud had from his earlier years a deep involvement with death as the obverse accompaniment of all that was good and happy in man's life, but the impact of certain deaths of loved ones, together with the terrific realizations about civilized mankind's unextinguished bestiality, provided him with occasion and example for developing his profoundly dualistic views. Already in his "Two Principles" (1911), Freud had begun to consider that opposed to the free course of the pleasure principle was not only a reality principle, but an unpleasure principle, which intervened when the pleasures themselves became excessive, leading the organism to retreat in order to decrease the quantity of stimulation.

By 1920, he had moved much further, to his famous formulation in *Beyond the Pleasure Principle*, in which he asserted that sometimes we repeat earlier experiences even when they are not pleasant. Furthermore, through considering the perpetual recurrence of wars, Freud arrived at his concept of a death instinct, an ingrained attraction for death and the aggressive in normal men, balancing the pleasure principle. The whole generation of optimistic post-Freudians miss the importance of this point for Freud when they find in his views hopeful signs that human nature can be molded to a better model, and that art, far from being either illusive or merely innocuous, was positively therapeutic. Thus Simon O. Lesser (1957), echoing Stokes's theories of restoration, concluded a long elegiac description of the pain, unpleasure, and guilt in reality, with the remark that people read fiction "to make good some of the deficiencies of experience"; later in the same book, he rebuffed Sachs's attempt to formulate a theory of aesthetic experience based on psychoanalysis because Sachs introduced the concept of the death instinct: "I cannot assent to his view that a feeling of sadness is a necessary constituent of the esthetic experience." And Norman N. Holland (1968), building on Lesser's book, updates Freud with the claim that "the key to the most successful literary works . . . is that their very defenses give me pleasure." This overlooks Freud's description of the course of the defensive neuroses:[78] there is a premature and traumatic sexual experience; on some later occasion when the experience is called to memory, it is repressed with the consequent formation of a primary symptom; there follows "a stage of successful defense, which resembles health, except for the existence of the primary symptom"; and, finally, a stage when the repressed ideas return, leading to a struggle with the ego and construction of fresh symptoms, which constitute the illness proper. A considerable literature has been produced exploring the defensive function of art in neurosis and in schizophrenia, where it seems to help ward off the disintegrating threat of psychosis;[79] but this defensive role only superficially resembles artistic production, and usually disappears with the anxiety, so that the art and the disease are "cured" together. Clearly, in Freud's view, the "pleasure" derived from defense stands on a very precarious base, and represents a moment in the evolution of a neurotic illness. The whole question is tied to the nature of defense, which Freud describes as "an aversion to directing psychical energy in such a way that unpleasure results."

When, at the beginning of his career, Freud hinted at the presence, along with *Lust*, of an *Unlust*—the one deriving from the pleasing discharge of tensions, the other from the painful increase of tensions of energy above a certain threshold—he was working within the same economic-mechanical model that he derived from Helmholtz and his associates, and which he applied to jokes. The central idea involved was the law of constancy, whereby any expenditure of energy on one side would have to be compensated for by an addition, and vice versa, or some significant and deforming excess or loss would result. (The often-discussed mechanism of homeostasis was introduced as a working principle in biology by Claude Bernard and others, parallel to the law of the conservation of energy in physics.) The most satisfactory condition of the organism, in Freud's view, seems to have been a steady state, an equilibrium of those awesome forces within and without on which the fragile ego rides or is ridden (a more dynamic and dramatic concept than Schopenhauer's momentary suspension of the will). While the pleasure principle, in the phrasing of Max Schur,[80] "regulates the need to re-create by action or fantasy any situation which has created the experience of satisfaction," the unpleasure principle operates "to eliminate disturbances of equilibrium arising mainly from excessive external stimulation."

As already pointed out, a major problem of arriving at a workable psychoanalytic aesthetics comes from its undue weighting of pleasure in its implied definition of beauty. Artists and critics alike have long overwhelmingly rejected this reduction of their experience to pleasure, which for some art forms like tragedy may not even be significantly relevant. In sum, then, a Freudian aesthetic would have to find ways to cope with the contemplative enjoyment of the spectator and the exhilaration of the creator before it could advance from a psychoanalysis of art to an aesthetic of art. Moreover, the position that the "deepest" level of any work is the one revealed by psychoanalysis has not been well received by critics for whom surface and depth in art are fused into the very texture of the work itself. Looking away from the work of art and toward its "essential" and measureable elements was the practice of the nineteenth-century scientific aesthetics of Fechner and others on which Freud's approach to art in good measure depends, and in some measure explains, the limitations of his art criticism.

Freud's coupling of the pleasure principle with a principle of equilibrium might prove adequate to account for limited areas of aesthetic appreciation, but would hardly do justice to the artist's powerful drives to express himself through organizing forms and colors. The psychoanalyst's conservative taste may have restricted his vision in this area and blinded him to artistic problems in which the artist rebels against conventional modes of seeing and making art. The limits of Freud's vision here are probably the same as those circumscribing his teacher Brücke's academic concept of beauty as pleasantly tranquil. Inevitably, Freud excluded from his own implicit definition of beauty not only movements favoring the grotesque, such as Expressionism, but any of the fresh and inventive styles beginning with Impressionism —all of which would be lumped together as "ugly." The moderating role of beauty in art corresponds rather well to the function of the ego in Freud's mental scheme: just as a successful composition would, in this view, stay on a humane middle ground between bare abstraction and excessive emotionalism, so the healthy ego would remain master of its own house, neither dominated by the severe super-ego nor swept into the wild currents of the id. In terms of creativity, the ego would function as a synthesizer of divergent and swarming energies. Freud could have found support for such a position in Fechner (1876); for in his book on jokes,[81] he quotes passages by Fechner such as one treating the "principle of the unified linking of multiplicities," which Freud shows to operate in the field of jokes according to the following formula: "where several pleasure-giving factors operate together we are not able to attribute to each of them the share it has really taken in bringing about the result." The same formula, known to romantic aesthetics as "unity in variety," seems to apply to Freud's model of the mind's division into interacting forces, with the ego (when not a passive observer) uniting or balancing the divergent and competing messages arriving from the instinctual id forces, from the super-ego and from perceptions of reality (internal as well as external).[82]

In Freud's dynamic system, the tendency of the ego's energy to remain constant along with its synthesizing capacities would correspond to "unity," whereas the charging and discharging energies of super-ego, id, and reality would clearly correspond to "variety."[83] My translation of Freud's diagram of the mental apparatus into aesthetic terms emphasizes the role assigned by Freud to the conscious (or preconscious) elements in the production of art, and the need to maintain a certain balance between conscious and unconscious forces. Understandably, to prove just this point, Gombrich (1966), following Kris, emphasized the interesting sentence he found in Freud's letter to Stefan Zweig of July 20, 1938 concerning Surrealist and other unusual art forms: "the concept of art resists an extension beyond the point where the quantitative proportion between unconscious material and preconscious elaboration is not kept within a certain limit." This formula, with its obvious affinities to the old ratios of "scientific" aesthetics dear to Fechner, placed art on a scale between total conscious control and psychotic surrender to the unconscious. The new, daring leaps of contemporary art into the unknown were anathema to Freud and his associates, and it is little wonder that the artists whom he did know and who were allowed to do his portrait were—with the exception of Dali, who produced a slick and virtuoso sketch Freud admired —all mediocre. Dali was "saved" by his technical mastery from being considered by Freud as a mere lunatic. The originality of Freud's views on the importance of the ego, which he expressed more frequently in his later writings, should not be overestimated, however, nor should these views be regarded as contributions to an aesthetic of modern art, as Gombrich evidently considered them. Freud's position grows out of the nineteenth-century romantic preoccupation with originality, and just as he viewed the artist as a dreamer, somewhat Bohemian and not completely respectable, so he was concerned to find a formula for incorporating fantasy and "free association" into a legitimizing and coherent framework. In this respect, his ego, at the center of a distracting chaos of impressions, seems to blend the two opposed aesthetic trends with which he was best acquainted: the neoclassic, with its insistence on order and "beauty," and the romantic, emphasizing originality and uninhibited expression. One is reminded here of the nearly contemporary work of Edward Bullough (1912), which aimed to find an optimal "psychic distance" for art—neither "over-distanced" (detached and uninvolved in a sense not quite the same as classical reserve) nor "underdistanced" (so close and emotionally involved as to lose perspective and separation); and more recently, of McLuhan, with his pretentious "hot" and "cool" media.

Freud's aim at a balanced, sensible, healthy art seems to surface quite clearly in his essay "Psychopathic Characters on the Stage" (1905). Ruminating on the relation of the author of a play to his audience, Freud finds the spectator "a poor wretch to whom nothing of importance can happen," who must be enabled by playwright and actor alike "to identify himself with a hero." In plays whose main character is psychopathic, the hero must not start out psychopathic, but "*become* psychopathic in the course of the action of the play." Applying his criterion to a play he had recently seen, Hermann Bahr's *Die Andere* (1905), Freud finds the play—in contrast to *Hamlet*—defective because it offers the spectator a ready-made neurosis and a heroine with whom he cannot identify. Freud concluded with a generalization on "the limits set upon the employment of abnormal characters on the stage," finding them determined by the combination of "the neurotic instability of the public [*sic*] and the dramatist's skill in avoiding resistances and offering forepleasures." The essay on Bahr contains what appears to be the prototype of the later formula for deciding the success of art on the basis of its proportions of conscious to unconscious material. It should be noted that Freud's formula, here applied with conservative strictness, is vague and flexible enough to permit a far more generous, even avant-garde interpretation of it: the forepleasures that Bahr failed to supply Freud might have been appreciated by other members of the audience with more advanced taste. Admittedly, Freud's criterion of identification, as he presents it here, need not exclude the most unusual psychotic character, *provided* his illness unfolds before us gradually enough to allow for continuous sympathy with him. However, unless joined to complementary criteria showing how the various proportions apply to actual examples (assuming that such proportions can be determined), Freud's ratio of conscious to unconscious leaves the work of art in a limbo of highly psychological, and perhaps irrelevant, criticism.

In our previous considerations of Freud's views on art, it became quite clear that the objective aspect of the work was neglected in favor of psychological considerations. This tendency really pointed up a weakness in Freud's psychology itself; for it has been noted that he never seems to have solved the intersubjective problems of social behavior that every psychology must confront. Thus, in his essay "On Narcissism" (1914), he asks from what source the necessity arises "that urges our mental life to pass on beyond the limits of narcissism and to attach the libido to objects," and answers that "we are so impelled when the cathexis of the ego with libido exceeds a certain degree." Then he notes that while a strong egoism is a protection against neurosis, "in the last resort we must begin to love in order that we may not fall ill, and must fall ill if, in consequence of frustration, we cannot love. Somewhat after this fashion does Heine conceive of the psychogenesis of the Creation." This paradoxical quality of the ego, whose greatest strength occurs when it is able to direct its surplus energies outward toward others, may be directly linked to Freud's view of artistic creation; for, in his last sentence he compares the whole process of turning love outward to a theory of cosmic creation, which, coming from a skeptical poet, must have more to do with poetic creativity than with Biblical genesis. The paradoxical position of the ego's libido in Freud's psychology is rooted in his uneven treatments of, on the one hand, the artist's psyche, whose subtlest motivations are catalogued, and on the other, the artist's behavior or his actual work, whose modes and media, forms and styles, are rarely distinguished or defined in most of his writings apart from the *Jokes*. Actually, Freud was less interested in the artist or writer *per se* than in the creator of genius. He never wrote on Rembrandt, the artist whom he may have valued above all others (especially for his portraits), probably because what is known of the artist has mostly to do with his art and not with his mentality. Nor was there any Rembrandt portrait corresponding to the Mona Lisa or to Michelangelo's *Moses* in having stimulated a large literature puzzling over its "state of mind" or over the sequence of its presumed feelings and gestures preceding the moment represented.

Another difficulty of Freud's aesthetics is the question of value: psychoanalysis could probe the depths of a work without ever indicating whether it was good or bad art. Of course, many modern aestheticians follow the skepticism of F. H. Bradley, who can't see how the study of art can be at all relevant to the question of value; for the most careful and penetrating description of art will not lead the critic from his mass of facts to an evaluation of the work of art. It seems that such evaluation is inevitable in criticism, whether explicit or implicit, merely in the act of selecting the piece for study, and in any case, Freud assumed criteria of quality when he chose "great" works to illustrate his Oedipal theme. Freud, in fact, tried vaguely to explain the greatness of Sophocles' play, and its later versions in *Hamlet* and *The Brothers Karamazov*, by somehow connecting them all to the same great theme; but he also indicates that modern treatments, such as in Grillparzer's *Die Ahnfrau*, are inferior to the great versions. His explanation does not convince, nor does it enable us to penetrate into the literary qualities of the works, since they are all reduced to a single dimension, which omits their qualities of language, rhythm, image, and so forth.[84]

One might conclude from this study that the chief value of considering Freud's theories of art is for the light they can throw on psychoanalysis and on his personality. This holds, perhaps, for his more narrowly aesthetic statements, rooted often in his own early biases and prejudices, but (as will be shown in chapter 4) Freud stimulated others through his powerful literary example in the great works such as *The Interpretation of Dreams* and *The Psychopathology of Everyday Life*, and through his impressive formulation of ideas and techniques, which were not primarily intended as aesthetic, but which have had a great impact on several generations of critics, artists and writers. Here one thinks of such ideas as overdetermination and condensation; his intimate description of the continuity between normal and neurotic experience; and his dramatic view of the mind in which a war, not of good and evil, but of ego, super-ego, and id forces occurs as a secular *psychomachia*. That Freud chose to emphasize the content of art, and the wish-fulfillment aspect of fantastic mental processes, does not mean that students building on Freud's insights cannot bridge the gaps toward the formal, perceptual aspects of art. Furthermore, while certain writers exaggerated the indiscriminate applicability of Freud's art theories to modern art, some of these theories do have a direct bearing on, and can elucidate recent styles in, art and literature. Finally, Freud's ideas have been a fruitful source for new, imaginative interpretations of old art, which are sometimes revealing, sometimes wildly off the subject, but frequently point the way to new interpretations of considerable interest.

Four

Freud's Influence on Art, Literature, and Criticism

By exploring the complications and inconsistencies, the strengths and weaknesses of Freud's ideas about art, and by considering their relation to psychoanalysis as well as to his personal life, we have secured a vantage point from which to scan their impact on twentieth-century art and literature. This enormous and varied impact can only begin to be elucidated when we understand, first, what Freud himself produced, and second, how some of these heterogeneous ideas suited certain artistic movements, corresponded to some of the broad trends or fashions, and stimulated others (as broadly outlined in the Appendix). Freud's ideas have seemed especially suited to the needs and ambitions of the Surrealists.

The relation of Freud to Surrealism is known to be inexhaustively complex to everyone acquainted with the literature;[1] however, a brief discussion of the history of this relation will be useful here, since it can help clarify some aspects of. Freud's aesthetics. The origins of Surrealism merge with the demise of the short, lively Dada movement, from which came many of its founding members. But Dadaism, launched in Zürich in 1916 amidst the anxieties and destruction of World War I, was international from the start: a dispute persists among scholars about the "discovery" of the name of the movement (a French children's word meaning hobbyhorse), the honor being given to Tzara (a Rumanian), Hülsenbeck (a German), or Arp (a bilingual

18. Claude Mellan, *Decorative Ornament*
    (seventeenth-century French print).
    Reproduced from Eduard Fuchs,
    Illustrierte Sittengeschichte (Munich, 1909–12).

19. *The Snake*
    (eighteenth-century
    French caricature).
    Reproduced from
    Eduard Fuchs,
    *Illustrierte
    Sittengeschichte*
    (Munich, 1909–12).

21. Indian portraits of
Alexander the Great, with
a composite photograph by
Francis Galton. Reproduced
from Karl Pearson,
*The Life, Letters, and Labours
of Francis Galton*
(Cambridge, 1930). Permission:
Cambridge University Press.

20. Title page of a
French novel.
Reproduced from
Eduard Fuchs,
*Illustrierte
Sittengeschichte*
(Munich, 1909–12).

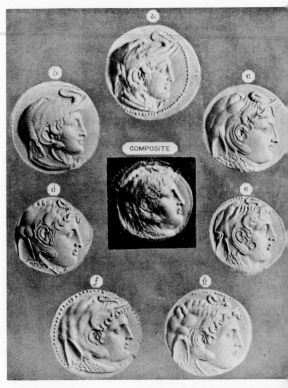

22. Caricature of "England"
by Jean Beber (1901).
Reproduced from
Eduard Fuchs,
*Geschichte der
erotischen Kunst*
(Berlin, 1908).

23. *Baubo.* Greek terra cotta
reproduced in
Salomon Reinach,
*Cultes, Mythes
et Religions*
(Paris, 1912).

24–25. Drawings after Michelangelo's *Moses*, illustrating Freud's essay "The Moses of Michelangelo."

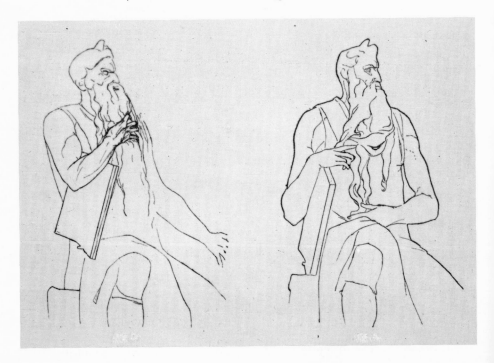

26. *Moses* (thirteenth-century statuette). Ashmolean Museum, Oxford.

27. Jacomo Rocchetti, *Sketch for the Tomb of Julius II,*
after Michelangelo. Berlin, Staatliche Museen.
Photo: Kupferstichkabinett und Sammlung der Zeichnungen.

28. Moritz von Schwind, *The Dream of a Prisoner*.
Munich, Bayerischen Staatsgemäldesammlungen.

29. André Masson, *Metamorphosis of Gradiva,* 1939.
Private collection. Photo: Galerie Louise Leiris, Paris.
Permission: A.D.A.G.P. 1971, by French Reproduction Rights, Inc.

30. René Magritte, *Le Viol*, 1934. Collection George Melly, London.
Photo: The Arts Council of Great Britain.

31. Marcel Duchamp, *L.H.O.O.Q.*, 1919.

32. Francis Galton, composite "all-round" photograph of a bust
in the British Museum. Reproduced from Karl Pearson,
The Life, Letters, and Labours of Francis Galton
(Cambridge, 1930). Permission: Cambridge University Press.

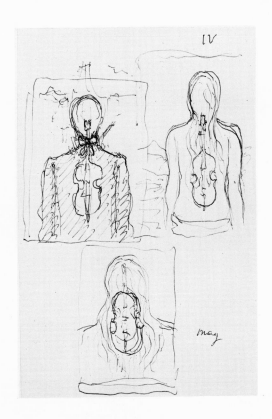

33–34. René Magritte,
Persian Letters,
1960. Drawings
for the painting
The Soul of Bandits.
Collection
Harry Torczyner,
New York. Photos:
The Museum of
Modern Art,
New York.

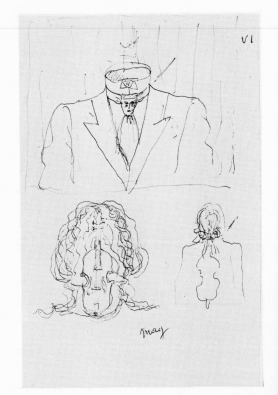

German born in France). Centered alike in Switzerland and Germany, with off-shoots in France and America, the German contingent of this wildly iconoclastic and nihilistic movement had sufficient contacts with the still-untranslated works of Freud, to have stimulated Wittels's contemptuous rejection of Dadaism, for claiming Freud as one of its models. (I am not referring to postwar Berlin, where the revolutionary attack on all order caused Freud, along with Jung and Adler, to be "consigned to the scrap-heap," as Hans Richter, the German Dadaist, puts it.)[2] There seems to have been some fascination among the Zürich Dadaists for Freud's work, so that the irrepressible iconoclast Tzara felt called upon to declare in his *Manifeste Dada 1918* (1924) that psychoanalysis is "a dangerous malady which puts the anti-real tendencies to sleep" and provides the bourgeoisie with a useful system (later Tzara was to become much more sympathetic to psychoanalytic ideas, and in his book *Grains et issues* of 1935, he revived the "experimental dream" and used Freudian jargon such as "sublimation"). Breton, in 1920, writing "Pour Dada," mentioned the vogue for the "systematic exploration of the unconscious," and noted that "spurious scholars" threaten to harm Dada by seeing in it "the application of a system which is enjoying vogue in psychiatry, Freud's psychoanalysis, an application foreseen, moreover, by myself. A very confused and particularly malevolent mind, that of H. R. Lenormand, was even prepared to suppose that we would benefit from psychoanalytic treatment . . . It goes without saying that the analogy to madmen is entirely superficial." Breton, after visiting Freud in Vienna in 1921, wrote a brief, critical description of the psychoanalyst,[3] which he later regretted as a Dadaist gesture.

The Surrealists, perhaps in part as a reaction against the Dadaists, responded favorably to psychoanalysis after the early 1920's; but this response is the opposite of what one would have expected when the term was first introduced. Compared to "Dada," the name "Surrealism" has a more certainly French pedigree, having been coined by Guillaume Apollinaire in 1917. Apollinaire, a militant Germanophobe, opposed all symbolism and romanticism, considering them tainted by German philosophy. He applied the word *Surréalisme* to his play *Les Mamelles de Tirésias* (*The Breasts of Tiresias*), in direct contradiction of Victor Basch, the French proponent of Lipps's *Einfühlung*, who claimed to have found symbolism in the play. Both in the style of his play and by the gesture of choosing a new name to describe it, Apollinaire joined other young Frenchmen who aimed for direct expression, a contemporary immediacy bypassing the old traditions.[4] At first, French Dadaists seemed to be following Apollinaire in associating themselves with the name *Surréalisme*; but Apollinaire's rejection of Symbolism was already being ignored or challenged, and some writers regarded Dadaism as essentially the Symbolist state of mind intensified to the point of insanity.

Through the complexity of the situation, in which the new and the old, the French and the German, the Symbolists and the Dadaists, were associated or opposed by variously motivated critics, the real history of the development often became clouded. By the time Breton was writing his first manifesto in 1924, he made a turnabout in his attitude both to Germany[5] and to Symbolism, and in part as a scandalous gesture, he threw the name of Freud at his French compatriots.[6] We must not forget that in the bitter aftermath of World War I, Freud's name would be equated with the German enemy; thus, the same Lenormand whose views on Dada Breton counter-attacked, insisted[7] that "Dadaism and its successor Surrealism" were a "regression to infancy" resembling hysteria and psychoneurosis, and he cites Henri Albert in the *Mercure de France* that "Dadaism was invented by the Germans with disordered nervous systems who wanted to restore their health by imitating the stammerings of early childhood." In humorously "psychoanalyzing" Dada poetry, Lenormand refers, not to Freud, but to Dr. Maeder, the Swiss writer who produced some of the earliest summaries of Freud's ideas in French, and who was personally known to Tzara and Breton.[8] Such summaries, despite their severe limitations, made Freud's ideas sufficiently accessible, so that slogans and phrases drawn from him could be introduced into some French intellectual circles; so, we must await further research to determine whether Clifford Browder,[9] who argues that Freud's works were translated into French only in the early 1920's and that Breton never learned German, and Michel Sanouillet,[10] who points to Breton's unfriendly account of his visit to Freud in 1921, are correct in minimizing Freud's influence on early Surrealism.[11] It seems to me that, their own claims to the contrary notwithstanding, the French Surrealists' version of psychoanalysis rarely coincided with Freud's: at their worst, they misunderstood his profoundly therapeutic intention, and at their best, they expanded the Freudian ideas of sex and the unconscious into new frontiers not foreseen by the great psychoanalyst, introducing elements drawn from French traditions. In support of this view, we may note the extent to which the Surrealists' ideas were continuous with those of earlier French poetry and psychiatry.[12] Freud himself, in a half-humorous interview with the Frenchman Raymond Recouly (1923), offered two explanations to account for his unpopularity in France: first, that "politics has something to do with it," and second, that "as my theories at least at their commencement were connected with those of your great Charcot, the French have been less than anxious to follow their development on foreign ground, in a foreign spirit and language."

How, then, account for Breton's seeming reliance on Freud's dream theories in his *First Manifesto* of 1924 (and his claim to have known those theories before 1919), in which Charcot's name does not appear? Breton, who prided himself on his acumen in the field of psychiatry, nevertheless, probably used Freud's name without fully understanding his theories at that time; for example, as early as 1923, Aragon, in "Max Ernst, peintre des illusions," suggested in a most general way that if one were to analyze Ernst's drawings "in the manner of Freud" one would find in them "a very simple phallic meaning." And Breton, in his *First Manifesto*, assumes, apparently unaware of Freud's opposite view, that dreams depend on the dreams of previous nights, and that they can "be used in solving the fundamental questions of life." Apparently he does not yet grasp the idea of the day-residues or of the wish fulfillment, and he does not refer to Freud's idea of sublimation as applied to art, a subject that he discusses briefly but with understanding in the *Second Manifesto* of 1930. Breton probably understated his debt to the French tradition of psychiatry for several reasons: French psychiatrists rarely sympathized either with Freud or with the Surrealists.[13] When we realize how much the technique of psychic automatism probably owes to Janet's writings (1889), we can only suppose that Breton's apparent indifference both to Charcot and to Janet[14] was due to their positions within academic psychology. Breton was probably much more favorably impressed by Jean Vinchon's little book *L'Art et la Folie*, published in Paris in 1924, just as

Surrealism was being consolidated. This book discusses the mentally disordered in terms of the ideas of Charcot and his followers at the Salpêtrière, applies Bleuler's term "schizophrenic," and uses Schopenhauer's notion that memories, instead of being wiped out, can remain isolated in the mind unconnected to any logical groups; but it completely ignores Freud's work.

Vinchon observes that among mentally disordered writers and artists "there is no longer an alternating of the life of dream and of real life as among the hashish-eaters of Moreau of Tours [the psychologist who wrote *Du Haschich et de l'Aliénation mentale*; Paris, 1845], but the tyrannic and definitive rule of the life of dream." This life of dream he calls "an automatic life," and he finds that "the dream, which the ecstasies of the delirious mystic and the states of trance of the medium resemble, can inspire the poet or the artist to elaborate his memories, from which he will derive surprising results, because it will escape the control of consciousness. This mode of inspiration represents the superior form of automatism." In that same year, 1924, Breton organized a Bureau of Surrealist Research, thereby approaching willy-nilly the experimentalism of Janet rather than Freud's therapy. This divergence from psychoanalysis becomes clear from Freud's own contrast of his views on hysteria to those of Janet, in his *Five Lectures on Psychoanalysis* (1910a): observing that Janet emphasized an unavoidable dissociation, whereas he accepted the possibility of synthesis, Freud concludes his essay with the point that a divergence between them was "inevitable, since I did not start out, like Janet, from laboratory experiments, but with therapeutic aims in mind." Only later, when Breton aspired to a therapy of sex and love, did Freud's theories become more significant for him.

In the *First Manifesto*, Breton translated Apollinaire's vague allusion to the novelty implied by his neologism *Surréalisme* into a monumentally assured definition:

Surrealism, noun. Psychic automatism in its pure state, by which one proposes to express—verbally, by means of the written word, or in any other manner—the actual functioning of thought. Dictated by thought, in the absence of any control exercised by reason, exempt from any aesthetic or moral concern . . . Surrealism is based on the belief in the superior reality of certain forms of previously neglected association, in the omnipotence of dream, in the disinterested play of thought.

This emphasis on the depth of thought, on imagination and memory, impelled Breton to look into older writers, especially those intrepid dream-explorers, the romantics; but Breton rejected the mysterious of the romantics in his quest of the "marvelous," and reduced the fuzzy edges and sentimentalism of the romantics to a more positivistic, psychologically informed discipline. It is too often overlooked that except for moments of excess the romantics tended to bracket dream and life. Thus, in Jean Paul's earthshaking "Speech of the Dead Christ," the author's terrifying vision is sandwiched between his falling asleep and his waking up, comforting his readers by means of the isolating frame as though to say, "It's not for real." In our own period, however, there is an increasing effort expended on tearing away the framing or barrier between the artist's feelings and sensations and the spectator's. E. T. A. Hoffmann's *Kater Murr*, on the other hand, comes complete with an explanation of its mixed-up pagination, so that the reader's anxiety is allayed in a manner that Surrealist texts do not permit. Even romantic humor, which in Börne's and Jean Paul's cases, at least, resembled the Surrealists' in pointing toward liberation—political as well as psychological—never went so far as the Surrealists' consistent *humour noir* and endless childish punning, both prefigurements of the Theater of the Absurd. Essentially, then, the Surrealists go beyond their forebears in bold and conscious exploitation of their minds, using guidelines from psychiatry and eventually psychoanalysis. Building on Freud's realistic approach to the unconscious, the Surrealists consider man's mind bound above and below by realities, not by mysteries, that is, by his experience, his memory, and his body: roughly, God becomes a super-ego, the soul becomes the unconscious, and religious ecstasy becomes the joy and pleasure of imagination in contact with the unconscious through dream or art. The establishment of real boundaries is accompanied by the dissolution of formal boundaries, as among life, dream and art, between adult and child, and between mind and mind, through the "exquisite corpse" games in which a group of Surrealists produce a poem by adding lines one after the other to a sheet of paper so folded that none knew what the others had written, or in drawings similarly produced.

Breton, departing from the more level-headed Freud, believed that these and other Surrealist games, taken together with such "sciences" as astrology, clairvoyance, and parapsychology, bring "out into the open a strange possibility of thought, which is that of its *pooling*." Such contacts of unconscious minds would contribute to realizing another of Breton's ambitions, the establishment of a collective myth. Here Breton, asserting his independence of Freud, attempts to add his own deities—women like Gradiva, Aurelia, and Nadja, who embodied the elusive love principle he pursued—to the Freudian pantheon, whose types had been limited to family members, above all (among the females), the dominant figure of the mother along with the sister. Breton disagrees with Freud on a number of other important issues: the relation of the conscious to the instinctual (Freud wishing the id to yield to the ego, Breton assigning to the id the role of liberator), the evaluation of neurosis (Freud wishing to cure it, Breton at moments promoting mental disorder, as when he encouraged the fascinatingly erratic and strange behavior of Nadja, a girl on the border line between reason and madness, who inspired a book bearing her name and illustrated with her drawings, in 1928), the relation of dream, life, and art (Freud insisting on their separation, Breton wishing to break down their barriers and mingle them), and even on approaches to the dream (Freud treating it clinically and positivistically, Breton as a marvelous phenomenon that, in contradiction to Freud's opinion, is even prophetic). The Surrealists in general approached the past with far less reverence than Freud, with his emphasis on verbal and auditory memory, had done; and, like the Futurists (to whom the Surrealists owe an unacknowledged debt), they exalted the new, the unexpected, and the shocking. Understandably, Gaston Bachelard,[15] sympathetic to Surrealism, opposes a phenomenological to a psychoanalytic approach to art, maintaining that "phenomenology liquidates the past and confronts what is new." Surrealist automatism, in reducing the importance of the visual and the verbal, tries to leave one blind and deaf in the interest of deeper unconscious truths and "in-sights," and tends to emphasize preimaginal kinesthetic sensations: when one sits down with pen idly meandering over paper, it matters little whether one is called artist or writer, since one is essentially making primitive *doodles* or word scrambles perhaps resembling the schemata of children at the point of learning the letters of the alphabet. The products of such activity are intended not to be "beautiful," but to shock, to upset the spectator or auditor and put him into a troubled state receptive to new, unexpected truths and realities.

The differences between Freud and Breton partly derive from the obviously dissimilar intellectual frameworks of the men, but also from a clash of these two powerful personalities, who were so alike in their common impulse to conquer and lead, in their self-control (Breton refused to fall into hypnotic sleep, just as Freud would never submit to being analyzed). The old gladiator and the young collided in an incident as revealing of their personalities as it was amusing. Breton wrote a book, *The Communicating Vessels* (1932),[16] in some ways his own *Interpretation of Dreams* (not only is Breton preoccupied with the dream theories of Freud's book, but he seems to have written it out of guilt feelings, like Freud: in Breton's case, for driving Nadja into psychosis; in Freud's, for his father's death), in which he summed up the more detailed knowledge of psychoanalysis he had been able to acquire through the translations into French of Freud's major works during the 1920's. In the course of his discussion, Breton made two criticisms of Freud's masterpiece; first, that although Freud had made use of the ideas of Volkelt, his bibliography remained "significantly silent" about this important predecessor (insinuating that Freud was perhaps motivated by envy of a competitor), and second—a criticism that seems particularly to have rankled Freud—that Freud was inconsistent, playing the prudent bourgeois in the analysis of his own dreams, as compared to those of others, since "sexual preoccupations apparently play no role in his personal dreams, whereas they contribute quite preponderantly to the working out of the other dreams (mainly of hysterics), which Freud submits to us." (Breton then follows this criticism with an analysis of one of his own dreams in which he says that "we shall try to be that imprudent and flawless observer.")

Freud read Breton's book, published at the end of November, 1932, and seems at once to have written the author two letters in rapid succession, on December 17 and 18, and a third on December 26, replying to Breton's criticism. Freud's first two letters elaborately justify the absence of the name of one of his sources from the bibliography of certain editions of *The Interpretation of Dreams*; but his third letter, of December 26, gets to the real issue for him, by way of a denial. Freud indicates that his excessively zealous response "is doubtless a form of reaction against the limitless ambition of infancy, happily overcome." (In his reply to this letter, Breton playfully questions whether this ambition has in fact been "happily overcome.") To Breton's second criticism, Freud replied:

> I believe that if I have not analyzed my own dreams as extensively as those of others, the cause is only rarely timidity with regard to the sexual. The fact is, much more frequently, that it would have required me regularly to discover the secret source of the whole series of dreams in my relations to my father, recently deceased. I maintain that I was in the right to set limits to the inevitable exhibition (as well of an infantile tendency since surmounted).

Breton sharply rebutted Freud's defense by noting that Freud's pretext about his father's death in 1896 seems rather shaky, since "the seven editions of his book since 1900 have provided Freud all the opportunities he could wish for to escape from his earlier reserve, or at least to explain it briefly." Breton's point agrees with our findings about Freud's responses to criticism of his *Leonardo*; and we might add that even the first edition of *The Interpretation of Dreams* was completed at least three years after the death of Jakob Freud, thereby invalidating Freud's description of his death as recent.

However incompatible some ideas of the French Surrealists of the 1920's were with Freud's, and in spite of the special tensions between Breton and Freud, from the late 1920's through the 1930's, one can find some quite significant attempts by the Surrealists to make use of psychoanalysis in their works, and they appear actually to have read the French translations of Freud. Breton, in particular, sought things in Freud that were not present in the French writers and psychologists accessible to him; for example, a justification for the Surrealist theories of love (as release from sexual inhibition enabling the lover to seek an ultimate mythic woman) and the comic (especially *humour noir*) as techniques of liberation, an elaborate metapsychology which made the human mind the center of politics, religion, and art, and a rationalization (mainly in *The Psychopathology of Everyday Life*) of their attempts to discover marvelous implications in the commonplace events and objects of everyday reality through a psychological determinism, which they could formulate as the "omnipotence of desire." In their emphasis on the psychological aspect of art, the Surrealists found as little place for formal questions as Freud had; [17] rather, they endeavored to use art not as self-expression but as a vehicle to rescue them from overvaluing their own egos, from falling into narcissism. Their project of a communal love, of getting out of one's own skin, was expressed poetically in notions of "mad love," "convulsive beauty," and the fusion of lovers in sexual ecstasy, which were realized by a variety of techniques, some derived from Freud's dream processes, some from the experimental techniques of avant-garde literature, such as the richly textured word patterns of Joyce's *Ulysses* and *Finnegans Wake*; and, plastically, by the intersection of the images of separate bodies (a technique learned from Cubism, but applied to the making of ambiguous, even androgynous forms and "exquisite corpses") or by the deformation of body images through stretching and intertwining them in the manner of some works of Chagall and Picasso. Art, or artistic situations, then, would act like "therapy," but a therapy seemingly less close to Freud (who emphasized a conventional social framework) than to Ferenczi or to F. H. Myers, who, becoming less skeptical than Freud, admitted parapsychological and mediumistic studies.[18] Pooling, the group games and spiritualism that were to draw individuals out of themselves, certainly borrowed from real or imputed analytic techniques: a version of free association translated into open, group situations became the paradigm of liberated creativity, displacing or even replacing automatism. The monstrous chimerical power of the unconscious, probed by intrepid artists and writers seeking their way through terrifying darks, using the light or thread of consciousness, was often symbolized in the 1930's by the minotaur and labyrinth.[19]

A final area of contact between psychoanalysis and Surrealism was the derivation of Surrealist imagery from Freudian symbolism. Obviously, sexual imagery takes pride of place, and we find phallic neckties (Breton), noses (Dali), and bones (Tanguy); fetishistic hair (Leonor Fini, Toyen, Félix Labisse, Meret Oppenheim); the sexuality of birds (Ernst); obsession with breasts (Paul Delvaux, Hans Bellmer);

and infantile sexuality (Dali, Balthus). The subject of dreams, of Oedipus Rex, of the Oedipus complex (as in Tanguy's *Mama, Papa Is Wound-
ed!*, representing a child's interpretation of his father's sexual
entry into his mother), and even of the "family romance" of the Holy
Family—all found their way into Surrealist painting or poetry. Dali's
"hand-painted dream photographs" attempted to capture the hallucinatory clarity of dreaming, as in his famous painting *The Persistence
of Memory* which suggests that time stands still within the
dreamer's mind, as it does in Freud's timeless unconscious, so that
metal watches go limp and functionless, rot and attract ants, and turn
into organic shapes, such as the watch drooping like an autumn leaf on
the otherwise bare limb of a tree. Not all of this can be attributed
uniquely to Freud's influence, of course, some being Dada—or
Futurist—inspired antitraditionalism, others biomorphic forms linked to
Cubism; but the presence of Freud's writings undoubtedly stimulated
the multiplication of such imagery, and demonstrably affected the content of a number of works.[20] One major image unquestionably inspired
by Freud was that of Gradiva.

Freud's essay on Jensen's *Gradiva* was translated for the first time
into French in 1931 by his old friend and follower Marie Bonaparte,
with an illustration of the ancient fragment of relief showing Gradiva
and two other figures, and it seems to have struck the Surrealists'
imagination more powerfully than any other of his works. Probably
Breton, always in pursuit of impressive females, fictional or real
(particularly those met by chance in the street), was the first to seize
upon the figure of Gradiva, which he was to return to more than once.
He placed the following passage from Jensen's book (the text of which
was included in the French edition) at the front of *Les Vases communicants* (1932) as a dedicatory quotation: "lightly raising her dress with
her left hand, Gradiva Rediviva-Zoé Bertgang, enveloped by the dreamy
glances of Hanold, with her soft and tranquil step, in full sunlight
on the tiles, passed on the other side of the street."[21] In 1937, the same
year that the Surrealist Galerie Gradiva opened in Paris with its glass
door by Duchamp, Breton wrote his essay "Gradiva,"[22] in which he
explains: "Gradiva? This title, borrowed from the marvelous work of
Jensen, signifies above all: SHE WHO ADVANCES."[23] He later remarks,
"From the child's picture book to that of the poets: / GRADIVA /

Over the bridge uniting dream and reality, 'lightly raising her dress with her left hand': / GRADIVA / At the border of utopia and truth, that is in the midst of life: / GRADIVA." In 1931, Dali, probably following Breton's lead, painted the first of a series of works treating the theme of Gradiva, which he was eventually to unite with the all-embracing figure of Gala, elusive and whimsical wife of Éluard and mistress of Max Ernst before becoming Dali's faithful muse, and receiving the name Gala-Gradiva. Impressed by the metamorphic images of Gradiva, Dali wrote in his *Secret Life of Salvador Dali*[24] that one could not tell "where Gradiva ends and where Zoe Bertrand [*sic*] begins in Jensen's *Delirium and Dream*." The enthusiastic Dali turned out numerous drawings of Gradiva, one foot of which seems to derive from the illustration showing the relief of Gradiva in the French edition; but he apparently missed completely (if he ever read) Jensen's point about the connection between the names Gradiva and Bertgang, and certainly seems not to have read Freud's interpretation of it, inasmuch as he consistently uses the incorrect name "Bertrand."[25] Dali must have produced his first Gradiva drawings in 1931 or later, in any case after the publication of the French edition of Gradiva.[26]

We are indebted to André Masson for a more important and interesting treatment of the theme: his *Metamorphosis of Gradiva* (*Fig. 29*), painted in 1939, brilliantly interprets Freud's essay. Following details of the story, Masson depicts a nearly nude classical figure, wearing toga and sandal on her left side, asleep on the steps of the Temple of Apollo before a characteristic Pompeiian fresco decoration. Other details, such as the erupting Vesuvius, the flies, and the crack in the wall with a lizard before it also illustrate Freud's presentation, as does the central theme of the tension between the parts of the body that are alive and those becoming petrified, a distinction clearly visible in the original, where one can see the contrast between the warm flesh tones and the spread-out legs (a position resembling a primitive mother-goddess) displaying a large vaginal form, and beside this a big thick slab of red beef covering the whole central trunk. With unrestrained sexuality, Masson interprets Freud's circumspect allusions; thus, the exploding volcano suggests an orgasmic breakthrough of repressed sexual material, the crack has obvious genital connotations, and the swarm of flies makes the sensual attractions of the meat toward which they move more palpable. The interesting question about this painting is the nature and degree of its dependence on Freud's discussion and on the illustration of the relief. Masson introduces a minor but striking change by substituting the red poppy (the French *coquelicot*), symbol of dream and death, for the asphodel alluded to in the story, but the artist imposes his own interpretation on the subject even more significantly in other details. The composition recalls that of *Woman*, a painting of 1925, and the form of Gradiva herself appears to be borrowed from the main figure in this painting.[27] The two figures resemble each other in the important detail of the dissected viscera (lungs? heart?), which becomes the slice of beef over the torso, in the definite profile of the left breast, and in their monumental scale. The whole left leg, and particularly the foot set on a tilted base with drapery above it in the *Woman*, reappear with slight changes—most significantly, the addition of the prominent right foot, whose posture derives from the illustration to Freud's book, and which serves to identify the subject. Apparently, in Masson's case at least, the influence of a book by Freud on a particular work of the artist must be taken in a very qualified sense: the artist was ready with a form that he could mold to fit a new iconography. Freud helped Masson to garnish his figure with symbolic attributes and with narrative color; but, the most important and interesting details depend upon the artist's personal iconography, which may or may not approximate the psychoanalytic.

From this discussion of the sources of Masson's painting of *Gradiva*, we may conclude that in some important instances even the Surrealist artist derived from psychoanalysis only what he was ready to apply and fit into his own development. But, since the movement passed through a phase in which efforts were made to produce psychologically interesting protocols, some writers have exaggerated Freud's influence; thus, Jean Cazaux[28] claimed that the Surrealist works are documents as valid for study as the records of psychological interviews or psychoanalytic sessions, and that therefore the Freudian approach can profitably be applied to them (it is ironic that Cazaux's description of psychoanalytic techniques is far vaguer than his comparatively extensive presentation of French psychiatric procedures). Kenneth Burke (1939) goes even further with his slogan, " In so far as art contains a Surrealist ingredient (and all art contains some of this ingredient), psychoanalytic co-ordinates are required to explain the logic of its structure." If we substitute for Burke's generalization, which is unprovable beyond the sense that all art has an emotional and motivational aspect, ranging from near zero to saturation, the more limited hypothesis that subjective or symbolic styles, rather than abstract or decorative ones, can most profitably be approached through psychoanalysis, I believe we will make psychoanalysis a more useful critical tool, and one congruent with the historian's viewpoint. Psychoanalytic criticism would, of course, be an essential key to the content of post-Freudian modern art and literature, which embody Freud's specific symbols and images, or his actual techniques. George Boas[29] has observed that, ironically, a new set of "hieroglyphs" has taken the place of an older, traditional one: "they are the symbols that the school of Freud has made popular." Comparing the Surrealists who borrowed Freudian symbols to older symbol-users, he notes that "the meaning of Surrealist symbols was hardly in the same domain as those of the emblem-writers, but what is of interest to us is that their meaning emerged entirely through visual shock, not through discursive thought."

Naturally, psychoanalysis can be applied to these borrowed symbols, if only to aid in defining them, but a harder question is whether there is an inevitable iconography and self-expression even in the work of so-called abstract artists, whose individuality may imply that part of their achievement entails identifiable marks of personality. There are periods when the artist strives for anonymity (or nonexpression, as the post-Dadaist John Cage and his followers do), but contemporary artists who realize their conceptions in mass production and who disdain to touch their pieces are anonymous only in a special sense; given the promotional role of their galleries and of the art journals, the one producing intricately professional *catalogues raisonnés* even for young artists and the other publishing full-blown analyses with sophisticated apologetics, nowadays there is a superabundance of artistic identities being defined, although many are soon quietly forgotten. For the virtuoso young formalist critics, psychoanalytic criticism of the old school, with its hunt for sexual and motivational data and its ignorance of formal matters, seems trivial and sophomoric. In combating attempts to psychoanalyze artists, formalist critics like Roger Fry had already pointed to artists like Matisse, with his unrevealing iconography, his evident immersion in formal pleasures, and his dull biography (exhilarating only if you follow his artistic evolution). But a new situation developed with two other giants of twentieth-century painting—Picasso and Duchamp—who seemed even more confusing for psychoanalytic critics.

Picasso, with his numerous dips into iconography, traditional as well as psychoanalytic, his ulcers, and his tempestuous love life, above all the notoriety of his Cubist style, stimulated various feeble attempts to "psychoanalyze" his art;[30] but the artist's amazingly protean quality, his adoption of a whole range of styles, past and present, has made him too elusive: the most sensitive studies of Picasso have been appreciations that accept the many-leveled diversity within individual works no less than from painting to painting. Even less accessible are the work and personality of Marcel Duchamp, who made his art a complex form of defense and who, like Joyce, found his aims to be "silence" (he stopped painting in 1923), "exile" (he hovered between France and America, without committing himself to either as domicile, being buried in France but leaving his major works to American museums), and "cunning" (his endlessly inventive gestures and his inscrutably complex ironies made him impervious to simple appreciation). While Duchamp (and the innumerable young men who emulate some aspect of his life or art) conceivably might prove accessible to psychoanalytic criticism, clearly the standard psychoanalytic formulas would have to be modified considerably. Although Duchamp, like all men, has a biography, the usual romantic notion of a personality directly "expressed" in his art is ludicrously inadequate for comprehending the man or his works; perhaps, moreover, Duchamp's excesses merely point up some home truths about a residual inaccessibility in all artists. Freud, beyond his own inhibitions, may have sensed a little of this, inasmuch as he avoided tackling the job of psychoanalyzing an artist; but he would have shuddered in abhorrence before the phenomenon of a Duchamp. Whether *any* psychoanalytic approach would help us come closer to this elusive being is too hard a question to answer here.

Despite the frequent complaints about, or piety before, Freud's musty nineteenth-century odor, Freud's ideas—or elements of them—have continued to survive as relevant to some contemporary writers and artists. The age of psychology foreseen by the romantics has become the age of the Freudian man, in whom neurosis and insight go hand in hand, and whose self-centered analyses apparently remove him from the values of politics and society. A characteristic (but not very insightful) complaint against this age has been made by the philosopher C. E. M. Joad (1948), who decries the " 'psychologizing' of morals and of thinking," and who insists that "to forget the self is—for all that psychoanalysis may say to the contrary—a better recipe for the good life than to know the self." But this self-centering and self-knowledge need not be attached to selfish bourgeois values; and there has been a persistent impulse among some contemporaries not only to "socialize morality" but to try to do so by uniting psychoanalytic and Marxian ideas of work and pleasure, in order to overcome the failures of the Western individual and of his society. The solutions of these writers, while starting from Freudian and Marxian ideas, and evolving dialectically as a clash between the bourgeois individualist psychology of Freud and the socialist collectivism of Marx, go far beyond either. This is quite evident with regard to art: "bad" academic along with controversial contemporary art, and non-Western along with primitive arts have been finding increasing space in museums, whereas the traditional "great art" has become bit by bit less visible.

Attitudes toward depth psychology itself and its relation to art have also evolved remarkably: at first, it seemed the key to understanding the hidden or repressed significance of art (hence the recurrent discussions of art and neurosis); then, it became itself a source for artistic techniques; next, it was widely rejected by writers and critics who felt that "depth" was irrelevant to the artistic surface, where everything of importance for art occurs; and, finally, there has been recently a renewed interest in the deep strata of art and of its experience as a series of surfaces with multiple layers of meaning linked to great myths but without the old hierarchical arrangement in which "early" meant "deep" and "late" meant "shallow." In this last phase psychoanalysis has been able to contribute to what is perhaps the most important aspect of modern art and literature: its search for a new secular mythology, one with which to replace the old lost religious center of the Western world, which was rooted in monotheism and the paternalistic family.

Granting that twentieth-century aesthetics is more concerned with irony and ambiguity than with beauty, and with new myths than with classical iconography, the significance of psychoanalysis and of the depth psychologies (such as Jung's) that can potentially explore these aspects of thought, is assured. With the disappearance of its nineteenth-century moral attachments, Freud's psychoanalysis has led to conclusions far afield from his own, but which nevertheless derive from aspects of his thought. Thus, the new emphasis on the validity of infant sexuality and the life-style of youth, the acceptance of the amoral nature of pleasure and the concentration on sensual satisfaction regardless of the sexual means involved—all borrow from Freud's (and his follower Wilhelm Reich's) exploration of the polymorphous-perverse sexual world of the infant, from his apparently permissive technique of free association, and from his constant reminder that sexual repression is unnatural and unhealthy for the individual. A similar relevance of certain of Freud's ideas for some modern art movements has also occurred, and seems at first surprising when one considers Freud's unperceptive responses to modern art.

We have already seen how little Freud thought of art from Impressionism on. On the other hand, he was excited by marginal works such as Rops's engravings, savored the humorous illustrations of *Die fliegende Blätter*, and was apparently impressed by downright inferior productions like Garnier's decorations of an edition of Rabelais, all of these examples providing useful corroborations of some point of his. His belligerently Victorian taste was almost identical to that of his admired mentors Lipps and Ernst Brücke, both of whom confined their taste mainly to the Renaissance and earlier art. We see this clearly in his letter of June 21, 1920, to Oskar Pfister. Commenting on the latter's book about Expressionist artists (1923), Freud ironically pretended to admire his follower's patience and fairness in writing such a book, which explains "clearly and exhaustively why these people lack the right to claim the name of artist." Freud himself admitted that he is "dreadfully intolerant of fools, sees only the harmful side of them," and refuses to treat seriously such " 'artists.' " Pfister's own discussion of modern art is hardly more sympathetic; for he finds the Expressionists introverts fortunate to be able to emerge from their regression to primitive patterns and to autistic behavior.[31] Slightly later, Fritz Wittels also abused modern art:

There is no doubt that the art of our times accords with Freud's psychology, because both are children of our times: art in the Dionysian channel; Freud, the scientist, in the Apollonian. Not all artists of the Freudian era are fabricators despite their comprehension of psychoanalysis. Expressionism in art reveals an outburst of the primitive, an attempt to externalize and represent the primary function with as little restraint as possible from the side of the secondary function. Dadaism—now a thing of the past—strove for severance from all reason, the regression to the infantile and beyond this to the animalistic. The Dadaists maintained that their theories derive from Freud . . . He would have sent them packing. His ideal of beauty is wholly different. . . . The Expressionists and the Dadaists are the anal daubers. The Cubists want to smear, but they allow themselves to be governed by the neurotic compulsion of the Superego. Daub? Sobeit, but only in geometric lines. [32]

Three decades later, Franz Alexander, another Freudian, wrote an essay showing how "The Psychoanalyst Looks at Contemporary Art,"[33] which is typical of orthodox psychoanalytic criticism. Alexander goes beyond Freud in being able to accept and even enjoy Impressionism, but he sees Impressionist art as a foil for the old bugaboo of Expressionism. Adapting (but without acknowledging) Worringer's opposition of *Einfühlung* to abstraction, Alexander finds that the "real difference between the two schools lies in their acceptance or rejection of the world," with the laurels for empathetic "warm attachment to the world" going to Impressionism, of course. Alexander handles the history of art with bold, simplistic strokes: the "fatal explosion" of 1914 burst "the bubble of [prewar] aesthetic culture," generating a "total rejection of the world which now so convincingly disclosed its sordid realities"; hence, abstraction in art, as an escape. Alexander makes a number of mistakes in his account of the origin of abstraction purely in terms of the mood of World War I nihilism. First of all, his skeletal account ignores the gradual emergence of abstraction among artists working after the heyday of Impressionism and before the advent of Dadaism: Gauguin, Seurat, Cézanne, the Nabis, the Fauves, and the

Cubists, all in different ways and to varying degrees explored decorative or structural aspects of their art, which were to be absorbed into later abstraction. Alexander does not understand that the complex interplay and blending of abstraction and empathy in their paintings demand far more than Worringer's elemental contrast to characterize, let alone to explain their art. In his one-dimensional psychological approach to history, Alexander actually rearranges chronology; thus, among the responses to the ugly realities of the war, the psychoanalyst lists the angry protests of the Blue Rider artists in Munich and the Futurists in Italy, without showing the slightest awareness of the fact that these groups emerged *before* the war. Perhaps the least satisfactory aspect of Alexander's discussion is his tracing the origin of Mondrian's highly serious and constructive art to the mood of Dadaist nihilism: in the art of "Mondrian, the nihilistic rejection of everything which even reminds one of the real world, is the main issue." Alexander's "real world" stands nakedly exposed: it is the world of the sentimental romantic landscape or, at best, familiar and pleasant Impressionist views; but it has nothing to do with the modern industrial world, nor with rectilinear cities like New York, which Mondrian loved.

Psychoanalysis as a technique has contributed little to the field of aesthetics, but as a technique it has had a most significant—and often stimulating—impact on some of the art and literature of this century. Of course, there are writers such as Meyer Levin (1953) who claim that the modern writer has acquired self-doubts from the encroachment of psychoanalysis, with its insights into human beings, the usual province and field of writers, and who blame the fact that "no 'great ones' have appeared in the last few decades" on the "struggle [with psychoanalysis] in which the energy of the writer is consumed in the effort to find again his own true area of function." This superficial view overlooks the fact that the absorption of some artists and writers in psychoanalysis is as much a symptom of their psychic responses to the larger sociocultural context as it is a "cause" of their sterility.

Clearly, psychoanalysts have done poorly in treating the history of modern art; yet their limitations have not prevented psychoanalysis itself from inspiring countless works more or less grounded in Freudian techniques or observations. If we take as a rich source of examples the magazine *transition*, particularly in the years 1927-30, when Surrealism was perhaps at its zenith of activity and growth, we find Kathleen Connell, in her "History of a Dream" (*transition* 18, 1927), inventing a dream game to be played with her friend, without any psychoanalytic intentions. "But," she acknowledges, "nowadays no one is innocent of Freud, and undoubtedly our method was inspired and, to some extent, directed by what we knew of Freud's theories." In the same magazine, Harry Crosby published his "Dreams: 1928-9," some of which have a transparently psychoanalytic character, as in this one:

> There is a tree too high for me to reach its top until the young girl with the blond hair and the white white skin (she wears furs and a veil) proposes that we take flying lessons whereupon I climb to the top of the tree and set at liberty my soul but when I slide down again to the ground the girl is disappearing out of sight on a tricycle and I am powerless to climb back again.

Interpreted psychoanalytically, this might read: I had trouble achieving erection and orgasm (tree top) until a seductive blonde showed me her pubic hair (furs) and offered to have intercourse with me (flying), whereupon I did achieve orgasm, with a feeling of playful regression (tricycle), followed by detumescence. Julian Trevelyan, who in his "Dreams" (*transition* 19) ignores Freud and cites Jung on the symbolizing function of the subconscious, proclaims that "TO DREAM IS TO CREATE"; but his examples don't always depart much from regulation Freudian symbolism, as in

> ... II. Women
> > Umbrellas up
> > > Umbrellas down.

(The closed, phallic umbrella is opposed to the open umbrella of orgasm.) Such arrangements of words on the page in terms of their visual impact were also practiced notably by Cummings and William Carlos Williams and by the recent school of concrete poetry, following a tradition which includes Mallarmé's *Un Coup de dés* and Apollinaire's *Calligrammes*.

In their antipathy to modern art, coupled with their affinity to classical art and their emphasis on symbolism, Freudian and non-Freudian psychoanalysts have distant cousins among many classical art historians, especially followers of the iconographic approach developed by Aby Warburg and his follower Panofsky.[34] The latter, a distinguished art historian with an antipathy to modern art, received a humanist education in Germany still allied to Freud's thirty-six years earlier in Austria; and in the words of an admiring colleague, he wished as a historian "to study and restore the heritage of the past, 'to endow,' as he said, 'ancient records with dynamic life.' "[35] Panofsky's analysis of a work of art in the spirit of the interpreter of secret texts is best defined in the introduction to his *Studies in Iconology* (1939). This Warburgian approach, which resembles Freud's interpretation of some art as hieroglyphic, comes right out of the rich and ancient tradition of Christian iconographic studies (from which romantic art and criticism also emerged). Here, a work of art is regarded not as a simply visible thing to be enjoyed, but as a many-leveled vehicle for hidden meanings.[36] A major task of Panofsky has been to trace the history of certain key conceptions of art, such as the Neoplatonic theory that the artist ought not imitate but surpass nature. This history has proved essential to the argument of the Viennese-trained art historian Ernst Kris, who attempted to work out an application of psychoanalysis to the history of art, especially in connection with his theory of the emergence of caricature, a theory in part resting on Panofsky's observation that, in passing from the Middle Ages to the Renaissance, the artist underwent a change in character, from imitator to creator, from disciple of nature to its master.[37] Although Kris's analysis of the origin of caricature is not quite convincing, his effort to unite the general history of aesthetic ideas and the specific history of a psychologically interesting phenomenon such as caricature, points in the right direction of interdisciplinary cooperation.

While the border line between art history and psychoanalysis had already been touched in passing by Panofsky as well as his teacher Aby Warburg, another art historian, more penetrating though less voluminously productive than Panofsky, Meyer Schapiro, has suggested a more concrete application of psychoanalysis in various of his studies. Starting from the ideas of Rank, whose work was so enthusiastically received in the mid-1920's in Paris, Schapiro was able to ground one of his points in that psychoanalyst's ideas. This occurs in his essay "From Mozarabic to Romanesque in Silos" (1939), which describes the transition from a style whose content is private and ritualistic to one that is public, monumental, and secular. In a long footnote concerned mainly with the potential for sexual symbolism in representations of ordinary objects such as a door, Schapiro suggests the compatibility of psychoanalytic and social interpretations—an attitude he has always maintained, with sensible reservations:[38]

> Thus, the presence of these implicit sexual meanings—if they are indeed such—in the particular scene of the Doubting Thomas would be less likely before the Romanesque period; they presuppose to some extent the conflicts and that secular tendency which arise mainly with the burgher class and the growth of the cities, and those very oppositions of faith and experience, ascetic repression and sensual enjoyment, expressed in the more overt meanings of the Doubting Thomas and the musicians in the city-frame.

The exemplary but cautious method followed here by Schapiro corrects the tendency by Freud and his followers to overgeneralize psychoanalytic principles and to project them wholesale onto history or biography without making the indispensable (but difficult) qualifications that detailed knowledge demands; thus, the surfacing here of psychoanalytically obvious sexual symbolism is not trivial (because external and universal), but takes on specific and cogent significance, because it marks a change from one moment to another in the history of Silos. Similarly, in another case, Schapiro felt justified (as Freud already had) to introduce a psychoanalytic interpretation when an unexpected incongruity was demonstrated in an artist's subject matter. This method might have yielded valid results, although in this case, unfortunately, the seeming difficulty has been explained without needing to resort to psychoanalytic methods.[39] Kris (1952) aspires at his best to Schapiro's method, without however quite achieving it. Much wilder are the results of the psychoanalytically minded art historian Adrian Stokes, who follows the uncritical line of Georg Groddeck when he exclaims, "How Gothic is the female genital,"[40] and who reduces architectural analysis to contrasts of smooth and rough textures, analyzed "in terms of the breast and nipple."[41]

In another study, Schapiro (1945) applied to a detail of a Flemish fifteenth-century masterpiece the same excellent method of analyzing the style in relation to its social and historical context and strengthening the analysis by observations of a psychoanalytical character (apparently modeling himself, as before, on Rank's analysis of the symbol). It is not surprising that, although occasional footnoting of Freudian insights is made in serious studies such as Julius S. Held's essay on Rembrandt (1969) or in the entertaining book of the Wittkowers (1963), Schapiro's work has not induced other art historians to produce significant psychoanalytically oriented studies of art; perhaps the talents demanded for tackling such interdisciplinary problems successfully are too rare—even Schapiro has been able to do so infrequently and in narrow contexts (limitation being the price of precision). But perhaps also the combined evidence needed to demonstrate points of intersection of three such diverse areas as art, history, and psychology may in most instances simply be impossible to gather.

It is a fitting irony that while Freud was a great analyst of humor, his own writings have, in their irritating directness, inspired a considerable number of parodies. But the psychoanalyst would probably say that he had attacked only delusions and ignorance, and that the parodies signified a resistance that has greatly declined since his ideas have become, if not wholly accepted, more assimilated into the texture of recent thinking. The resemblance of his analyses to the allegorical interpretations of solemn Christian exegetes contributed to some of these parodies. It is interesting to observe how often the parodies of psychoanalysis border on new directions of art that Freud has unintentionally pointed toward; for example, Adolph Wohlgemuth (1923), a hesitant follower of Freud at first who turned later into a fanatic antagonist, wrote extensive satirical analyses of dreams and of Freudian symbolism, especially taking pains to refute the phallic symbolism of the snake. To show the arbitrariness of the psychoanalyst Silberer's "anagogic" interpretation of the hidden symbols in a story, Wohlgemuth produced his own tongue-in-cheek version, treating the elements of the story as meat (beef, mutton, pork) and the hero or dreamer as a butcher (hence his naming of the new method "kreopolic" from the Greek for butcher). This burlesque of psychoanalysis suggests—without the artistic genius, to be sure—the domestic comedy of Joyce's *Ulysses* and of some of Eliot's metaphors of this period. At about the same time, Aldous Huxley played with psychoanalytic words like "trauma" and the Jungian "complex", and satirized both amateur psychoanalysts and the popular topic of the sexual instincts (1923). American psychologists critical of Freud have indulged in parodies; for, as has recently been shown,[42] Knight Dunlap produced "a parodic reinterpretation of classic nursery rhymes"; and Titchener probably wrote "An Attempt at Freudian Analysis," a symbolic interpretation of the motives of a "favorable reviewer of recent Freudian literature."

The numerous parodies of Freud were probably, in part, irritated responses to the unstable mixture in psychoanalytic interpretations of art and literature of enriching complication and of a parodically simplistic reduction. At first, many writers retreated from psychoanalytic methods as from an obtrusively scientific instrument; for they shared the sentiments of Max Jacob:[43] "La poésie moderne saute toutes les explications." Of course, the idea of clear and simple communication had been seriously questioned by both the ironical Dadaists and the earnest Expressionists, who intentionally obliterated obvious meaning and even traces of their personality (except in the psychoanalytic sense of Theodor Reik, who noted that even criminals apparently wishing to escape detection left behind traces of themselves, though sometimes in the form of their own feces); thus, the Dadaists produced incomprehensibly confused simultaneous readings of their poetry accompanied by unrelated noises. Many of the strange and apparently incomprehensible Expressionist products were probably made with the expectation, in the words of Walter H. Sokel[44] speaking of Wedekind, that "distortion reveals essence"; and some German novelists used simultaneity, or *Doppelbödigkeit*, with the hope that the discontinuities of human experience might—in the wake of a Joycean epiphany or a Proustian flashback—be momentarily transcended. This hope could be supported by Freud's investigations of the hidden meaning of dreams, free associations, and other seemingly jumbled, distorted, or meaningless expressions.

The notion that complication and the unexpected leaps of comparison that lead to surprise rather than to clear statement form the basis of poetry, was already formulated by Apollinaire, but others applied this criterion to visual art. Simultaneity became, for example, with Eisenstein, a central constituent of all art, which he called "juxtaposition,"[45] finding not only cinema but painting, sculpture, and even literature past and present to be founded on it. Northrop Frye considered metaphor itself as "simple juxtaposition," [46] and cites Pound's famous explanation of this aspect of metaphor in the figure of a Chinese ideogram that throws a group of elements together without predication. Pound's two-line poem, "In a Station of the Metro" reads: "The apparition of these faces in the crowd; Petals on a wet, black bough." Roger Shattuck (1958) daringly inflates these ideas to cover the whole modern period, which he sees as one lacking in transitions and characterized by sudden, disjunctive juxtapositions. He senses the connection between juxtaposition and irony discussed by Frye and others, but instead of finding this unfortunate, he rather exalts the phenomenon and speaks of ambiguity as a "high style," of the pun as a form once considered "vulgar," but now elevated.

Juxtaposition as a formative principle joins the trivial to the important with surprising inversions or distortions of value and meaning in the manner of those dream processes described by Freud; hence D. H. Lawrence, disturbed by Freud's dream theories, directed his criticism precisely at the psychoanalyst's overvaluation of these trivia:

Usually . . . the images that are accidentally swept into the mind in sleep are as disconnected and as unmeaning as the pieces of paper which the street cleaners sweep into a bin from the city gutters at night. We should not think of taking all these papers, piecing them together, and making a marvelous book of them, prophetic of the future and pregnant with the past. We should not do so, although every rag of printed paper swept from the gutter would have some connection with the past day's event. But its significance, the significance of the words printed upon it is so small, that we relegate it into the limbo of the accidental and meaningless. There is no vital connection between the many bits of paper—only an accidental connection. Each bit of paper has a reference to some actual event: a bus-ticket, an envelope, a tract, a pastry-shop bag, a newspaper, a hand-bill. But take them all together . . . and they have no individual sequence, they belong more to the mechanical arrangements than to the vital consequence of our existence. And the same with most dreams.[47]

This astonishing, sweeping rejection of the accidental in art, like Wohlgemuth's spoof of the *Gradiva*, points to a number of advanced artistic procedures, notably that of the collage, the pasting of cut-out pieces of paper (and of other materials eventually), practiced since the Cubists, with variants introduced by many artists, including the Surrealists and even writers such as Bryan Gysin and the novelist William Burroughs (whose use of collage to represent his dreams may owe something to the Surrealist Ernst's collage novels).

Attempts to produce works reflecting a direct interplay of the visual and the verbal (beyond the theoretical identification of painting and poetry from the ancients on, signified in Horace's famous simile *Ut pictura poesis*) have been made from the Mannerists to Mallarmé, Apollinaire and Cummings in poetry, and among the Cubists, Futurists, Dadaists, and Surrealists in painting. The Surrealists, in particular, made use of "games" employing punlike repetitions of sound, but even less coherent than the worst pun, and resembling instead some highly neurotic expressions, as in echolalia (the senseless repetition of words by mentally disturbed or hypnotized subjects) or even the jumbled "word salad" of the schizophrenic. The dissolution of rational limits, which the Surrealists found in such hypnotic and psychotic states and which they tried to emulate in their productions, is a characteristic Freud also found in the dream and in some neurotic expressions. Freud's analyses moreover, cross the boundaries of the visual and the verbal in his search for deeper significance; thus, the process whereby compound words are produced in some jokes (Heine's joke, cited by Freud, about the familiarity with the millionaire becoming "famillionaire"; Brill's Christmas season being described as "alcoholidays") closely resembles the construction of the mixed-figure (*Mischfigur*) of dreams.[48] We have seen how Freud's analysis of the image of the face on Baubo's abdomen helped him to unravel the seemingly meaningless neologism *Vaterarsch* and to penetrate to the important but latent meaning of the compound word. This fusion of the visual and the verbal has, in varying degree, been practiced often by the Surrealists, aiming to attain to the "marvelous," a state that, as Aragon (1965) put it, "is the eruption of contradiction within the real."

The interpretation and full appreciation of works embodying such complicated techniques demands a key that will unlock otherwise buried riches of the imagination; condensation and displacement can often provide that key. I do not mean that the critic should indulge in the subjective or even mystical acrobatics of some impressionist criticism founded on free association; for example, Gaston Bachelard [49] proposes that a critic should take "the image just as . . . the poet created it, and make it his own . . . He brings the image to the very limit of what he is able to imagine." Such far-fetched free associations would probably be more a historical counterpart than a genuine elucidation of poetry. A better critical model would be Freud's subtle analyses tracing philologically the meaning of phrases or words, as in the Boltraffio-Botticelli example discussed in chapter 2. There, Freud showed that when one treats an expression on more than its surface level and in terms of condensation, decomposition, and so forth, one can find a host of allied associated ideas, which share deep latent content—in the Boltraffio example, sex and death. It seems to me that this method has great relevance for certain twentieth-century art and literature, and in fact can provide clues to perceiving the great excitements and the wealth of ideas in works that may be either disarmingly simple or discouragingly complex. Using Freud's approach, I should like now to analyze an example of the first kind in a painting by Magritte, and of the second, in a passage by Joyce.

Le Viol (*Fig. 30*) by Magritte was from its creation in 1934 valued as a powerful and characteristic statement of Surrealism, and an engraving by the artist representing the main features of the painting was placed on the front cover of Breton's important lecture published as the pamphlet *Qu'est-ce-que le Surréalisme?* (Brussels, 1934). Breton continued to be interested in Magritte's art as late as 1952, and in his book of essays of that date,[50] he compared himself as a poet making a *poème-objet* to Magritte as an artist "who detected what could result from relating concrete words of great resonance (the word 'mountain', the word 'pipe' . . .) with forms which deny, or at least do not rationally correspond to them." Breton was willing to let the matter rest, and not seek out hidden meanings or quasi-rational correspondences, nor did he think to apply Freudian analysis, although he had attempted in his *Les Vases communicants* (1932) to prove himself up to the great dream interpreter himself. However, an approach enriched by analytic insights, but tempered and controlled by a careful study of the background of Magritte's work, might help us to understand it better and to appreciate it all the more.

The fusion of face and torso in *Le Viol* shocks us like Duchamp's graffito moustache drawn over the revered face of Leonardo's Mona Lisa (*Fig. 31*), or like Freud's Baubo, who provoked surprised laughter on lifting her dress. Image fusions can be seen in Galton (*Fig. 32*), and they also appear in some cartoons of the early twentieth century with proto-Cubist mergings of frontal and profile views of the face,[51] in works of the Cubists, and later of the Futurists, Dadaists, and Surrealists.[52] In his remarkable painting *The Pregnant Woman* (1913), Chagall implied the sexual fusion of man and woman (like the Siamese twinning of Adam and Eve, whose groins merge in a painting of 1911) by using such facial intersections. The painting shows a large standing woman whose child is displayed inside her belly and whose face, looking out at us, is overlaid on the left side by the profile of a man with a projecting beard.

But what can the *viol* signify? Surely this carefully painted and static "portrait" set before an expansive, well-lighted landscape seems innocuous enough, displaying neither an obvious rapine, nor even Masson's interweaving movements—of bodies, in his *Metamorphosis of Lovers* (1938); of lines, in *The Rape* (1941). However, the irreverent imposition of an attractively shaped face with well-groomed hair upon a torso with a prominent pubic mouth, over a suggestively phallic neck, already indicates that there is more to the picture: this equation of a public face with private parts usually withheld from view *does* violate our habits of etiquette and propriety, perhaps even about the deceptively ornamental and pleasing content of art (it was Degas's observation that "art is a vice, one does not wed it—one rapes it"). Possibly Magritte's point is that the "rape" of an attractive face encountered on a street occurs each time a man superimposes his own image of the woman's body, an obvious wish fulfillment, on the exposed face. (Magritte earlier represented a "collage rape" in his oil *Les jours gigantesques* of 1928, which blends into a single image—like some contemporary paintings by Picabia—a man in a dark suit over a naked woman struggling in his grasp.)

But there is more. First, the name. In his useful article "On René Magritte" (1966), Roger Shattuck instructively cites Paul Nougé's remark that "the *word* serves as a source of Magritte's poetic invention"; while he applies this remark to other works of Magritte, Shattuck fails to do so for *Le Viol*. The tip-off to this typical misunderstanding of the painting is his translation of the title into English. The key, however, is in the name *Le Viol*. The subtle Duchamp had already in 1921 punned on the words *violette-voilette*, when he posed as a veiled woman on the label of a bottle of toilet water called "Eau de Voilette" and this well-known pun was doubtless remembered by the Surrealists when they produced an important but little-known book on the young criminal heroine Violette Nozières, who, presumably tormented by an incestuous attachment to her father, murdered both her parents. In their book celebrating her monstrous crime, *Violette Nozières* (Brussels, 1933), a number of major Surrealists collaborated, including Breton, René Char, Benjamin Peret, Arp, Giacometti, and Magritte. Alluding to the violent act, Breton wrote that "M. Nozières was a provident man . . . especially because he gave his daughter a Christian name in the first part of which his intentions can be read psycho-analytically"; Peret in his poem stated that the father "violait . . . Violette"; and Gui Rosey employed the words "dévoilée" and "inviolable," and referred to "le sexe de la femme à barbe" ("the genital of the bearded woman"). Magritte's contribution seems unrelated to *Le Viol* and showed a man with a girl on his lap placing his hand under her dress; but I am sure that *Le Viol*, painted one year later, was in part stimulated by his experience with the name Violette and her awful crime.

Yet the title contains still more than an allusion to this sick young girl. It also alludes literally to violins, instruments with notoriously sexual connotations. Freud in 1906 [53] referred to the idea often used by cartoonists of representing "the violin as a woman, and the violin bow as a penis"; and later, in *Totem and Taboo*, he cited the French phrase *jouer au violon*, which, he points out, represents onanism. [54] In a photograph he called *Violon d'Ingres* (meaning a hobby, like the painter Ingres's violin-playing), Man Ray displayed a nude woman with two f-holes painted on her back, emphasizing her violin shape. Doubtless a different sort of playing with the nude, who resembles an Ingres *Odalisque*, was also intended. In their so-called analytic phase, the witty Cubists, Picasso and Braque often painted musicians in such a way that the performer's body merged with his instrument; the violin, with its gracefully curving contours and its well-defined configuration, was among the most popular instruments so treated. We may note that already in 1926, Magritte's collage *Les notes musicales* had contours ambiguously suggesting either a curvy female figure or a violin, and also that a biomorphic abstraction by the ex-Dadaist Arp, called *Woman* (1927), is so ambiguous that it can be considered to be either a body or a head. The possibility that a torso or head not reduced to an abstraction might allude to a violin was established by one of the "exquisite corpses" on which, among others, Breton, then in close touch with Magritte, collaborated. The drawing, executed in 1934,[55] shows a six-breasted female whose neck expands not into a head but into a violin with a clump of hair and a small breast growing from its right margin.

Magritte's intentions in *Le Viol*, and his way of realizing them, would be best revealed by study of his preliminary drawings; unfortunately, I know of none. However, an earlier painting of 1932, *L'Attentat*, associates a prominently displayed female torso with a title suggesting violence; moreover, the sketches for a later painting, *L'Âme des bandits* (1960),[56] perhaps reveal Magritte's thought, and above all corroborate my interpretation that the violin served as his bridge from a head covered with hair to a torso (whose sexual exposure constituted its "rape"). In a series of seven drawings, Magritte played freely with a series of words, which he illustrated.[57] Among these drawings I find two that bear most strongly on *Le Viol*: the three drawings in number IV (*Fig. 33*) showed the violin (which in some drawings resembles a man with a moustache) surrounded by a woman's long hair, first attached to the queue of a man's eighteenth- century coiffure,[58] then placed tentatively in a woman's hair, and finally situated at the height of the woman's head (somewhat suggesting a face, though her back is turned). The second drawing, number VI (*Fig. 34*), shows the hair-violin-face clearly and frontally, and also presents a most interesting headless torso (a few lines only suggest a phantom face above the collar), with a head at the knot of the tie, perhaps an allusion to the *viola d'amore*, which often has a head of Amor, but almost surely connected to an "exquisite corpse" by Breton that shows a head on a tie, unmistakably illustrating the Freudian symbolism of the phallus. What results from all this is that without the psychoanalytic mode of seeing, we would miss Magritte's special way of packing complex associations into what seems to be his simple image in bad taste. Any further insight into the dense and difficult humor of *Le Viol* would require access both to preparatory drawings for it, and to biographical information about the artist's thought and activity in 1933–34.

Although the work of Joyce apparently contains many devices analogous to those employed in psychoanalysis, both Joyce and the psychoanalysts spent much energy attacking one another and denying an affinity: on the one hand, Sten Selander's review of Freud's influence on modern literature denied such an influence on Joyce, whose *Ulysses* made "boring" use of a stream of "stinking intellectual toilet water lacking coherent thoughts";[59] on the other hand, Joyce, infuriated at being constantly associated with the psychoanalysts, was engaged in a continual polemic against them. Still, a pun (or a cluster of puns) entirely in the verbal medium, which I believe is of a similar kind to Magritte's, also has much in common with certain Freudian dream mechanisms. This pun stands (among a myriad of others) on the first page of *Finnegans Wake* in the passage reading, "Sir Tristram, violer d'amores, had passencore rearrived from North Armorica." Without detailing the dense array of meanings any bit of Joycean text contains, we may note[60] that the relevant story concerns two heroes: the Tristan of Arthurian legend, whose love-death with Iseult is so famous; and a historical Sir Almeric Tristram, founder of Howth Castle, musician of love, the Anglo-Norman conqueror of Ireland who had a morbid, unconsummated marriage to a second Iseult. Tristan's love for Iseult introduces a classic example of love as dying, comparable to the link between sleep and death, which forms the axis of this whole book about Tim Finnegan's "wake"—a festive Irish funeral ("funferall") ending in revival of the corpse who gets up from sleep (hence the cyclical form of the book and its title: Fin- end, Egan- again). The book involves several basic polarities—male and female, love and hate, life and death—which, like a latent dream wish, underlie the many diverse passages of the book. In the passage cited, the phrase "violer d'amores" has no simple obvious meaning, and in fact combines or condenses several, directly linked to the events occurring in the strange dream world of the book. A few of the meanings will help, if not to explain the passage, at least to open its potential for appreciative exploration. (My basis for analyzing Joyce's macaronic word-plays is limited to the French language, and allusions to Gaelic and other languages are not considered. Other clues for appreciating Joyce's verbal inventions can be found in Freud, 1910b.)

"viol aid(e) amour": an ironic therapy for Tristram's unfulfilled love;

"viol aid(e) à mort," or "viol aida mort": the other side of the coin —death aided by the rape;

"violer d'amour": to play the violin (or viola d'amore) from enjoyment of the instrument, or play with love, at worst from narcissistic motives as in *jouer au violon*, or at best for the sake of the loved one;

"violé d'amour": violated by the unfulfilled love of the neurotic and frigid Iseult.

Northrop Frye,[61] aware of the techniques of both Freud and Joyce, found in a phrase of Poe's the potential for a Joycean word-play: "In Poe's line 'the viol, the violet and the vine,' we have a fusion of two opposed qualities . . . *Finnegans Wake* is a very funny book . . . There may well be buried in it some such word as 'vinolent,' intended to express everything in Poe's line at once." It seems to me that a similar fusion of meanings occurs in the phrase I have just considered, and that each of the readings of it may be valid for one of the several currents flowing through the book; for the intense and complex style of Joyce resembles not so much a single "stream of consciousness" as a series of intertwining currents that mingle and part in their flow along a river bed. Nor is Joyce content with keeping the significance of the dreamer's imagery restricted to the private world described by Freud; rather, he aims to relate the personal to the cosmic. This aim, which amounts to an effort to discover a mythological dimension in everyday life, looks back to some suggestions of Freud, and forward to some interesting recent critical speculation.

The ambiguous and ironic content of the works of Magritte and Joyce demands new methods of criticism, often philological in character. Freud has often supplied the technical means to effect this criticism: his idea of condensation helped us to penetrate the sense of Magritte and Joyce, and his ideas of overdetermination and displacement of symbols can also serve as clues to new critical frameworks applicable to modern ironic art forms. We have noted that some major critics such as Northrop Frye worry (in contradiction of Shattuck's complacent optimism about the dominance of irony) about our being in an age of decline. Frye, in line with Hegel's prophetic pessimism about the decline of art in a world where religion is increasingly secularized, sees our ironic age as at the end of a cycle. Less comfortable with nature than the romantic theorists of *Einfühlung*, Frye seeks no sympathetic harmony with the nonhuman to heal the ironic split, and instead looks to myth-making to lead to a new upward movement of the cycle, which will be one dominated by a renewed sense of symbolism. Although, as Frye observes, "for the critic there is no such thing as a private symbol," he distrusted the vague mysticism of Jung's archetypal symbolism, preferring Freud's approach for its concreteness, in starting out from individual experience rather than from quasi-religious or metaphysical notions. But he reverses Freud's judgment on art as escape by insisting that in art and literature the "world of desire" is not "an escape from 'reality,' but . . . the genuine form of the world that human life tries to imitate."[62] In an important discussion,[63] Frye advances arguments resembling those of Rank and Sachs (1916) on the infinite potential of the changeless unconscious, with its apparently limited range of symbolism. Frye shows that originality in art is not a break with convention as such, but that the artist is actually obeying "an obscure but profound impulse to revolt against the conception established in his own day, in order to rediscover convention on a deeper level." Perhaps the most interesting aspect of Frye's work has been his effort to show that modern man can break through the conventions in which he is inevitably immersed, thereby in a sense restoring the conventional to the ritual. In this respect, he adds a romantic interest in the unexpected, which fits into his mythologically "religious" system, somewhat as miracles fitted into the old Christian vision of a world order.

Freud's idea of displacement was especially valuable to Frye for enabling him, in the words of Geoffrey Hartmann,[64] "to revalue what grosser histories of literature see merely as secularization. For the movement from myth to realism does not infer the sad decline of hero into anti-hero or of an ancestor's great seal rings into Belinda's hairpin. We discover that secular man is not devoid of mythical attributes." Frye's concept of the epiphany (whose most familiar example is the star appearing in the sky to the three kings of the Nativity) also depends in part on Freudian displacement; and it is crucial to him, for as Murray

Krieger[65] has observed, "his notion of epiphany does permit Frye to leave open the possibility of a momentary break-through of the desired into the real, of Utopia into the resistant world of things." This notion of a sudden illumination without conscious preparation has appealed to many others among Frye's contemporaries, and especially among those preoccupied with the relation of conscious to unconscious aspects of mind. The Surrealists, aiming (as Breton made clear in the *manifestos*) to turn art into a collective myth, and not a personal one in Freud's terms, nonetheless apparently applied some of the ideas Freud outlined in *Totem and Taboo*, especially in connection with the over-determined meaning of the magically potent fetish or the magical quality of the chance encounter. While Freud always sought a deter-mining motive in the experience of his patients who hallucinated, or in those who experienced mental telepathy and allied phenomena, his whole fascination with the intrusion of the unexpected and irrational into ordinary life made his own discussions immensely rich and sugges-tive; and some writers who shared Freud's naturalist framework, such as Joyce and the Surrealists, made use of the breakthrough moment of epiphany as the last frontier of the marvelous. The Surrealists antici-pated in the chance encounter with ordinary things or with people on the street and elsewhere (*l'hasard objectif, l'object trouvé*) a "magic" enriching the familiar and mundane with other dimensions of meaning. As Breton understood, this magic was dependent on the role of over-determination, which invests dream images with rich symbolic content.[66] It seems to me that the many-layered mind described by psychoana-lysis has somehow come into the service—despite Freud's cautious and skeptical approach—of a modern "secularized" religion of art, which recalls in some ways the medieval and Renaissance tradition of levels of meaning in the interpretation of symbols, passing from the literal to the allegorical to the tropological to the anagogical.

These recent applications of Freudian techniques are often diamet-rically opposed to his archaeological emphasis;[67] for example, to Freud, overdetermination meant an inevitable association with past experiences, whereas many younger theorists, regarding the past as irrelevant and the future as dim or frightening, tend to emphasize the present, the here-and-now experience of joy (perhaps comparable to the Nietzschian idea that joy yearns for eternity). André Malraux shared with Frye a tendency to make artistic form autonomous, to make it stand above history; thus, in his well-known study *The Voices of Silence* (1953), he flattens art history by taking the works out of chronological sequence and by making various anachronistic distortions of the images through photographic tricks of blow-ups of details and odd-angled shots. His recent *Anti-Memoirs* (1965) applies an analogous approach to the field of autobiography, in which his reminiscences, freely associated and set free from a biographical context, densely overlay and interpenetrate one another like Galton's superimposed photographs. It is as though Malraux aimed to touch that great timeless region designated by Freud as the unconscious—a region, we must add, that for Freud is inaccessible to our efforts consciously to enter it. An aim similar to Malraux's animates the Swiss school of critics, with its romantic efforts to make time stand still and to reach "eternity" through the romantic experience of *paramnesia* or the sense that what is recollected is actually present. The anthropologist Lévi-Strauss (1963) also sees a "synchronic" transcendence of time and a cross-cultural identity between certain elementary patterns or structures of social behavior, and— apparently harking back to *Totem and Taboo*, with modifications perhaps in part suggested by Lord Raglan's famous study *The Hero* (1936)— finds the Freudian unconscious the magical source for a modern mythical or ahistorical time: "The modern version of shamanistic technique called psychoanalysis thus derives its specific characteristics from the fact that in industrial civilization there is no longer any room for mythical time, except within man himself."

Developments within New York painting of the 1940's and 1950's paralleled the literary shifts already noted, from an emphasis on an individualized unconscious to a more universalized realm of myth. In the early 1940's, works like the Surrealist Max Ernst's *Vox Angelica* combined the old Surrealist device of grouped tableaux embodying images with personal associations (as in Magritte's *The Bold Sleeper*, 1927; the tablets of Dali's *Accommodations of Desire*, 1929; the boxes of symbolic signs in Torres-García's paintings and in Joseph Cornell's assemblages) with the universalizing structure of Mondrian's rectilinear networks. Such works surely influenced Adolph Gottlieb's pictographic boxes, as in his *Oracle*. Young Americans like Barnett Newman, inspired by the Surrealists in New York in the early

1940's, found a way to transform their delicate but conventional realism into an art combining the personal and the monumental, and to bypass Cubism, then the dominant form of modernism. By the late 1940's, Surrealist content is commonly found along with forms influenced by Picasso, Mondrian, Kandinsky, Miró, Tanguy, and Ernst. Barnett Newman's *Genetic Moment* and *The Death of Euclid* (both 1947) share with some of Ernst's frottages (rubbings) of the 1920's (especially his forest scenes) the combination of a regular form with irregular "automatic" forms.

Despite their affinities to Surrealism and to some aspects of Freudian psychoanalysis, the American artists, exhibiting the same shrewd independence with which they had successively denied all of their other influences, rejected Surrealism and its attachment to Freud's psychology of the individual dream. Instead, they turned to the archetypal mythology of Jung. This was a logical step for these artists, on their way to an art aiming to make impersonal, abstract signs into personal expressions.

Recent attempts to make use of psychoanalysis have often transformed Freud's concrete interpretations of the symbolism of dream and neurosis into a generalized psychology of language; in fact one writer sympathetic to psychoanalysis[68] declared that "much of Freud's work was really semantic, and that he made a revolutionary discovery in semantics; viz., that neurotic symptoms are meaningful disguised communication." Critics who build on this unquestionably valid aspect of Freud's contribution, an approach in which structural linguistics runs away with the emotional specifics of a work of art, seem to me to be intensifying one of the initial difficulties built into a Freudian aesthetics: its non-specificity for a given work of art. As the thoughtful structuralist Michael Riffaterre[69] acknowledges, "there may well be strictly poetic structures that cannot be recognized as such by an analysis not geared to the specificity of poetic language," a point applicable to psychoanalysis and to any approach that superimposes a critical system on a work of art without finding a way to meet the work on its own ground. But the reduction of psychoanalytic aesthetics to a semantic criticism and to technical formulas such as overdeterminism and condensation, while leaving out the rich insights of psychoanalysis, amounts to a truncation from below. Thus, Lévi-Strauss,[70] who regards any myth as consisting of all its versions, translates Freud's Oedipus myth into the generalized problem "of understanding how *one* can be born from two" and then finds many examples of it. It seems to me that in multiplying the parallels of the myth among different cultures, he divides its rich concrete meaning for western man.

In the end, with all of the writers I have just been discussing, we may have returned to questions of taste; for they have all moved very far from the humanist Western values of beauty and of individual personality. When the young structuralist art historian Sheldon Nodelman,[71] modeling himself on the Roman archaeologist Guido Kaschnitz von Weinberg, states that it is only after a structural description "undertaken with the aid of the bracketing method, that the interaction between work and spectator can be usefully discussed," we can understand that he, like his model, was fascinated by Roman portrait busts. The problem posed by a large number of anonymous heads in a similar style demands grouping and ordering processes which can safely postpone till later (or never, if the data are lacking) questions of psychological or biographical content in relation to the artist. The "interaction between work and spectator" is a preoccupation of much recent criticism of art, and there is a real coherence between Nodelman's taste for ancient Roman stones and his interest in current hard-edge painting.[72]

We have come far from the projects of some psychoanalytic criticism to delve into the psychogenesis of a work of art, to explore the individual artist's development, and the relation of his art to his childhood experiences. These projects were by no means crowned with success. Nor are we any closer to answering the important problem of value posed by psychoanalysis, and which Freud avoided as outside the scope of his work. The recent interest in psychoanalysis by some structuralists leaves little of the genius of Freud visible, and extracts only certain useful insights. Still, Freud's ideas seem to find their way into the changing scene: their flexibility and fecundity assure them a part in whatever trends may emerge in the foreseeable future.

Conclusion

Our efforts to define the nature and impact, the significance and the limitations of Freud's views on art and the artist have demanded that we explore not only his psychoanalytic theories, but his most intimate biography. Freud's worlds of art and literature, which we have seen displayed in his collections of art and books and in his own writings, bore the stamp of his unorthodox Jewish background and of the combined humanist and scientific education that the creator of psychoanalysis absorbed in Vienna from the 1860's to the *fin de siècle*. If this study of Freud's ideas on art has emphasized the biographical and personal dimension, it is not that these ideas have no intrinsic interest or even merit in themselves, but that they provide a major source of material for gaining an insight into this amazing mind. And I feel that if his psychoanalysis provided a key to no other literature than his own, it would have value enough; for his writings invite us to enter and experience his fantastic psychoanalytic universe imaginatively as we share the vision of great novelists like Dostoievsky, who make the sublime, the ridiculous, and the despicably criminal palpably human and immediately real to us. In a sense, his whole production, but especially his sensitive writings on art and the artist with their secret identifications and biases, mirror his attempt through an endless psychoanalysis to transcend his own problems.

This paradoxical personality—strong and courageous in some things, neurotically inhibited in others, boldly inventive, yet bound to nineteenth-century scientific materialist theories—groped with rare honesty toward a truth about himself he never quite reached; but Freud's problems are less important than his uneasiness about them, and his restless search to liberate himself. Along the uneven path of that quest Freud stumbled continually on new ideas, each discovery liberating him for a moment before memory closed in, tieing him to his childhood "family romance" with mother and father. Sometimes, when he felt inadequate to his tasks, he made Martha his scapegoat and unjustly reproached her. The artist, too, served a role as carrier of his prejudices and problems; rather, not the average artist (whom he usually regarded as dominated by his desires), but the geniuses, father substitutes like Shakespeare and Goethe with whom he identified in various ways and degrees throughout his life. The high value of Freud's struggle with his own dirt and sickness, his own ugliness and meanness, is visible in the great monument of *The Interpretation of Dreams* and the numerous later offshoots of it. Freud has given to a whole generation a rare example of searching and insightful self-discovery; and the futile efforts by this paternalistic genius to find a satisfactory model with whom to identify made sense to many young persons struggling with their own crises of identification: perhaps no writer of comparable stature reveals such a combination of the indomitable creator and the pathetically human being.

Freud's "aesthetics" essentially continued one side of romantic art theory—not those aspects of romanticism concerned with the modern, the new and the original, but with the unconscious of buried wish and feeling, allied to the old concept of imagination. Major tasks of this aesthetic were to outline the access routes, especially the symbolism, whereby the mind of the artist came into contact with the unconscious, and to show how this mental process was "embodied" in the objective work. Here the various notions of projection and *Einfühlung* were highly important; and if my analysis was correct, Freud's undeveloped suggestion of an "ideational mimetics" would have crowned his theories of art with a device allowing essential contact between the psychological workings of the individual mind and the external world of other people and of things, including art. There is an unexpected parallel between these projective and expressive theories and the early statements of Freud's contemporaries, artists such as Kandinsky groping toward an abstract art, who associated feelings and ideas to certain colors and abstract forms. But Freud ignored abstract art, not only because he demanded art (as in the classical or Renaissance periods) with a content capable of interpretation by a hermeneutic approach along the lines of psychoanalysis, but because he never appreciated the "musically expressive" qualities of nonmimetic, abstract art.

Freud's concern for interpreting symbolic and expressive languages in art has not fared well with many post-romantic aestheticians, who do not try to uncover what personal feelings the artist "expressed," nor to "explain" the self-rewarding activity of aesthetic enjoyment, and professional critics of modern art hardly ever ask Freudian questions about the art or the artist any more. The tendency has been to seek emergent or "creative" qualities in art, not in terms of its inspired maker, but in the coherence of its self-sufficient formal pattern or structure. The humanist Freud, on the other hand, has emphasized the role of memory in art, and has had little to say about the artistic act as a creative gesture, beyond finding it ineffable. Clearly, no comprehensive aesthetic applicable to wide areas of art can be derived from psychoanalysis without major infusions from the areas of perception, form, and value. Freud's theories in the state he left them are chiefly useful for interpreting symbolic art, or for comprehending the artist of neurotic vision, and their greatest achievement was to create a context in which Symbolist and Surrealist productions could be understood and appreciated. Moreover, many first-rate twentieth-century works containing dreamlike elements but not obviously indebted to Freud's technical analyses reveal an essential side of their ironic and seemingly irrational content to those aware of psychoanalysis, as I have tried to show in the cases of Magritte's *Le Viol* and of Joyce's *Finnegans Wake*. Of such works the critic often asks first, not "is it good?" but "what does it mean?" or "what verbal and visual puns does the work hold?"

In some advanced fields of Western art criticism, Freud's ideas, in a modified form, have continued to be relevant. The anxious emphasis by many modern critics on the "created" objects of art and their nervous but futile search for an elusive vocabulary for the new objects have perhaps quasi-religious overtones, reflecting the loss of the stable framework that supported a whole establishment of Western culture, with its religion, educational methods, and philosophical systems. The search for symbolic substitutes for the loss of such comforts has turned "creation" from the psychological sense of romantic genius to a coolly impersonal one in which the object takes precedence. Here, Freud's work takes on a curious relevance; for the modern "created" work, like the found object of the Surrealists, has the quality of hidden and symbolical significance, and these recondite objects speak to us like the symbols and images that rise from the unconscious Freud examined. Psychoanalysis in this context does not address the artist's momentary feelings expressed in the work but the universal myth he has tapped in this unconscious memory. Since the Jungians have particularly developed the universality of unconscious myth, their version of psychoanalysis has recently stolen the limelight from the Freudians among some young artists. But Freud has triumphed among other young writers and artists involved with semantic questions: his engagement with the mechanisms of dream and neurosis enabled him to work out techniques for exploring layers of meaning by semantic (mainly etymological) means, which are independent of his baggage of psychological assumptions. Young French structuralists, following the lead of men like Lévi-Strauss and Alcan, have not been slow to apply Freud's analyses to literature, adapting them to their old school methods of the *textes commentés*.

The grandeur of Freud's production transcends his own limits as a man and outruns its real and even its potential influence. Freud, stimulated by the "resistances to psychoanalysis" that he may well have relished and that spurred him on to ever more daring challenges to his public, called himself a conquistador. This self-description seems to fit his achievements, at least in the aesthetic domains into which he boldly intruded; but though he has stormed some real castles and penetrated into some dark and forbidding regions, he has also, like the chivalrous character Don Quixote, left behind him more than one bruised windmill. And like Don Quixote, he has been, in Unamuno's words, "an awakener of sleeping souls." But what will survive long beyond the real and shadowy debris of his speculations about art, the dream, and neurosis may well be the novelistic world he charted, and to some extent fabricated in his writings.

Appendix:
A Survey of
Freud's
Influence, by
Decade and in
Different
Countries

The impact of Freud on art and literature has changed over the decades, partly mirroring changes in his psychoanalytic theories. The basic notions (or even preconceptions) about the artist were already significantly shaped in the "prehistoric period," before the mid-1880's when Freud pioneered his psychoanalysis, and were based on his childhood background. Thus, in the grandly expansive "heroic period" of the 1890's through 1914, when he produced his major discussions of artists in terms of sex, the dream, and the unconscious, Freud deviated little from his earlier opinions and tastes in art. He regarded the artist as somewhat eccentric and a bit neurotic, a failure in reality saved by his fantasy of success from feeling his failure. As discussed in chapter 2, the almost lyrical quality of Freud's writings about himself and his own dreams during this period gives way to a more austere, a drier discussion of theory and refinements of techniques. Perhaps the change was brought about as a response to the major criticisms of former disciples such as Adler, Rank, and Jung, which he may have wished to answer, despite his reticence about them and their ideas (except for his great polemical blasts against them in the *History of the Psychoanalytic*

Movement of 1914). In his last years, from the mid-1920's to his death in 1939, he broadened his metaphysical bases of religious speculation and faith, especially in connection with his discussion of Moses. The earlier writings had a far greater impact on twentieth-century art and literature, a fact that becomes clear when we study this impact, first, as part of broad historical developments and then in terms of the specific artistic and literary activities of the major countries affected.

The first group of Freud's disciples was drawn into the master's circle shortly after the publication of *The Interpretation of Dreams*, and in the wake of his discussions of art, they produced their own works, more or less interesting, but rarely adding much of fundamental importance to what Freud had advanced. Thus, Karl Abraham wrote a study of the Italian artist Giovanni Segantini (1911) that is clearly modeled on Freud's *Leonardo*: Abraham studied Segantini's childhood and found, among other parallels to Freud's book, the Leonardesque theme of the two mothers central to his artistic activity. Studies proliferated: Jones wrote on Andrea del Sarto; Alice Sperber on "Dante's Unconscious Soul-Life"; and Lenau, Kleist, Gogol, and other great figures were explored psychoanalytically.[1] Everywhere the Oedipus complex was discovered, and from Rank and Sachs's basic work (1916) and Jones's impressive essay on *Hamlet* to more recent and less important writings, this concept has stimulated art no less than literary criticism. It will be, in fact, a peculiar problem for future literary historians to distinguish spontaneous and "mannered" examples of the various neurotic syndromes so incisively presented by Freud.

Inevitably, Freud's brief *History* barely hints at the beehive of activity in artistic and literary circles of many countries affected by his theories; for even the earlier survey of *The Significance of Psychoanalysis for the Mental Sciences* written by Rank and Sachs (1916) could not comprehend the whole wealth of productions up to that time. In its first decade, the impact of psychoanalysis was mainly on German letters, naturally, and a series of novels in that language offered more or less bizarre interpretations of the theory, intended for a wide market. The Expressionist Leonhard Frank also popularized the young movement, but with less superficiality (*Die Ursache*, 1915; *Der Mensch ist gut*, 1917). The decade 1910-20 seems to be one of confusion, not only because of the war years, but because of the emergence of competitive schools of psychoanalysis, beginning with Adler's defection in 1911, and continued by Jung's in 1913 (Rank's occurred in the next decade). During this period, an increasing number of artists actually were psychoanalyzed, and the debate about the value of the treatment for the creative personality stimulated Hesse to write an essay in 1918, "The Artist and Psychoanalysis," defending the usefulness of the technique, which nonetheless cannot replace the essentially intuitive talent necessary for all creativity. It is characteristic of Hesse—then in analysis with Jung, who had rejected Freud's emphasis on sexuality—to ignore questions of sex in his discussion of Freudian psychoanalysis, and to dwell on a version of the unconscious that he could legitimately compare to nineteenth-century models.

During the 1920's, while Freud fretted over complicated refinements and niceties of his theories and passed *Beyond the Pleasure Principle* (1920), an expansive postwar temper seized on psychoanalysis and its derivatives. Many more writers and artists had direct contact with the psychoanalytic techniques of free association and dream interpretation handled by analysts trained on Freud's earlier, more sex-oriented theories. Especially in the United States, England and France, Freud's notoriety as a German Jew lent a touch of the recondite professor to his image, and probably intensified the thrill of cathartic release and sexual liberation anticipated from psychoanalytic treatment, even by his followers. Novels and biographies "deepened" by a prurient psychoanalysis (of "normal" persons as well as of neurotics) abounded at this time, exerting an immense attraction upon a public tempted to escape from its own stereotypes and to follow the new models of behavior. However, formalist critics, including Roger Fry and Clive Bell, as well as Samuel Beckett and other associates of James Joyce, vociferously rejected the psychologizing biographies as irrelevant to the experience of art. The hectic period of the 1930's, with its intellectual and cultural, along with its economic and political, rearming, brought with it sharper ideological formulations in all areas, including the arts. Upsurging nationalism, masked by international socialist pretensions, characterized the totalitarianism of the Soviets, the Italian Fascists, and the National Socialists; but a nostalgia for its truly international and humane beginnings still gave the Soviets an edge with some of the most advanced artists, a few of whom refused to become disillusioned even after the Moscow trials of the mid-1930's. Apart from the innumerable individual artists cajoled by the popular front into mock-heroic radicalism, the major thrust at this time among mature artists working together to realize socialist ideals came from the Surrealists. This group, led by the gifted and dogmatic André Breton, perhaps epitomized the diverse ideological tendencies of the period in its attempt to unite psychoanalytic ideas and techniques to Marxian ideals, and through special psychological and artistic strategies to realize a utopian society.

The 1940's were dominated by the war and its anxious aftermath, the cold war, a period that looked back to mass murders and forward to threats of atomic holocaust. With the collapse of the verbiage and the paper utopias of the 1930's, many disillusioned artists and writers turned inward, to develop their personalities (in an odd way analogous to the 1920's without the hope and exhilaration of that decade, and now to the 1970's). Some psychoanalysts turned to developing an "ego-psychology" (see chapter 2) to replace the old emphasis on the determinism of the unconscious forces and of the tribal instinct, which even the late Freud began to modify. The death of Freud in September, 1939, in the same month as the outbreak of World War II, somewhat muted the impact it might otherwise have had around the world, but did open access to some of the previously unpublished materials, and thereby enabled several fine scholars to gain a deeper and more intimate knowledge of the man and the formation of his ideas. During the 1950's, certain postwar tendencies began to prevail that challenged the basis of psychoanalysis from different directions: as a science (some of whose theories had become commonplace among students of personality), on the one hand, and as a useful guide to creativity on the other. Attempts were made to validate Freudian concepts like repression, and even to reinterpret Freudian theories of personality in general in terms of modern behavioral theory.[2] As other schools of psychoanalysis emerged (this time developed by young men without the European roots and education of the older psychoanalysts), a new emphasis on the surface phenomenon, on the quick cure, and on the role of group therapy prevailed. The notion of ego psychology came more and more to stand for one progressive wing of the already declining school of orthodox psychoanalysis. The United States, which had welcomed the refugee analysts during the years just before and during the war, became the land most involved with psychoanalysis, and so also the site of a massive rejection of, or bypassing of, Freudian theories.

A surprising development was the rejection of older leftist critics of Freud, such as Erich Fromm, who regarded Freud as a bourgeois insensitive to social values, and the discovery of the revolutionary implications of Freudian psychoanalysis by members of the New Left, such as Herbert Marcuse (1955), and by the oracular historian Norman O. Brown (1959). Both Marcuse and Brown based their reappraisals on the late works of Freud. Brown apparently followed in the footsteps of Trilling's *Beyond Culture* (1955), which noted that Freud's greatest claim to praise was his placing "at the very center of his thought" the idea of the existence of "the self apart from culture." What had been attacked as bourgeois romanticism in Freud by Marxists became the basis for a new radical individualism to those troubled by the repressive aspect of modern society and its culture. Marcuse, like Brown, found in Freud's *Beyond the Pleasure Principle* and *Civilization and Its Discontents* attractive speculations resting on Freud's dualistic idea that Eros the life-force (generalized from the earlier, purely sexual libido, perhaps in response to certain critics) was inevitably associated with and opposed to an aggressive or death instinct. Neither writer was content to regard this state of affairs with the fatalistic pessimism of Freud, and so each concocted from various writings of Freud and others a "dialectical" approach to man's splits both internal (life versus death) and external (individual versus culture), in which the repressive reality principle would be at last overwhelmed by the libertarian pleasure principle. The earliest phase of life, viewed by Freud as "polymorphus perverse," in which all sexual potentials are present, become for these the paradigm to move back toward, and one immensely influential with certain branches of the radical youth of today. No wonder the critic Kenneth Burke was provoked to proclaim in print [3] against recent works whose aims he reduces to the slogan " 'Down with politics, up with apocalypse.' " In Burke's eyes, ingenious writers like Brown, "feeding the appetite" for such slogans, are "Freudian in Utopian ways that would doubtless have vexed Freud sorely."

Following the new directions of the 1950's, and right through the late 1960's, important changes in the response to psychoanalysis have become evident: those aspects that had earlier shocked and scandalized proved acceptable to many strata of society now exposed to a wide spectrum of ideas through mass media like television; but while "the unconscious" or the sexual theories of infancy became platitudinous, innovating critics of art and literature began to discover a value in sides of Freud that had heretofore been ignored, and some artists began to absorb these ideas, albeit usually without knowledge of their debt to him. Moreover, not only did Freud become the object of a psychoanalytic scrutiny free of older biases, but his whole movement began sympathetically to be examined by anthropologists like Lévi-Strauss, who compared such techniques as free association to the magic and religious practices of other, including primitive, societies (turning upon Freud an approach that the psychoanalyst himself had sponsored with regard to the roots of Western religion and culture). Finally, Freud's analytic methods for interpreting symbols—detached from their therapeutic significance—served as stimuli or even models for certain students of linguistics and of aesthetic questions. The transformation of psychoanalysis and its changed impact can be more sharply defined if we add to this general outline a complementary discussion of the specific national influences.

The home site of psychoanalysis and of Freud's first intimate circle of followers was, of course, Austria, or—to be more precise—Vienna, the intellectual center of the country. The complex early situation of psychoanalysis in Vienna we have already discussed: since Freud matured within the same academic and cultural tradition as contemporaries such as Schnitzler and von Hofmannsthal, it is very difficult to isolate or measure the impact of Freud's ideas on their styles. Although Freud's ideas were frequently contested or aggressively ignored in Austria (as in Germany) before World War I, the battle for medical recognition seems to have been even harder to win after the war, when the republic was formed. Certainly the political uncertainties of the period, with the extreme polarities between left and right, as well as the dismemberment of the Austro-Hungarian Empire, lessened the chances for the dissemination of his ideas in that part of Europe. Nevertheless, the postwar attractions between the two German-speaking countries, and their tendency toward *Anschluss* (with Germany's intellectual and economic dominance), made it possible for German intellectuals, wishing to express their admiration for Austrian genius, to honor Freud in 1930 with the Goethe Prize for literature. Only with Hitler's takeover did Freud's Jewishness rather than his contribution to German letters become the main issue, in both countries. But the 1930 prize suggests how important Freud had been in literary circles during the 1920's. Especially the Austrian Expressionists considered problems that Freud himself touched in his writings of the 1920's on group psychology, the nature of war and religion. Novels such as Franz Werfel's *Not the Murderer but the Murdered Is Guilty* (1920) express a central insight clearly enunciated by Freud (and passed on to certain writings of Theodor Reik); and Jakob Wassermann, a German living in Austria, produced strange situations and perverse characters often with Freudian overtones. A self-tortured Jew, Wassermann constantly exposed and criticized his Jewish characters, and presented in *The Maurizius Case* (1928), his most Freudian effort, a detective novel that relentlessly removes one veil after the other until the "truth" (in this case, whether the hero actually committed the murder for which he has been punished) is revealed, and we learn that he is in fact guilty. Max Mell, in *Seven Against Thebes* (1931), continued the line of von Hofmannsthal's Freudian transformations of Greek plays, but more significant was Robert Musil's profound novel *The Man Without Qualities* (1930-33), which describes the prewar Austrian as a featureless being shaped by custom into passivity and loss of individuality. In fact, he touches deeply on the pre-Hitler desperation of the early 1930's in Austria and Germany. With the advent of Hitler, of course, Freud's influence went underground or emigrated with political refugees. The wasteland for psychoanalytic studies of those years of Nazi bookburning can be gauged today from the nearly complete absence of original editions of Freud's books in the main libraries of Vienna and Munich; but many post-World War II books on Freud, including new German editions of the collected works, are beginning to fill the library shelves. The impact of Freud has been hotly contested, however, by the new school of Catholic psychologists led by Viktor Frankl (1949), who blended existentialism, bits of Jung and Freud, and his unshakable religious convictions into a "Logotherapy." Yet Freud is not to be denied in Vienna and after a great celebration, it is planned that Berggasse 19 will become a national monument; but he has in fact always loomed like a distant mountain behind Viennese culture. Of course,

Freud's return to respectability cannot serve as a ground for good and interesting literature unless the young Viennese themselves are readying a new period that can restore some of the old *fin de siècle* glory.

German attitudes to psychoanalysis evolved in a manner comparable to the Austrian development. In his *History* (1914), Freud indicates that by 1914 psychoanalysis was talked about everywhere in Germany —but as something to *reject*. The public image in Germany of the procedures of the psychoanalyst can be gauged from Grete Meisel-Hess's novel *The Intellectuals* (Berlin, 1911), which describes the session of a middle-aged neurotic woman. Inevitably the psychoanalyst in this novel, regarded then as a somewhat esoteric and powerful figure, as well as one who delves into sexual mysteries, acted both as hypnotist and as gynecologist. The uprooted situation of the postwar Weimar Republic resembled that of its counterpart in Austria, in providing a background forming the greatest diversity of political and cultural positions. The cult of individual power (*Machtmensch*) and the militant confrontations of groups of the left and right created a tension-filled atmosphere conducive to Expressionist violence and distortions. The perversions and sexual crises of many of the Expressionists seem like caricatures of Freud's neurotics, whose bizarre dreams became here waking realities; for the Expressionists tried to turn the plumbed depths of their unconscious into conscious norms: in his uninhibited representation of the Oedipal theme of blinding, the Hamburg novelist Hanns H. Jahn filled his *Medea* (1925) with violent excesses such as the tearing out of eyes. By 1931, Sten Selander could hardly review the literary influence of Freud comprehensively and concentrated on countries dominated by his influence: Germany, France, England, and America. According to Selander, Freud so fascinated the Germans that they "slavishly" submitted to his ideas (he cites Leonhard Frank, Franz Werfel, and Thomas Mann). But he noted an opposition to Freud developing: "Young, radical talents can't warm up to Freud for these revolutionaries (as a rule communists) are basically optimists who come out of Rousseau's optimistic idealism, and Freud's view that man from birth on is an evil, aggressive and egoistic being stands dramatically opposed to that utopianism."

This utopian mood of the radicals was travestied by the emerging nationalistic groups such as the Nazis, who rejected Freud more from anti-Semitism than from optimistic idealism. Chanting their simple-minded folk hymns to health, the Nazis would hear nothing of sickness or neurosis, certainly not from a Jewish psychologist. Although the Expressionist intensities had abated, the Nazis, bypassing the cooler mood of hard-headed realism (*Neue Sachlichkeit*), which briefly succeeded it, beat the drums for mass hysteria grounded in the romanticism of blood and soil (*Blut und Scholle*). During the economic and political crises of the early 1930's, the Nazis naturally exploited the paranoia about "international Jewish conspiracies": Freud eventually joined other Jewish scapegoats, who were either silenced or forced to flee during the 1930's in Germany. In the expansive, rejuvenated postwar Germany, Freud, a representative of cosmopolitan thought, has returned to ever-growing favor and influence. His impact on German letters will probably resume its earlier importance, in a climate yielding the sensitive *bizarreries* of Günter Grass and the Expressionist intensity of Peter Weiss.

The Swiss early manifested an interest in psychoanalysis, according to Freud's *History*. Jung knew his work in 1902, and by 1903 psychoanalysis already was a main topic of discussion. After their meeting in 1908, Freud and Jung founded a journal jointly expressing the views of the groups in Vienna and Zürich. Soon Zürich became the center of the movement and most of Freud's later followers, as he himself acknowledges, came to him via Zürich. An early divergence between the groups arose, however, Freud's sexual interpretation being opposed by the Swiss's strictly organic theory of neurosis (Bleuler). Coupled with a rejection of Freud's narrow interpretation of sexuality was a tendency to employ a theory of the "collective unconscious" to explain the similarity of myths and symbols in different cultures. Consistent with this turn to the "spirit" as essential, Jung emphasized the religious aspect of man's life, meaning his need for faith, hope, love, and insight. Jung's version has dominated Swiss psychoanalysis, and characterized its incessant quest for symbols as guides to a collective unconscious. The development of Hesse is characteristic: from an interest in Freud and Jung, he passed through a Jungian analysis to a heightened interest in symbolism, ending in the Oriental mysticism typical of his later works (a similar development may be occurring among young American writers and artists of the 1970's). Swiss psychoanalytic literary criticism has also preserved strong attachments to religious—often Christian—interpretations, linked to Jung's religious emphasis. Thus the noted pastor Georges Berguer, with no breach of pious proprieties, applied a Jungian psychoanalytic method to the personality of Christ (1917), and Charles Baudouin, another Swiss, in his numerous aesthetic studies, found Freud's idea of overdetermination a valuable road leading from the individual work to larger symbols and creative influences. The first translation of Freud's works (the *Five Essays* delivered in America) appeared in the *Revue de Genève* in 1921. A Geneva school of psychoanalytically oriented critics has emerged, including Albert Béguin (1939), who sees romanticism as ultimately religious, and who compares poetic states to religious revelations, and Georges Poulet (1950, 1952), who turned psychoanalysis to metaphysical use, in seeking Kantian categories of space and time to account for interior experience. Freud's old analysis of the Swiss trend to religion, or at least to metaphysical speculation, seems still to hold true.

In France, the characteristic split between Cartesian intellectuality, accompanied by academic restrictions on one's life style (even to the control of language through the *Dictionnaire française*), and an impulse toward absurd humor, obscurity, and Rabelaisian exaggeration, produced a corresponding difference between the responses of official psychology and of many writers and artists. Nineteenth-century French psychology had more than one representative of unorthodox views that anticipate Freud's; aside from the school of hypnotists following Charcot, the famous Taine's *L'Intelligence* (1870) advanced concepts that strongly suggest Freud's: chains of ideas and *association d'images*, repression, the ego as the stable interior of the self, and the notion of a repressed image (*image refoulée*) corresponding to a preceding sensation. No wonder Freud praised the book so highly in a letter of February 13, 1896, to Fliess. As Ellenberger (1970) has shown, late-nineteenth-century French psychology already accepted infantile sexuality; yet, when Freud's views on the Oedipus complex were made known, great and uncomprehending opposition met them, as is evident from a perusal of contemporary journals of psychology. Against Freud's view of the origin of incest (in *Totem and Taboo*), French psychiatrists accepted Westermarck's common-sense opinion that persons who had grown up together from childhood would not be sexually excited by one another, since they were "used" to each other. More interesting are the many productions among the French Symbolists, Freud's contemporaries, dealing with unconscious and obscure areas of experience, of which we have already spoken; but after 1900, a wave of opposition to the artificialities of the Symbolists passed over some French writers rediscovering the powerful spontaneity of the unconscious,[4] and others opposed to all forms of *passéisme* and moving toward Marinetti's Futurism.[5]

In line with the rejection of Symbolist mystery, the dominant psychology became the academic behavioral and rational one of Babinski, rather than Charcot's, regarded as vague and unscientific. The official and academic repudiation of psychoanalysis may have been connected to the powerful resurgence of a Catholic-military reaction centered around the Dreyfus trial. Typically, a prominent anti-Dreyfusard, Abbé L.-Cl. Delfour,[6] could write that "France, tired of the Anglo-German domination, aspires to intellectual and religious independence. But will it have the force to overcome the triumvirate of Jew, Protestant and Free-Mason ?" As a German-writing Jew, Freud would have come under the attack of the numerous anti-German chauvinists wishing to keep France free of the "Boches"; for example, Apollinaire lauded the Diaghilev-Cocteau-Picasso ballet *Parade* for its break with German romanticism in "The New Spirit" (1917). Freud was only slightly consoled that in place of being accepted in scientific circles, he became after the war the hero for some young adventurously cosmopolitan writers, a number of whom must have been stimulated by Mme. Sokolnicka's lectures on psychoanalysis in Paris in 1921. Although (as Freud observed in his foreword to the *Introductory Lectures* of 1917) a good introductory survey of psychoanalysis was already available in E. Regis and A. Hesnard's *La Psychanalyse des nevroses et des psychoses* of 1914, even established writers like Albert Thibaudet (1921) rather misconstrued Freud's meaning.[7] The split between official psychology and some avant-garde writers seems to have reached a head in the mid-1920's, when the Surrealist movement, under Breton's leadership, made Freud into an idol, the more valuable for his being rejected by the establishment.[8] Charles Blondel (1924) considered Freud less a scientist than a contributor to the history of ideas; he singled out "The Dream of Irma's Injection" for special sarcasm about Freud's associating chemical formulas to Irma: "Our language doesn't treat women like alkaloids"; and the Botticelli-Boltraffio analysis of *The Psychopathology of Everyday Life* annoyed him since, in Blondel's opinion, Freud had "suggested to the young man the very ideas he claimed to have discovered in him."

Despite such continuing rejection by psychologists, in 1924 the Parisian journal *Disque vert* produced an issue devoted to psychoanalysis (stimulating Freud to write a sympathetic letter to the editor); and in his *Autobiographical Study* of a year later, Freud contrasted the "violent objection to the acceptance of psychoanalysis" evident in current newspapers and the tendency to claim that Freud's ideas were borrowed from Janet, to the "interest in psychoanalysis growing among men of letters." [9] Freud may have had in mind such writings as Gide's *Counterfeiters* (1925), a "polyphonic plot" whose characters diverge from sexual norms; or Jacques de Lacretelle's *La Boniface* (1925), a story of a woman with lesbian tendencies isolated in a small provincial village. New impetus was given to Freudianism by the founding of *La Société Psychanalytique de Paris* in 1926, and of *La Revue française de psychanalyse* in 1927 (by Laforgue). Breton's Second Surrealist Manifesto of 1930 gave Freud pride of place as a model, although some defectors from the movement such as Aragon in the same year demanded at the Soviet Writers' Congress the condemnation of Freud's bourgeois ideas. Aside from Breton's group, and the interesting blend of Catholicism and Freudianism in P. J. Jouve, [10] who saw man torn between his sexual instinct and his need for spirituality, there was a rather diffuse interest among French critics in the Freudian notion of the unconscious during the 1930's when a series of romantic novels were written. During the 1940's a new sense of realism prevailed, accompanied by the metaphysical explorations of the Existentialists, and these tendencies fused in the 1950's in the *nouveau roman* of Robbe-Grillet and Sarraute, whose anti-novels emphasized a phenomenological immediacy. For these writers, the psychoanalytic "profundities" seemed insincere melodrama. As late as 1966, Simone de Beauvoir ridiculed those who overvalued the past (implied alike by Proust's cup of tea and *madeleine*, and by Freud's repressed sexual experience of childhood). [11] But the main trend of the 1960's and beyond has been the French Structuralists' project to recover a link between depth and surface, and their exploration of an abstract and many-leveled mythology joining past and present, similar to Freud's psychoanalysis.

Psychoanalysis had apparently slight impact on Italy, probably for the same reasons that deprived Italy of a romantic movement comparable to the ones in England and Germany. Thus, the Futurists spent half of their time directing their scorn at the museums and academies, from which they could not really escape, finally transforming their opposition to classical Italian culture into hysterical support of Fascist nationalism. In his *History*, Freud notes that after some positive starts in Italy, nothing more was heard of psychoanalysis in the country. In fact, some Italians responded favorably as early as 1907 in brief notes, and in more extensive articles from 1908 on;[12] perhaps the case of Sante de Sanctis best sums up the situation alluded to by Freud. Sante's early study *I Sogni* (1899) so impressed Freud that he cited it in *The Interpretation of Dreams* as a fine survey of pre-Freudian dream theories; but Sante produced little more touching on psychoanalysis until as late as 1924. In 1928, Freud praised Sante's volume: "I may refer to an admirable volume on the subject (the psychology of conversion) by Sante de Sanctis (1924), which incidentally takes all the findings of psychoanalysis into account."[13] Sante's unusual interest in psychoanalysis was not picked up by younger psychologists, nor did Sante himself feel able or willing to follow Freud's more elaborate treatment of the unconscious. Whether or not, as claimed by Michel David,[14] anti-Semitism formed an important obstacle to the diffusion of psychoanalysis in Italy, it is certainly true, as David observes,[15] that Freud's *Gradiva* had little success in Italy, though translated into Italian, and David expected only hostile responses to Freud's *Leonardo*, still not translated into Italian. It would hardly have gratified Freud to learn that Leonardo's romantic eulogist Giuseppina Fumagalli,[16] while rejecting Freud's analysis of Leonardo's sublimation, justified his mistaking a kite for the vulture of Leonardo's fantasy, on the grounds that the kite, identified with mother nature, was a fitting symbol for Leonardo's genius, which conquers in its battle with the wind, "and lifts him up glorious above all other men."

Despite, or perhaps because of, the general indifference or hostility toward Freud in Italy from the early 1930's through the postwar period, some of the best avant-garde writers found psychoanalysis liberating for them, even though they tended to ignore the unconscious and to concentrate on the sexual component of Freud's theories.

Although in his *La Coscienza di Zeno* (1923), Italo Svevo takes little details from Freud rather than the essential theory of neurosis, Freud provided the initial impetus for the author, at least to the extent of inspiring him with a sympathy for and understanding of the neurotic in man.[17] Alberto Moravia, who used Freud as an antidote to Croce and to his own naturalism, seems to be the most Freudian of the Italians, especially because he wrote at the low point of interest in Freud among the Italian avant-garde, in 1944–54. Cesare Pavese, whose "Freudian period" occurred about 1939–41, was particularly drawn to the psychoanalyst's idea of an all-pervading sexuality.[18] Certainly the main funnel for psychoanalytic ideas coming to Italy was the cosmopolitan center of Trieste, where Freud's theories were widely known even before the World War I. This was mainly due to the presence of Viennese psychoanalysts made possible through Austria's possession of the city up to 1914, and through the large Jewish colony there. We are surprised to learn that while the Viennese still commonly considered psychoanalysis in terms of traditional medical therapy, many writers residing in Trieste diffused Freud's ideas not as therapy but for their insights into culture.[19] Evidently Joyce's *Ulysses* (1922) as well as Svevo's *Zeno* owed much to their authors' exposure to Freud's ideas in Trieste.

In the United States, Freud's five lectures delivered at Clark University in 1909 won him a good reception (those same lectures, translated into English, now form the substance of most readings of Freud in American universities), and several influential supporters, including Clark's president, G. Stanley Hall. Characteristically, psychoanalysis became for Americans one more frontier to cross and a means to progress toward a truly democratic education; and Max Eastman in 1915 already called for practical new educational approaches grounded in Freud's views on repression and sublimation: "Education must be thought of as a kind of *emancipation*." As we know, Freud felt little agreement with his American interpreters; but this was not the first time that the American tendency to combine an excessive pragmatism with an expansive idealism had resulted in the distortion of a European concept. The tense straining toward an egoistic freedom, with backs to Europe and faces to the frontier has been associated with a crusading puritanism. (Only recently has this "Yankee" spirit of conquest begun to yield—as in the late Roman empire—to what one might term a "domestic cosmopolitanism" in which a diversity of subcultures challenges the rule of a homogeneous majority whose "melting-pot" caused identity crises among those unable or unwilling to conform.) This puritanism is even visible in the writings of G. Stanley Hall, who in 1912 considered the patient who frees himself from a mental disease to be like "a sinner [who] extradites guilt or a Freudian patient an inner trauma by confession." Perhaps the puritanical psychiatrist in T. S. Eliot's *Cocktail Party* (1949) whose insights seem both prescient and morally wholesome best epitomizes this quality of the American mind. Inevitably, psychoanalytic theories of sexuality provided a basis for a host of novels whose "liberated" characters were usually not so much insightfully probed as indecently exposed.

Much of this misreading of Freud began to be corrected during the 1930's, with the great influx of psychoanalysts emigrating from a Nazi-dominated Europe. During the 1940's and 1950's, these analysts gave sensitive Americans the chance at last to be psychoanalyzed. Very soon, writers and artists began to raise the same problem that Hesse and Thomas Mann had already posed on the relation of creativity to neurosis. This was the central problem treated by a series of articles, mainly from the 1940's, published in the pages of the magazine *Partisan Review*. These articles (and others mainly by European writers in translation touching on analogous questions) were collected in an anthology by William Phillips (1957), whose introductory discussion of "Art and Neurosis" matches Trilling's essay bearing the same title, which closes the book. In his dialectical exposition Phillips asserts first that art can be neither neurotic nor healthy (these being different domains from art), and then, observing that much modern writing is, after all, neurotic ("obsessive"), he asks what it can mean "to say that Swift's or Kafka's writings contained some central distortion of experience traceable to the neuroses of the authors?" He answers that "their neurotic impressions of the world coincided with impressions that were not neurotic and served to organize and energize the latter." Unfortunately, his discussion does not enlighten us very much about the boundaries of the neurotic in the writer's work, nor are we told just what mysterious process allows the "neurotic impression" to "energize" the "non-neurotic impression." Nor will we find an answer in the essays by psychoanalysts included in the anthology, for they relentlessly track down the neuroses of great writers such as Kafka, Poe, and von Kleist, with little concern for the root problem of the relation of art to neurosis posed by the editor. In the postwar period of the cold war, the changed relations between the United States and Russia provoked a crisis among disillusioned writers who had once wished to establish a rapport between psychoanalysis and Marxism; and the chief "revisionist," from the early 1930's on, of Freud's thought with respect to its pessimism about society and politics—Erich Fromm—found his efforts to unite Freud and Marx less and less popular. By the 1950's, sensitive critics like Richard Chase and Lionel Trilling were already rejecting Fromm's liberal confusions, and pointing toward the biological and naturalistic in psychoanalysis as its essence.

With the vogue for Wilhelm Reich and the proclamations of Herbert Marcuse and N. O. Brown, the tide began to turn back to a radical sexualism and emphasis on the body as the source of emotional and mental life. This materialist and sensual emphasis has restored the Enlightenment hopes that Freud's pessimism denied, but the humanist element has seemed less and less relevant to the concerns of many contemporary youth who sympathize with Gay Power and Women's Liberation and who consequently reject the slow ripening to *man*hood as a submission to one superior stable tradition. The preference for instant satisfaction (the drug culture, replacing the old cult of experience, has undercut the Freudian idea of long searching analyses that "excavate" remote infantile experiences in order to achieve "maturity"); the new values and fashions that young middle-class whites have been adopting from aggressive minority groups; the renewed emphasis on religion as shown by numerous independent cult groups and by widespread mysticism in the form of numerology and astrology—all this seems even post-Marcuse and -Brown (in bypassing Freud's rational humanism, a number of young artists and writers have moved closer to Jung). Nevertheless, aside from the many "hinterland" mentalities among the bright youth, who each year pass through Freud on their way to Marcuse and Brown and beyond, some recent critics in the United States and Europe have begun to find a new relevance for Freud's ideas.

Although Freud could practically ignore England in his *History*, the response to psychoanalysis has since grown there tremendously. England was potentially a fertile soil for psychoanalysis, since Freud derived much from the English literature he so admired and was influenced by Spencer, Darwin, and Galton; moreover, the psychologist Grant Allen had already introduced the phrase "stream of consciousness," which the Bloomsbury group (including Leonard Woolf, the critic, and his wife, Virginia, who together published Freud in England) later adopted. Ever since Ernest Jones moved from Toronto University to London in 1911, Freud has been staunchly represented in England, and Havelock Ellis also wrote often and sympathetically (at first) on psychoanalysis, while the psychoanalyst Edward Glover briskly defended Freud against academic British psychology and Jung. The best early literary parallels to psychoanalysis occurred in the delicate works of "stream of consciousness" writers like Katherine Mansfield, Elizabeth Bowen, and Virginia Woolf, and in the masterfully subtle treatment of ambiguity by the critic William Empson (1931). Sex and the unconscious of Freud seem to have had less attraction among English writers except as objects of satire, or in the ecstatic anti-Freudian tirades of D. H. Lawrence. A rich literature appeared in the 1930's, straddling if not uniting the views of Freud and Marx, as in the poetry of Auden and Spender. Freud's presence has been felt in British art especially since the big London Surrealist exhibition of 1936 helped Herbert Read to launch Surrealism in England on a large scale. The brisk little school of English psychoanalysis has kept Freud's ideas alive there, so that the old skimpy surveys of his influence in books such as Hoffman's (1957) are even less valid today: we await a thorough and comprehensive study that will do justice to Freud's impact on England.

By 1914, Freud could announce in his *History* that almost all of his works had been translated into Russian; but he adds that little real understanding of them had yet been evident among Russian psychiatrists. However, Freud makes no mention of A. Kostyleff, a professor in the École des Hautes Études in Paris, who tried to unite a Pavlovian theory of poetry as a verbo-motor discharge to Freudian psychoanalysis.[20] Kostyleff's attempted synthesis points to a deep split in Russian thought between behavioral and spiritual viewpoints: side by side with the uncanny insights into the human soul of Tolstoy and Dostoievsky emerged Pavlovian reflex psychology, and an aesthetics of classical simplicity. In nineteenth-century aesthetics, already the famous Belinsky's circle of "enlighteners" (Herzen, Chernyshevsky, Dobrolyubov, Pisarev) strongly inclined to the rational and functional, and won the admiration of twentieth-century Marxists for making art a pure result of the historical process. His follower Pisarev wrote as a naturalist in 1865 on "The Destruction of Aesthetics," and promoted the aim of reducing art and beauty to psychology and mental hygiene under the slogan, "Every healthy and normal person is beautiful." The Marxists derived from such nineteenth-century Russian criticism the idea that art should be useful and serve a social function, including propaganda. The old Russian intelligentsia, isolated spokesmen of progress with values that were cosmopolitan rather than nationalist, atheist rather than religious, and radical rather than conservative, only felt at ease in their own country for a few years at the beginning of the great revolution, before the Soviet bureaucracy replaced the czarist.

Lenin, a major influence on Marxist criticism, derived his ideas in part from the nineteenth-century functionalists, and emphasized that art at once reflects social reality and should be used to influence it. Puritanical, and with a rather philistine taste, his ideas on art served as a proper model for the provincial mentality of the Georgian Joseph Stalin. None of the major Soviet politicians expressed interest in psychoanalysis, aside from Trotsky, perhaps the most sensitive and creative personality produced by the revolution. Although he basically shared Lenin's functionalism and social utilitarianism and wished to make art a weapon in his doomed political struggle toward a socialist Russia, Trotsky was open to new ideas and attempted to apply some Freudian concepts to his Marxist theories. The attempt to reconcile Freud and Marx by his comrade, Radek, was probably a political expedient, and he made indiscriminate rejections of "bourgeois" writers for whom he found no use, calling Joyce's work "a heap of dung." Trotsky was somewhat less obsessively political in his significant *Literature and Revolution* (1925), in which he used psychoanalysis as a polemical weapon against "reactionary" psychologists ignoring sex, and the great school of formalist criticism of Shklovsky and Jakobson (who, in Trotsky's view, ignore the psychological aspects of art, which, like the sociopolitical background, are necessary accompaniments to the origin of form), meanwhile praising the work of the Austrian psychoanalytical school (Freud, Jung, Adler). He singled out Freud for his contribution to "the question of the sex-element in the forming of individual character and of social consciousness,"[21] a position that the prudish Lenin would have rejected vigorously. Again, he predicts[22] that the force of competition, in "the language of psychoanalysis, will be sublimated (i.e., will assume a higher and more fertile form)."

Trotsky's acquaintance with psychoanalysis was rather superficial (his idea of sublimation is closer to Nietzsche's than to Freud's) and by no means exceptional: at this very moment the diffusion of psychoanalysis among nonpolitical circles in Russia reached its high point. Alexander Luria, an eminent psychologist, conducted experiments at the State Institute of Experimental Psychology, between 1923 and 1930, that supported some basic Freudian assumptions about the unconscious, repression, and free association,[23] and wrote favorably about psychoanalysis as offering "the materialistic basis for constructing a really Marxist psychology."[24] The Soviets, officially never very friendly to psychoanalysis, refused to accept psychoanalysts or others among the many brilliant German and Austrian intellectuals exiled for political reasons or as Jews during the *Nazi-Zeit*. This blind hostility helped shape the famous remark in the postwar *Short Philosophical Dictionary of the U.S.S.R.* (1951): "Scientific psychology categorically denies the existence of the Freudian 'subconscious' . . . The German fascists have availed themselves of Freudianism."[25] The situation has not changed much in recent years, to judge from Priscilla Johnson's book (1965); for the name of no major psychoanalyst, nor of psychoanalysis itself, is mentioned in the long discussions of Soviet cultural activity during the early 1960's.

The attempt to unite the theories of Freud and Marx seemed on the verge of becoming pan-European in the mid-1920's; in 1929, such projects disappeared abruptly. The intensified competition and struggle within the Communist Party, which started even before Lenin's death in 1924, was squelched (publicly, at least) when the iron hand of Stalin seized power and expelled his rival Trotsky from Russia in 1929. The dictator, with his parochial, bureaucratic resistance to new ideas, opposed psychoanalysis and dropped the short-lived Institute of Psycho-analysis in 1929. Sadly, no major literature or art stimulated by psychoanalysis appears to have been produced in Soviet Russia, and those trying to assimilate *any* advanced Western culture whatever became a sort of underground—at best ignored, but never encouraged. However, it was still possible for the Surrealist Breton who sympathized with Trotsky, to hope that a new period of productive synthesis between psychoanalysis and Marxism was dawning, since Bukharin in his address to the First Congress of Soviet Writers in August, 1935, concluded that "there is no antagonism between the image (the recourse to the irrational) and the idea, between the 'new eroticism' and the 'meaning of the collectivity' within the framework of a 'socialist realism.'"[26] André Malraux's applauded speech at the same congress seemed to Breton another favorable "sign of the times," since it contained the sentiment that "Art is a conquest . . . of feelings . . . about the unconscious . . . Marxism is the consciousness of the social; culture is the consciousness of the psychological." Breton agreed, adding that Freud would replace "consciousness" by "pre-consciousness," and would answer the question "How can we bring repressed elements into (pre)-consciousness? by reestablishing through the work of analysis those intermediate preconscious members, verbal memories." Breton notes that these verbal memories, or representations—mnemonic traces derived from acoustic perceptions, according to Freud—are the raw material of poetry. Surrealism's whole effort, in Breton's view (borrowing from *The Interpretation of Dreams*), "has been to obtain from the poet the instantaneous revelation of these verbal traces whose psychic charges are capable of being communicated to the perception-consciousness system (and also to obtain from the painter the most rapid projection possible of optical mnemonic traces)." These projects—prefiguring and perhaps influencing Abstract Expressionism—he finds can be realized through automatism, which alone allows "passage from the unconscious to the preconscious."

The most interesting English Marxist to be concerned with Freud's theories was the influential critic Christopher Caudwell, who, in passing from an early involvement with psychoanalysis to revolutionary politics, converted whatever traces of Freudianism remained into his new Marxian ideology. Thus, while comparing poetry to the dream in his *Illusion and Reality* (1937), he insisted that Freud's dream is bourgeois, a latent content that must be reinterpreted in terms of Marx's manifest content. Like Breton and Malraux, Caudwell sought to maximize social awareness, and regarded Freud's pessimism about man's instinctual limitations as a conservative undermining of revolutionary progress. Unobserved by Caudwell and his colleagues was the fact that Marxian and Freudian criticism shared certain problems and shortcomings: both lacked (except perhaps in the thought of the great Marxist literary critic Georg Lukács) a framework in which to appreciate properly great writers rather than mediocrities embodying the main ideas of a class or a neurosis; both abused the artist for his lack of seriousness—his devotion to the pleasure principle and his "escape" into illusion and fantasy; and both dispensed a salvation in terms of a return to reality (for Caudwell, the poet's "magic" can be effective in motivating men to work, as in the old fertility rites).

More recent efforts to synthesize the ideas of Freud and Marx, especially in the United States, have aimed to reverse the old value system, which placed conflict, work, and productivity—the values dominant in the 1930's and 1940's—above play and pleasure. Characteristically, in the 1930's, the critic Kenneth Burke (1939) thought that Freud and Marx could be combined in a theory of drama, "the one worked out in terms of personal conflicts, the other in terms of public conflicts." While this view is quite in line with Freud's pessimistic opinion of man's instinctual aggressiveness, other theories linked sex and politics in terms of love rather than aggression. Fourier, early in the nineteenth century, already thought of sex as a social glue, but without the specific apparatus Freud introduced. Breton's admiration of Freud's ideas for helping to emancipate men—an optimism Freud did not share with his romantic forerunners—seems to have been picked up by N. O. Brown (1955), who apparently effects a dialectical inversion of the relation of Marx's historical and economic factors to Freud's psychological ones: in his view, the economic does not cause or condition the sexual habits and social or cultural forms, but the reverse; consequently, changed sexual habits will lead ultimately to new social relations and freedom for individuals. Specifically, Brown compares genital (phallic) to patriarchal dominance and bourgeois technological specialization, and recommends that the human organism open itself to all sensual possibilities—the condition described by Freud as polymorphous perversity. Brown's book, in line with its subtitle, "The Psychological Meaning of History," reduces time to a psychological dimension and is essentially unhistorical, as has been shown in a trenchant critique.[27]

The concept of polymorphic perversity (aside from its obvious links to Plato's famous myth) has affinities to the romantic image of the androgyne, a symbol whose decline in the nineteenth century was traced by Mario Praz (1951), and by Mircea Eliade (1965), who emphasized that in the nineteenth century and later the androgyne degenerated from a symbol of wholeness to a purely sensual, mundane creature. Perhaps this decline is part of a broader loss of self-esteem by Western man, the *fin de siècle* myth of the corrupt civilized man being a sad descendant of the eighteenth-century Rousseauan myth of the noble savage. Breton and the Surrealists addressed the problems of civilized man's shrunken vitality, and—taking hints from Freud—they defined freedom to mean, above all, the abolition of sexual and political repression (a possibility Freud never strongly affirmed) and, going beyond the suggestions of Wilhelm Reich, they advocated the restoration of pregenital sexuality, the return to the infantile emotional and all-loving mentality. And play becomes the psychotherapy of child and adult alike! In the nineteenth century, only the genius could play, but twentieth-century Surrealists like Breton have discovered the possibility (known already to Dadaists like Arp) that everyone can play. He finds the point of contact between Marx and Freud to be their agreement that "the human physical senses must be emancipated from the sense of possession, and then the humanity of the senses and the human enjoyment of the senses will be achieved for the first time."

Herbert Marcuse approaches Freud from a more securely Marxian, or Hegelian, angle than Brown. Following Fourier's socialism, he specifically sets the goal for a utopian society to be the transforming of labor into pleasure, and like Brown, he feels that the enemy of gratification, "time" (which Brown connects to guilt and repression), can be overcome by play. Following the old aesthetics of play propounded by Schiller, Marcuse asserts that play can liberate man. In ascribing to Freud the optimistic ideal of changing men, rather than simply curing his neuroses, Marcuse returns to views once popularized by lectures at the Bauhaus in 1930 and 1931 by Dr. Karlfried Count von Dürckheim, the Gestalt psychologist: "Phenomenon eroticism—love: it is more than momentary satisfaction. Freud did not fully recognize this higher aim of Eros. Freud was too much a rationalist; but in his later years he changed, wanting not only to free people from complexes but to mold them."[28] One senses that it is but a step from Marcuse's emphasis on the joys of living and the pleasure of labor to nineteenth-century romantic socialism as represented by William Morris's arts and crafts movement, which opposed to industrial art and inhuman machinery the simple joys of handicraft. Both Brown and Marcuse advance from Freud's idea that there has never been a nonrepressive civilization to the utopian vision of a society freed through psychoanalysis. But they forget that the political order need not be transformed, and may in fact remain as repressive as ever, even though the moral code becomes highly permissive; for as Rieff has well pointed out, "The combination of a repressive political order with a permissive moral order is not unheard of in human history."[29]

These recent efforts to fuse Freud and Marx in the political sphere were anticipated by the Surrealists, whose ideas also form perhaps the most interesting attempt of all to bring psychoanalysis into relation with poetry. While Marcuse understood that "the Surrealists recognized the revolutionary implications of Freud's discoveries ... in demanding that the dream be made into reality,"[30] Brown seems unaware of what he probably derived from them, although the Surrealists before him employed such basic ideas as the power of love to affect politics, the unity of opposites, and the liberating quality of infantile sexuality.[31] Some of the parallels between Brown and the Surrealists are brought out in criticisms of the Surrealists from the Marxist and psychoanalytic viewpoint: the Marxist Caudwell[32] called the Surrealists bourgeois for believing they can become free and realize themselves in opposition to society (not a wholly accurate representation of their position), whereas Marxists believe that the individual can become free only through society. From the psychoanalytic viewpoint, Emilio Servadio[33] criticized the Surrealists for showing a tendency to regress from adult genitality to a pregenital undifferentiated sexuality, thus opposing to the psychoanalytic effort to integrate the self their goal of disintegrating the self.

Notes

In works cited by author and date, refer to Bibliography.

Introduction

1. For a critical review of attempts to gain insight into Freud through his self-analytic writings, see Ernst Kris, in Freud, *Origins of Psychoanalysis*, p. 34, n.

2. *Modern German Literature, 1880–1938*, 2d ed. (London, 1946), pp. 338–39.

Chapter 1

1. See the writings of the Bernfelds, L. L. Whyte, and Henri Ellenberger.

2. Philip Rieff, 1959, p. 66.

3. Ernest Jones, *The Life and Work of Sigmund Freud*, 1:2.

4. Letter to Fliess, 19 September, 1901.

5. According to a remark in *The Interpretation of Dreams*, he read his first modern novel at the age of thirteen—probably the Reverend Charles Kingsley's *Hypatia*, 1853. See Alexander Grinstein, 1968.

6. Vol. 1, ch. 1.

7. Letter to J. Braun-Vogelstein, 30 October, 1927.

8. *Confessions d'un Auteur Dramatique*, p. 271.

9. Pseudonym of E. D. Dekker, well-known Dutch writer (1820–87).

10. A work on which he lectured to the B'nai Brith Society on 27 April 1900.

11. Called the "Shakespeare of the novella," a student of the great Ludwig Feuerbach.

12. E. Grosse, *Die Anfänge der Kunst* (Freiburg im Breisgau, 1894); Theodor Lipps, *Grundtatsachen des Seelenlebens* (Bonn, 1883); Burckhardt's *Vorträge* (1844–87, Basel, 1918).

13. Baudouin's books, except for his first, *Études de Psychanalyse* (Neuchâtel and Paris, 1922).

14. Jakob Burckhardt's *Die Cultur der Renaissance in Italien* (Leipzig, 1896), or his *Der Cicerone*, or Gustav Fechner, *Vorschule der Ästhetik* (Leipzig, 1876) in the 2d ed. of 1897.

15. Zweig's book *Die Heilung durch den Geist* (Leipzig, 1931).

16. Cf. the essay by Emil du Bois-Reymond, 1890.

17. S. C. Bernfeld, 1951.

18. According to Professor Otto Brendel of Columbia, an eminent authority on classical antiquity.

19. See Hanns Sachs, 1944, pp. 101–2.

20. Joseph Wortis, 1940, p. 84.

21. *Minutes of the Vienna Psychoanalytic Society,* 19 February 1908.

22. Max Eastman, 1942, p. 264.

23. Whose importance for Freud's views on art was already mentioned by Fritz Wittels, 1931, p. 43.

24. In Professor Brendel's opinion.

25. Hence not brought back from Paris by Freud in 1886, as Jones states, but probably in 1889.

26. And so probably late nineteenth century, according to Professor Brendel.

27. See Jones, *Sigmund Freud,* 1:67. For a later reference to Kaulbach, see Freud's *The Ego and the Id,* 1923.

28. Perhaps this, or the aforementioned engraving by Dürer, is the one presented to Freud as a gift by Emmanuel Loewy, as mentioned in Freud's letter to his son Martin, dated 16 August 1937.

29. Freud cited a passage from *Max und Moritz,* in a letter of 6 August 1878.

30. S. C. Bernfeld, 1951.

31. See ch. 8 of *The Psychopathology of Everyday Life.*

32. Arthur Koestler, 1949, p. 216.

33. The lectures Pierre Janet published in 1925 tell of finding in the German writer Friedländer a description of Vienna as having "a peculiar sexual atmosphere."

34. See Ellenberger, 1970.

35. See Leopold Rosenmayr, 1966.

36. "Politics and the Psyche in *fin-de-siècle* Vienna: Schnitzler and Hoffmannsthal," *American Historical Review,* July 1961, pp. 930–46.

37. Joseph S. Bloch, 1923.

38. Carl E. Schorske, 1961, p. 934.

39. And also non-Jewish ones, like those in *Simplicissimus,* the Munich comic paper, which he "regularly enjoys," he says in a letter to Fliess, 11 September 1899.

40. Theodor Reik, 1954, pp. 13, 16.

41. Ibid.

42. *Studien zur Kritik der Moderne.*

43. Bahr, 1894.

44. Jones, *Sigmund Freud,* 1:183–84.

45. *Der Fall Böcklin, und die Lehre von den Einheiten* (Stuttgart, 1905).

46. Eastman, 1942, p. 264, describing Berggasse 19, which he visited in 1926, remarked: "I was not surprised to see hanging beside Rembrandt's *Anatomy Lesson,* without which no doctor's office would be recognizable, a picture of *The Nightmare*—a horrid monster with a semievil laugh or leer, squatting upon a sleeping maiden's breast."

47. A detailed study of the nightmare as a subject of folktales, art, and literature was made by Freud's follower Ernest Jones, who had doubtless seen the engraving

hanging in Berggasse 19; H. W. Janson wrote an article on the painting, and Nicholas Powell is completing a book on it.

48. See n. 46, above.

49. "La Foi qui guérit," *Revue Hebdomadaire*, December 1892, pp. 112–32.

50. It is not clear whether this copy of the Louvre statue—visible in the illustration facing p. 29 in Martin Freud, 1958—is one of the "plaster casts of the Florentine [*sic*] statues" adorning his room in Vienna, according to a letter to Fliess, 6 December 1896.

51. See Ary Renan, *Gustave Moreau* (Paris, 1900).

52. Doolittle, 1956, p. 91.

53. Jones, *Sigmund Freud*, 1:ix.

54. Burckhardt, 1893, p. 2.

55. Letter of 1885 cited in Jones, *Sigmund Freud*, 1:182.

56. Jones, *Sigmund Freud*, 3:158.

57. *On Judging Works of Visual Art* (Berkeley and Los Angeles, 1949, 1st ed. 1876).

58. *The Problem of Form in Painting and Sculpture* (New York, 1907, 1st ed. 1893).

59. Cf. André Chastel, "L'Interpretation ésotérique de l'art de la Renaissance à la fin du siècle dernier," *Umanesimo e Esoterismo. Archivio di Filosofia* (Rome, 1960), pp. 439–48.

60. Praz, 1951, p. 206.

61. "Réponse à une Enquête," in Jacques Hurel, *Enquête* (Paris, 1891).

62. Cited in Rewald, *Post-Impressionism* (New York, 1962), p. 452.

63. See Michel Decaudin, 1960, p. 59.

64. H. Henel, *The Poetry of C. F. Meyer* (Madison, Wis., 1954).

Chapter 2

1. Jones, *Sigmund Freud*, 1:110 ff.

2. See Siegfried Bernfeld, "An Unknown Autobiographical Fragment by Freud," *American Imago*, August 1946, pp. 3–19.

3. *S.E. (Standard Edition)*, 4:xxi–xxii.

4. In "The Subtleties of a Faulty Action," *S.E.* 22:234.

5. Grinstein, 1968, p. 46.

6. For Freud's later comments on chemical explanations, see the last page of the *Leonardo*.

7. Freud's perception that geometric and mathematical events may have sexual implications is fully in step with those humorists who burlesqued sexual apparatuses with quasi-scientific descriptions and nomenclatures: in the late nineteenth century, Villiers de l'Isle-Adam's *Ève future*, Alfred Jarry's "pataphysical" inventions, and Raymond Roussel's inventions in *Impressions d'Afrique*; and, in the early twentieth century, Duchamp's brides and Picabia's love machine.

8. See the discussion of Michelangelo's *Moses*, pp. 64–68.

9. His library contains books on Leonardo by Franz M. Feldhaus (Jena, 1922), Wilhelm von Bode (Berlin, 1921), and Kurt Zoege von Manteuffel (Munich, 1920).

10. In a letter to M. Schiller, 26 March 1931.

11. "The Historical Interpretation of Literature," in D. A. Stauffer, ed., *The Intent of the Critic* (Princeton, 1941).

12. *Leonardo da Vinci. Psychoanalytic Notes on the Enigma* (London, 1962). Incredibly, Eva M. Rosenfeld's eulogizing review, in the *International Journal of Psychoanalysis* 44 (1963): 380–82, of Eissler's book never mentions the article that the book debates.

13. Nunberg and Federn, vol. 2, p. 341.

14. Merezhkovsky, 1903, p. v.

15. George Boas, 1950, casts considerable doubt on the possibility of Leonardo's having known this source.

16. Mâle, 1947, pp. 367–68; a psychoanalytic interpretation of the devil as mother would surely be farfetched.

17. Letter to Fliess, 3 October 1897.

18. Jones, *Sigmund Freud*, 1:316–17.

19. See also Vincent Brome's more detailed description in *Freud and His Early Circle*.

20. Jones, 1959, p. 222.

21. *Reich Speaks of Freud*, M. Higgins and C. M. Raphael, eds. (New York, 1967); Paul Roazen, 1969.

22. *S.E.*, 5:400.

23. Cf. the end of ch. 1 for further discussion of burial alive in relation to Freud's collection.

24. Freud to Weiss, 12 April 1933.

25. Jones, *Sigmund Freud*, 3:368.

26. Hermann Keyserling, 1950.

27. Ellenberger, 1970, p. 816.

28. See the chapter entitled "If Moses was an Egyptian."

29. Klein, 1968, p. 74.

30. See his essay "On the Beautiful and on Aesthetics," *Selected Essays* (London, 1909), p. 313.

31. Freud discussed this hypocritical reversal of hostile feelings toward the father in 1910. See *S.E.*, 5:398 n.

32. See his letter to Martha, 15 November 1883, ridiculing John Stuart Mill's writings on this subject.

33. Jones, *Sigmund Freud*, 1:102.

34. Slochower cites the "coca episode" discussed in Erich Fromm, *The Forgotten Language*, p. 92.

35. As noted by Jones in *Sigmund Freud*, vol. 1.

36. *The Interpretation of Dreams. S.E.*, 4:265.

Chapter 3

1. A position developed by Otto Rank. See also William Phillips, "Introduction: Art and Neurosis," in Phillips, ed., 1957, for a critic's defense of neurotic distortion in some modern literature.

2. S. E. Hyman, 1962, p. 351.

3. This is the sense of his argument with Havelock Ellis over the possibility that Leonardo's "fantasy" was actually a memory of a real event, in a note added to the book in 1919. This problem resembles those that preoccupied Freud's forerunners in the study of dream symbolism, and in fact a great number of romantic writers were convinced that the products of their imagination were not merely subjective fantasies, as noted by C. M. Bowra (1950). I. A. Richards (1934) felt that the problem of the truth-value of the imagination raised by the romantic viewpoint is "the most comprehensive problem of philosophy."

4. In L. C. Knights, 1951, pp. 1–40.

5. On this changed view of the Greeks, see especially the various works of Pierre M. Schuhl, and also Dodds, *The Greeks and the Irrational* (Berkeley, 1951). In her challenging essay *From Sophocles to Sartre* (New York, 1969), Käte Hamburger, aware of Freud's theories, attempted to explain the modern preference for the Elektra over the Oedipus legend. She notes that the Elektra legend and the Greek tragedians' interpretations of it "contain neither the factor of unknowingness nor the committing of incest," and concludes that the modern writer would be more attracted to the "latent possibility rather than the fact," as offering "more scope for literary creativity." For the Surrealists' fascination with Elektra, see Nicolas Calas, "L'Amour de la révolution à nos jours," *Minotaure*, vol. 2, 1938. Excerpts from a number of texts dealing with the theme of Oedipus can be found in M. Kallich, A. MacLeish, and G. Schoenbohm, eds., *Oedipus: Myth and Drama* (New York, 1968).

6. See Jones, 1910, p. 74.

7. A. W. Levi, 1963, p. 328, n. 3.

8. Cf. ch. 1, n. 18, and also E. Rosenfeld, 1956, and Ricoeur, 1970.

9. Jones, *Sigmund Freud*, 1:56.

10. Mill, "Plato's Doctrine of Reminiscence Epitomized in Meno," in *Dissertations and Discussions* (New York and London, 1874), vol. 4, pp. 302, 314.

11. Freud, 1905a, *S.E.*, 8: 21–22.

12. Loewy first touched on this area in 1891, but his major work, *The Rendering of Nature in Early Greek Art*, appeared the same year as Freud's *Interpretation of Dreams*, 1900. In order to explain the small number of typical shapes and their stylized, schematic quality, which he found in archaic Greek art as well as in primitive and child art, Loewy maintained that art evolves both for whole cultures and for individuals from abstract generalized forms to natural ones, and "in the direction from the psychological to the physiological, the retinal image, the objectively perceived segment of nature with all its accidents and irrelevancies." His explanation of the stylizing of archaic art "is based on the more and more fully recognized

role which memory plays in the creation and acceptance of art. [Cf. Fechner, *Vorschule der Ästhetik*, vol. 1, 86ff.] As the result of the visual impressions which we have received from numerous examples of the same object, there remains fixed in our minds a memory-picture, which is no other than the Platonic Idea of the object, viz., a typical picture, clear of everything individual or accidental. The graphic expression of this would be a schema of lines and planes approaching as nearly as possible simple geometrical forms: this is stylisation." This schematization can produce curiously unrealistic images: "In the mental image there can coexist elements where in reality the one would be excluded by the other; e.g., two eyes in the profile view of the face." Not only would Freud have been receptive to his friend's use of the Platonic theory of reminiscence, but to his linking of early stages of artistic realization to processes that parallel those of the dream-work and of regression in their removal from realistic perception to a more "primitive" condition of mental work. The interesting idea that the memory may contribute creatively to art, allied perhaps to older academic notions, wherein exercises of memory played the major role in learning drawing (for example, in the French artist Boisbaudran's methods), was deeply ingrained in Freud's approach to art, but never made explicit.

13. *S.E.*, 5:528, n. 1.

14. *A General Introduction to Psychoanalysis*, 1917a, Lecture 11.

15. J. J. David, *A Poet?*, Zola, *L'Oeuvre*, etc. Alexander Grinstein, 1968, has tracked down many of them.

16. Following Freud, Jones (1955, p. 149) formulated the idea of a process the inverse of condensation, "de-composition," whereby the writer invents various attributes of different characters by deriving them from the attributes of one original character.

17. Gustav Bychowski, 1951, p. 391.

18. He would surely never have gone so far as Daniel Schneider, 1950, who, misconstruing ideas expressed in Freud's book on jokes, declared: "The dream-work of the unconscious is the consummate art to which conscious art work aspires."

19. *S.E.*, 5:345.

20. *S.E.*, 5:685.

21. Cf. Rorschach, 1912, p. 675.

22. Quoted in Wyss, 1966, p. 394.

23. *The Meaning of Meaning* (New York and London, 1927), pp. 199–200.

24. "What the Freudian has done is to propose a theory as to why the individual finds it difficult to formulate the signification of certain of his signs and indeed why he actively resists such a formulation by himself or others. This theory, insofar as it is sound, is a contribution to the understanding of pathic signs; there is nothing in it which in principle cannot be translated into the terminology of behavioral semiotic." (1946), p. 276.

25. Jones, *Sigmund Freud*, 3:411.

26. *Sex in Psychoanalysis*, p. 277.

27. In a footnote to his *Three Essays* of 1905, added in 1915.

28. The aesthetician Max Dessoir challenged Freud's reduction of aesthetics to

sex in the *Zeitschrift für Aesthetik und allgemeine Kunstwissenschaft* (Stuttgart, 1914), vol. 10, no. 2.

29. Cf. the famous biologist Wilhelm Bölsche's assertion that "Poetry is produced by the genitals," or Przybyszewski's remark in the 1890's that "Art is nothing but a game that sex plays with the brain."

30. Alfred Espinas, *Des Sociétés animales* (Paris, 1877); Heinrich Steinthal, *Einleitung in die Psychologie* (Berlin, 1881); P. J. Moebius, *Über Schopenhauer* (Leipzig, 1899); George Santayana, *The Sense of Beauty* (New York and London, 1896); Gustav Naumann, *Geschlecht und Kunst* (Leipzig, 1899); Yrjö Hirn, *Origins of Art* (London, 1900); and Rémy de Gourmont, "La Dissociation des idées" (Paris, 1900). Even earlier, romantics like Tieck in *William Lovell* (1796) could state, "Poetry, art and even devotion are only disguised hidden lust," while Novalis in *Schriften*, vol. 3, p. 171, summed up the position elegantly: "The brain resembles the testes."

31. Paul Souriau, in *La Beauté rationnelle*, p. 212, affirmed that "not only is the sexual instinct rich in aesthetic emotions, but it is in fact the creator of beauty." Later, Charles Lalo in *La Beauté et l'instinct sexuel* treated the relation of beauty to sexuality.

32. "The Theory of Symbolism," in *Papers on Psychoanalysis*, p. 137.

33. This romantically derived position, common in late-nineteenth-century Europe, has continued to preoccupy some contemporary critics (a whole debate raged in the pages of *Partisan Review* on the "Art and Anxiety" theme, during the 1950's), although studies, some dating back to the 1930's, have exploded the idea that the artist is temperamentally unlike other men.

34. 1913b, *S.E.*, 13.

35. Norman N. Holland in *The Dynamics of Literary Response*, p. 85, believing himself correctly Freudian, cites a paper of 1888 and then goes completely off the track with the remark that "the most exact analogy to the literary situation is hypnosis," a position Freud would never have accepted, certainly not in his mature writings.

36. For Freud's technical objections to hypnosis, see "Freud's Psycho-Analytic Procedure," 1904, *S.E.*, 7:252.

37. Freud, 1954, p. 373.

38. One is reminded of Freud's description of Leonardo, son of an accountant, who kept detailed financial accounts in a diary, a point whose significance was overlooked by Freud in his efforts to minimize the father as a model. Cf. Schapiro, 1956.

39. Hesse, 1951, pp. 575–78. For a highly speculative attempt to interpret Leonardo's literary and artistic productions in terms of sublimation, see Raymond S. Stites, *The Sublimations of Leonardo da Vinci* (Washington, D.C., 1970). Stites concludes that Leonardo's ability to sublimate ensured his normality and mental health.

40. *Insight and Outlook*, pp. 214–15.

41. See Freud, 1905b, *S.E.*, 7 : 156.

42. Freud, 1925, *S.E.*, 20 : 65.

43. Freud, 1905a, *S.E.*, 8.

44. Jones, *Sigmund Freud*, 3:411

45. Jones, *Sigmund Freud*, 3:412.

46. In a letter to Stefan Zweig, 7 February 1931.

47. Jones, *Sigmund Freud*, 3:414.

48. In Kris, 1952, p. 175. Phyllis Greenacre, in *Swift and Carroll: A Psychoanalytic Study of Two Lives* (New York, 1955), pp. 269–70, cites with approval Kris's theory that "caricature is a combination of regression and aggression" within a situation providing "a considerable degree of security and mastery, i.e., of control as a background. Otherwise the drop to regression does not entail pleasure."

49. Kris, 1952, p. 194.

50. "Duquesnoy's 'Nano di Crequi,' " in *The Art Bulletin*, June 1970, p. 144, n. 75.

51. Morris Philipson, 1963, p. 164.

52. *The Ego and the Mechanisms of Defense*, p. 193.

53. The English psychoanalyst Hanna Segal, 1952, maintains that "our wish is to find in art evidence of the triumph of life over death; we recognize the power of death when we say a thing is ugly."

54. Jones, *Sigmund Freud*, 1:3.

55. *Freud: The Mind of the Moralist*, p. 80, n.

56. One thinks here of Wundt's notion that play, especially in animals, can occur only when there are renewed memories to which are associated pleasurable feelings. See his *Vorlesungen über der Menschen-und-Thierseele* (3d ed., Hamburg and Leipzig, 1897).

57. Eastman, 1936, p. 23.

58. It is no wonder that the psychologist Karl Bühler, in his volume *Die Krise der Psychologie* (Jena, 1927), ignored Freud's still-born hint about aimless pleasure in technique, and developed a theory of "pleasure in functioning" specifically opposed to the simplistic theory he attributed to Freud of art as catharsis and tension release.

59. Bosanquet, 1957, p. 183.

60. Rank and Sachs, 1916, p. 27–28.

61. See Wolfgang Köhler, *Gestalt Psychology* (New York, 1947).

62. *System der Ästhetik*, vol. 1, p. 145ff.; in Freud's library.

63. See Jack Spector, 1969.

64. There is a curious justice in the fact that the Surrealist leader Breton found the true predecessor of Pfister's analysis in Alfred Jarry's whimsical commentaries on paintings: Jarry had read into older art, images obviously not intended by the artist, but which Jarry found by tracing continuous contours along the edges of adjacent but distinct forms. Breton felt that Jarry penetrated directly into the latent content of the works ("Alfred Jarry, initiateur et éclaireur," October 1951, published in *La Clé des champs* [Paris, 1953], pp. 254–63): "Nothing shows this better than [Jarry's] commentary to the *Martyrdom of Saint Catherine*, from which we reproduce the most significant passage by masking out the rest. The attitude of Jarry,

investigating Dürer's engraving in this way, prefigures that of an Oscar [*sic*] Pfister discovering in Leonardo's *St. Anne* in the Louvre, the contours of the obsessive vulture from which Freud extricated the psychoanalytic sense. It initiated the paranoiac-critical method established in its main lines by Max Ernst and systematized by Dali. Jarry, doubtless the first, proceeds from the conviction that 'indefinite dissection always exhumes from works something new' (*Les Minutes de sable mémorial*; avant propos)."

65. See Karl Pearson, 1930.

66. We might observe a curious prefiguring of Galton's method in the great eighteenth-century English artist Joshua Reynolds's notion that each species has its own "central form, which is the abstract of the various individual forms belonging to that class." See his *Discourse* No. 3. Galton's method seems to have been applied by Rank (1909, probably following Freud) to the problem of creating an archetype of the mythic birth. The method was widely publicized among German scientists by du Bois-Reymond, 1890.

67. The work of contemporary anthropologists such as Desmond Morris (*The Naked Ape*, London, 1967), who does not refer to Freud in this context, seems to point to similar attitudes among the ancestors of Freud's modern hysteric: "the protuberant breasts of the female must . . . be copies of the fleshy buttocks, and the sharply defined red lips around the mouth must be copies of the labia."

68. Erwin Panofsky, 1939, p. 178, n. 18, suggested that the sculptor's characteristic "movement without locomotion" might be connected psychoanalytically to his self-isolation and to his inactivating of an impulse to approach others lovingly.

69. An interpretation strongly asserted by Panofsky, 1939, an essay omitted from Janson's discussion.

70. For brief discussions of the stylistic factors determining the posture of this corner figure, see Panofsky, 1939, p. 188, n. 56, and Hartt, 1968.

71. In his great *Treatise on Physiological Optics* (Leipzig, 1856–66), Helmholtz, like Freud, insisted on the interdependent role of memory and visual perception, cautiously concluding from his researches that "at all events it must be conceded that, even in what appears to the adult as being direct apperception of the senses, possibly a number of single factors may be involved which are really the product of experience; although at the time it is difficult to draw the line between them."

72. From Anthony A. Cooper, third earl of Shaftesbury, *An Essay on Painting* (London, 1713), ch. 1, p. 10.

73. Cited and illustrated by Freud in *The Interpretation of Dreams*, from Rank, in the 4th–7th eds.

74. This view of artistic illusion originated at least as far back as Coleridge, and has more recently been affirmed in Vaihinger's "Philosophy of As-If."

75. Rank, 1924, p. 160.

76. *The Archetypal World of Henry Moore* (New York and London, 1959), p. 101.

77. Norman O. Brown, 1955, p. 50.

78. Draft K, 1 January 1896, in *Origins of Psychoanalysis*, pp. 146–55.

79. See, for example, Harry B. Lee, "Poetry Production as a Supplemental

Emergency Defense Against Anxiety," *Psychoanalytic Quarterly*, vol. 7, pp. 232–42; and Margaret S. Mahler, John R. Ross, Jr., and Zira De Fries, "Clinical Studies in Benign and Malignant Cases of Childhood Psychosis (Schizophrenia-like)," *American Journal of Orthopsychiatry*, vol. 19, pp. 295–304.

80. *The Id and the Regulatory Principles of Mental Functioning* (London, 1967), p. 8.

81. Freud, 1905a, *S.E.*, 8 : 124, 135.

82. Despite important differences in detail, one might compare this approach to the harmony of impulses or *synaesthesia* propounded by Charles Ogden, I. A. Richards, and James Wood, 1925.

83. In a succinct statement of Stokes, 1965, we find a recent attempt to approach art in the terms close to those of unity in variety: "The felicity of art lies in its sustaining power, in a markedly dual content, in multiple forms of expression within one boundary that harmonize." At various points in his book, Kris, 1952, discusses this question of the ego and unification in art, as Helene Deutsch already had done (1927).

84. The psychoanalytically oriented critic Norman N. Holland, 1968, feels that he can actually set up criteria for literature based on psychoanalysis. He has essentially two criteria; first of all, a "central or nuclear fantasy known from clinical evidence, in which all the separate elements of the text play a role." A psychoanalytic reading will reveal this central phantasy, but throughout his book Holland shows how his judgment is guided by a second criterion, his "gut response," which is as legitimate a tool of the informed critic now as among his nineteenth-century forerunners. Assigning a privileged status to the "central fantasy" is of a different order. It sneaks back, under the guise of clinical realism, an almost metaphysical entity serving as an explanation, and is all the more objectionable when it is extended to all literature; for some works may not have one nuclear fantasy, and others may not easily be analyzed at all in terms of such sharply defined clinical entities without procrustean abuses of the text.

Chapter 4

1. Ray Ellenwood, a former student of mine, is completing a doctoral dissertation on the nature and extent of Freud's influence on Breton.

2. See Richter's retrospective *Dada : Art and Anti-Art* (New York, 1965; London, 1966), p. 112.

3. In *Littérature*, March 1922, p. 19.

4. Cf. Max Jacob, *Cornet à dés* (Paris, 1917); the unanimists such as Pierre-Jean Jouve, in his *Les Directions de la littérature moderne* (Paris, 1912), and the writings of Jules Romains, calling for *poésie immédiate* and of Georges Duhamel for "l'expression nue."

5. Cf. his approval of Lipps in *Point du Jour* (Paris, 1934), pp. 242–43.

6. Later, with militant internationalism, Breton wrote, "We Surrealists do not

love our country." See his "Speech to the Congress of Writers" of 1935, in *Manifestos*, pp. 234–41.

7. In Lenormand's *Les Confessions d'un auteur dramatique*, p. 314ff.

8. Letter of Breton to Tzara, 12 June 1919, in Michel Sanouillet, 1965, p. 446.

9. *André Breton, Arbiter of Surrealism*, pp. 16–17.

10. Sanouillet, 1965, pp. 126–27.

11. It should be noted that while Freud surely had an important impact on Surrealism, evidently the common opinion that the Surrealists used Freud's free-association techniques (for example, in Kris, *Psychoanalytic Explorations in Art*, p. 30) or that the "Surrealist automatic writing ... is a transcription of the verbal content of a particular form of thought ... brought to light by Freud and his school" (Jean Cazaux, *Surréalisme et psychologie*, p. 11; Breton might have agreed with Cazaux's remarks), demands thorough reexamination. As Ellenberger (*The Discovery of the Unconscious*, p. 837) puts it, whatever Breton's debts to dynamic psychology, his "dictation from the unconscious [was not] identical with Freud's method of free association."

12. Sanouillet, 1965, p. 123, corroborates his opinion that French sources dominated early Surrealism by citing Philippe Soupault's account of his collaboration in 1919 with Breton on what has often been called "the first Surrealist work," *Les Champs magnétiques*, of which Soupault writes: "We agreed to adopt what the psychiatrist Janet called 'automatic writing.' "

13. Breton mockingly placed at the head of the *Second Manifesto* an excerpt from a report of a meeting of the *Société Médico-Psychologique* published in the *Journal de l'Aliénation Mentale*, in which Professor Janet, among others, comments critically on the artistic methods of the Surrealists.

14. Mr. Ray Ellenwood has observed to me that Janet's overconfident and narrowly exact scientific manner must have actually repelled Breton.

15. *The Poetics of Space* (New York, 1964; 1st ed., 1958), p. xxxvii.

16. Breton sent Freud a copy with his dedication, but I did not come across it in Freud's library in London. The annotations, if any, by Freud would be of the greatest interest.

17. See Breton's definition of Surrealism, p. 150.

18. Cf. Jean Starobinski, "Freud, Breton et Myers," in Marc Eigeldinger, ed., *André Breton* (Neuchâtel, 1970). Starobinski tends to exaggerate the importance of Myers to Breton at Freud's expense, and overlooks the significant parallels between the two personalities; for example, Freud and Breton shared an experimental openness toward all new experience, including the occult, without either one's thereby becoming a mystic. A similar misinterpretation of Breton, coupled with an overestimate of Janet's importance for Breton, can be found in Anna Balakian, *André Breton, Magus of Surrealism* (New York, 1971). A review of the book is being prepared by Professor J. H. Matthews. In his forthcoming dissertation at Rutgers University, Ray Ellenwood discusses these questions at length.

19. Cf. Picasso's cover for the first issue of the magazine *Minotaure*, 1933, and his

famous etching *Minotauromachy*, 1935; and a number of works on the theme by Masson and other Surrealists.

20. Cf. Lawrence Alloway, "De Chirico, Tanguy and Freud," *Art News and Review*, 28 April 1956.

21. Breton's prefatory quotation apparently inspired Dali's later dedication of the *Diary of a Genius (1952–63)* (Paris, 1964) to "Gala-Gradiva, etc."

22. "Gradiva," reprinted in *La Clé des champs* (Paris, 1953), pp. 25–28.

23. *Ibid.*, p. 25; characteristically, Breton takes a contrary stand to Freud's in reversing the psychoanalyst's harsh judgment of the quality of Jensen's work.

24. Dali, 1942, p. 240.

25. Dali might have mistakenly transcribed "Bertrand" through hearing Breton's pronunciation of Bertgang: the hard "g" in French sounding perhaps to one who spoke such bad French as Dali like the trilled "r," and the nasalized "ng" sounding exactly like "nd"; hence, assuming that Breton did introduce Dali to the name Gradiva, and that Dali did not at first read the book—or with little understanding— then Dali might very easily have assimilated "Bertrand," a familiar French family name, to the actual "Bertgang."

26. I disagree with Whitney Chadwick ("Masson's *Gradiva*: The Metamorphosis of a Surrealist Myth," in *Art Bulletin*, December 1970, pp. 415–22), who accepts the rather questionable testimony of the fantastic Dali, who dates to 1930 his earliest drawings of the subject. Chadwick makes no allusion to the French edition of the book, which unquestionably was the source for the Surrealist's interest in Gradiva, and not the German edition of 1907 cited by Chadwick, which few— certainly neither Breton nor Dali—could have understood. Ignoring the French edition of 1931 also caused him to make the anachronism on p. 416, n. 18, of claiming that Breton's *Second Manifesto* (1930) derived in part from Freud's essay.

27. Reproduced in William Rubin, *Dada, Surrealism and their Heritage* (New York, 1968; London, 1969), p. 73; Chadwick ("Masson's *Gradiva*: The Metamorphosis of a Surrealist Myth") compares Masson's *Gradiva* to his *Pygmalion* of 1938, but the paintings seem to have little in common.

28. Cazaux, 1938, p. 55.

29. Boas, 1950, p. 41ff.

30. For example, Daniel E. Schneider, "Picasso's Innovations," in *The Psychoanalyst and the Artist* (New York, 1962; 1st ed., 1950).

31. In my opinion, Pfister reveals the shortcomings of his viewpoint most clearly in his choice of an artist to analyze, namely, a twenty-three-year-old French Expressionist named "José," whose mediocre talent—visible in the illustrations— hardly merits his choice to represent the work of so many powerful and accessible artists.

32. Wittels, 1931, pp. 401, 403–4.

33. In *Explorations in Psychoanalysis*, Robert Lindner, ed. (New York, 1953).

34. For a proposed collation between the Institutes of Warburg and Jung as an aid to tracing the history of symbols, see Eugenio Battisti, *Rinascimento e Barocco* (Turin, 1960).

35. Rennselaer W. Lee, "Erwin Panofsky," *Art Journal*, Summer 1968, p. 370. Lee adds that most twentieth-century art did not attract Panofsky since it was cut off from tradition and "lacked complexity and richness. . . . It had, as he once humorously said, no iconography."

36. Panofsky distinguishes the following "strata" (as he calls them) in the work of art: "formal perception"; the "factual meaning" (together with the "expressional" meaning); the secondary or conventional subject matter; and the "intrinsic meaning or content," which must be apprehended through the "underlying principles which reveal the basic attitude of a nation, a period, a class, a religious or philosophical persuasion—unconsciously qualified by one personality and condensed into one work." Freud's contemporary, whose work he knew, Salomon Reinach, wrote on the "iconological method" in "De l'Influence des images sur la formation des mythes" (published in Reinach, 1912). The founders of the modern science of interpretation, or "hermeneutics," applied alike to literature and art, were Friedrich Schleiermacher and Friedrich Schlegel (cf. Paul Ricoeur, *De l'Interpretation*, and Richard E. Palmer, *Hermeneutics* . . . [Northwestern University Press, 1969]).

37. Kris, 1952, p. 198.

38. Contrary to Michel David, 1967, p. 187, relying on Eissler's misunderstandings, Schapiro's "Leonardo and Freud" is not "a severe criticism from a sociocultural point of view with a decided rejection of the instrument of psychoanalysis." Schapiro is, however, not a devout Freudian, and was inspired both by Rank and by the important work of his friend, the independently minded psychoanalyst Paul Schilder, whose ideas in some respects agreed with Kris's (1952). Through Schapiro's brilliant discussions of van Gogh and Cézanne, Schilder's ideas, best represented in his book *Image and Appearance of the Human Body* (London, 1935), have indirectly stimulated a number of studies by Schapiro's colleagues and students at Columbia University.

39. See Schapiro, *The Parma Ildefonsus. A Romanesque Illuminated Manuscript from Cluny* (College Art Association, 1964), p. 11, n. 27, for a psychoanalytic interpretation of a romanesque artist's sexual projection implied by his placement of an *open* door beneath the Virgin. This was exceptional on the artist's part; for in medieval commentary, the universal attribute of the Virgin is the *porta clausa*, symbolizing her virginity. But in his important review of Schapiro's book, Walter Cahn, in *The Art Bulletin*, March 1967, p. 75, points out that "the psychoanalytic hypothesis offered as a tentative explanation is not very convincing. The scene is perhaps best explained as an illustration of Ildefonsus's Vision of the Virgin . . . (in which, as its medieval author notes) . . . as Ildefonsus was nearing the church to celebrate Mass, the portal suddenly opened . . . and he beheld the Virgin seated in the place of the bishop on an ivory throne."

40. *The Invitation in Art*, p. 42.

41. *Smooth and Rough* (London, 1951). While Stokes may here contribute little to art history, he may prove to be the ideal psychologist of Pop art; for this trend seemed at one moment to have fulfilled his hope that art would return to the warm enveloping environment of the breast, and he describes the "flood of happiness I

felt when it was represented that Pop art showed affecting warm contact with the urban environment" (*The Invitation in Art*).

42. David Shakow and David Rapaport, 1964.

43. *L'Art poétique*, p. 17.

44. *The Writer in Extremis*, pp. 67–75.

45. Eisenstein, 1942, p. 11 and passim.

46. Frye, 1957, p. 123.

47. *Fantasia of the Unconscious*, p. 239ff.

48. In the first paragraph of his *Art of Poetry*, Horace observed that such mixed figures in painting and poetry would be absurdly comic, and compared them to "the dreams of a sick man." On the psychotic fusion of image and word, see Kris, 1952, p. 100 and passim.

49. *The Poetics of Space* (New York, 1964; 1st ed., 1958), p. 227.

50. *Entretiens, 1913–52*, p. 162.

51. See Aaron Scharf, *Art and Photography* (London, 1968), p. 210–11, showing an illustration from *Le Rire* of 1901.

52. Cf. Robert Rosenblum, *Cubism and Twentieth Century Art* (New York, 1961; London, 1968), p. 242, and p. 176, illustration.

53. Nunberg and Federn, vol. 1, p. 66.

54. For the passionate fiddling of a cello that swells from one scene to the next, see Rops's *Phantasy on a Violoncello*.

55. See Sarane Alexandrian, *Surrealist Art* (New York, 1970), illustration 42.

56. The work is in the tradition of Breton's *Nadja*: her drawing "L'Âme du blé" puns on "the soul of wheat" and "double blade" or "lame doublée," as well as "l'âme doublée" ("the doubled, or understudied, soul").

57. Cf. Shattuck, 1958.

58. Probably a pun on Montesquieu, whose *Lettres persanes* provided the first title to the painting; there is a vague mount or *mont* in the background.

59. In contrast, Breton, perhaps envious of Joyce's genius, found in his essay "On Surrealism in its Living Works" of 1953 that Joyce's interior monologue was too artistic and conscious, an imitation of life lacking the total spontaneity of the Surrealists, who get back to "true life."

60. Following Joseph Campbell and H. M. Robinson, *A Skeleton Key to Finnegans Wake* (New York, 1944), pp. 26–27.

61. Frye, 1957, pp. 276–77.

62. *Ibid.* 1957, p. 184.

63. *Ibid.* 1957, p. 131.

64. "Ghostlier Demarcations," in Murray Krieger, ed., *Northrop Frye in Modern Criticism* (New York, 1966), p. 126.

65. "Northrop Frye and Contemporary Criticism," in Krieger, ed., *Northrop Frye in Modern Criticism*.

66. With regard to overdetermination, one may note parenthetically that neo-Marxist theoreticians such as Louis Althusser (*Lire le Capital* [Paris, 1966]) make

this process axiomatic in their efforts to synthesize Marx and Freud: "overdetermin-ation *always* occurs. The retrograde movement of the true . . . For this see the *Psychopathology of Everyday Life*."

67. An exception is the writings of Jean-Paul Weber, for example his *The Psycho-logy of Art* (New York, 1969), which approaches art through "themes" derived from the artist's childhood. Weber makes free use of Freudian and non-Freudian psychoanalysis, but tries to go beyond them and to do justice to the work as a phenomenon valuable in itself, apart from its psychological origins.

68. Charles Rycroft, "Introduction: Causes and Meaning," in Rycroft, ed., *Psychoanalysis Observed* (New York and London, 1966), p. 14.

69. "Deriving Poetic Structures: Two Approaches to Baudelaire's *Les Chats*," *Yale French Studies*, October 1966.

70. Lévi-Strauss, 1963, p. 216.

71. "Structural Analysis in Art and Anthropology," *Yale French Studies*, October 1966.

72. Jack Burnham, in *The Structure of Art* (New York, 1971), has tried to apply certain structuralist ideas to art, using examples from the nineteenth century to the present (but also including Stonehenge). Burnham generalizes from clues he picks out of Duchamp's work to an optimistic vision perhaps closer to Breton's or Tzara's than to the sly old Dadaist's.

Appendix

1. For a list of such studies, see "Psychoanalytic Studies of Genius," *American Journal of Psychology*, vol. 27, pp. 363–416.

2. See N. E. Miller and J. Dollard, 1950.

3. *The Philosophy of Literary Form*, p. viii.

4. Cf. Jacques Jary, "La Psychologie de l'Inconscient," *Akademos*, 15 June 1909.

5. René Arcos, *La Tragédie des Espaces* (Paris, 1906).

6. *Catholicisme et Romanticisme* (Paris, 1905), p. 23.

7. Thibaudet's article was severely criticized in *Imago*, vol. 7, p. 355.

8. Impeccably iconoclastic, Breton loudly proclaimed his sympathy for Germany (though he never learned its language) and married a Jewish girl, Simonne Collinet. It is interesting that while singling out Freud for attention, the Surrealists remained indifferent to Rank, then in Paris; to Jung, with his symbolism; and to Wilhelm Reich, with his synthesis of Freud and Marx.

9. Several years later in the pages of the scientific journal *Isis*, edited by the great scholar George Sarton, appeared a review of Jean Laumonnier's hostile *Le Freudisme, Exposé et Critique*, which noted that whatever success psychoanalysis has had in France has largely been among "novelists and playwrights, who exploit a convenient new tendency without always knowing what lies at the bottom of it."

10. See Jouve's preface, "Inconscient, spiritualité et catastrophe," to *Sueur de Sang* (Paris, 1934).

11. In her novel *Les Belles Images* (Eng. ed., New York, 1968), the heroine's archaeologist (shades of *Gradiva!*) father, confronting Greek antiquity, makes "mental snapshots" to insert into a sort of memory album; whereas the heroine can disdainfully point out: "For my part I had neither album nor museum: I had come face to face with beauty."

12. See, for example, L. Baroncini, "Il fondamento e il meccanismo della psico-analisi," *Rivista Psicologica*, March 1908, pp. 211–13.

13. Freud, *S.E.*, 21:171–72.

14. David, 1966, pp. 6 ff.

15. *Ibid.*, p. 272.

16. *Leonardo, Omo senza Lettere* (Florence, 1952), p. 115, n.1.; she used the French edition of Freud's study published in 1927.

17. See Michel David, 1966, for an extended discussion, and also B. Freedman, "Italo Svevo, A Psychoanalytic Novelist," *Psychoanalytic Review*, 1931, pp. 434–38.

18. Pavese's complex personality has prompted ill-informed "psychoanalyses" of the writer, but a three-volume study of Pavese and his works being prepared by my colleague Umberto Mariani should provide us with a reliable insight into this important figure of modern letters.

19. A. Spaini, *Autoritratto triestino* (Milan, 1963), p. 215; cited in David, *op. cit.*, p. 376.

20. Cf. Michel David, 1967, p. 252.

21. Leon Trotsky, 1960, p. 42.

22. *Ibid.*, p. 230.

23. Francis Bartlett, *Sigmund Freud: A Marxian Essay*, p. 26.

24. Cf. Enrico Morselli, *La psicanalisi* (Turin, 1926), vol. 1, p. 19.

25. For the astonishing view that the Freud-influenced Surrealists helped prepare the way for Hitler, see Herbert Muller (doubtless a follower of Stalin), "Surrealism: A Dissenting Opinion," *New Directions in Prose and Poetry* (Norfolk, Conn., 1940), p. 553.

26. Use of the latter phrase was a political bow to Stalin, who nevertheless purged Bukharin in 1938 and who, maintaining Lenin's puritanism, eradicated the "new eroticism."

27. Frederick C. Crews, "Love in the Western World," *Partisan Review*, Spring 1967, pp. 272–87.

28. Cited in Hans M. Wingler, *The Bauhaus* (MIT Press, 1969), pp. 159–60.

29. Philip Rieff, 1959, p. 338.

30. Herbert Marcuse, 1955, pp. 148–49.

31. See Herbert Gershmann, *Bibliography of the Surrealist Revolution in France* (Ann Arbor, Mich., 1969), p. 180, n. 48, for the favorable reaction of Surrealists to Brown's book.

32. Caudwell, 1937, p. 137.

33. "Il Surrealismo: Storia, dottrina, valutazione psicoanalitica," *Psicanalisi* (1946), p. 77.

Bibliography

ABRAHAM, KARL. *Giovanni Segantini; Ein psychoanalytischer Versuch.* Leipzig, 1911.

ALEXANDER, FRANZ. "The Psychoanalyst Looks at Contemporary Art." In ROBERT LINDNER, ed., *Explorations in Psychoanalysis.* New York, 1953.

ALLERS, RUDOLF. *Existentialism and Psychiatry.* Springfield, Ill., 1961.

ALLOWAY, LAWRENCE. "De Chirico, Tanguy and Freud." *Art News and Review,* 28 April 1956.

ANDERSON, HAROLD H., and GLADYS L. ANDERSON. *An Introduction to Projective Techniques.* Englewood Cliffs, N.J., 1951.

ARAGON, LOUIS. *Les Collages.* Paris, 1965.

BACHELARD, GASTON. *La Psychanalyse du feu.* Paris, 1938.

BAHR, HERMANN. *Burgtheater.* Vienna, 1920.

—— "Die neue Psychologie." In *Die Überwindung des Naturalismus.* Dresden, 1891.

—— "Symbolisten." In *Studien zur Kritik der Moderne.* Frankfurt, 1894.

BARTLETT, FRANCIS. *Sigmund Freud: A Marxian Essay.* London, 1930.

BÉGUIN, ALBERT. *L'Âme romantique et le rêve.* Paris, 1939.

BELL, CLIVE. "Dr. Freud on Art." *The Dial,* April 1925, pp. 280–81.

BERGUER, GEORGES. *Quelques traits de la vie de Jésus.* Geneva, 1917.

BERNFELD, SIEGFRIED. "Freud's Scientific Beginnings." *American Imago* 6 (1949): 163–96.

BERNFELD, SUZANNE CASSIRER. "Freud and Archaeology." *American Imago* 8 (1951): 107–28.

BERTALANFFY, LUDWIG VON. "On the Definition of the Symbol." In J. R. ROYCE, ed., *Psychology and the Symbol: An Interdisciplinary Symposium.* New York, 1965.

BITHELL, JETHRO. *Modern German Literature, 1880–1950.* London, 1959.

BLOCH, JOSEPH S. *My Reminiscences.* Vienna, 1923.

BLONDEL, CHARLES. *La Psychanalyse.* Paris, 1924.

BOAS, GEORGE. *The Hieroglyphics of Horapollo.* New York, 1950.

BONAPARTE, MARIE. *Edgar Poe, étude psychanalytique,* Paris, 1933.

BOSANQUET, BERNARD. *A History of Aesthetic.* 2d ed. New York, 1957 (London, 1904).

BOWRA, C. M. *The Romantic Imagination.* London, 1950.

BRETON, ANDRÉ. *Entretiens, 1913–52.* Paris, 1952.

——— *Les Vases communicants,* Paris, 1932.

——— *Manifestoes of Surrealism,* Ann Arbor, Mich., 1969.

BRETON, ANDRÉ, et al. *Violette Nozières.* Brussels, 1933.

BROME, VINCENT. *Freud and His Early Circle.* New York, 1968.

BROWDER, CLIFFORD. *André Breton, Arbiter of Surrealism.* Geneva, 1967.

BROWN, NORMAN O. *Life Against Death.* New York, 1955; London, 1959.

BRÜCKE, ERNST. "Die Darstellung der Bewegung durch die bildenden Künste." *Deutsche Rundschau* 26 (1881): 43 ff.

——— *Schönheit und Fehler der Menschlichen Gestalt.* 3d ed. Vienna, 1905.

BRÜCKNER, PETER. "Sigmund Freuds Privatlektüre." *Psyche* 15 (1961–62): 881–902, and 16 (1962): 721–43, 881–95.

BULLOUGH, EDWARD. "Psychical Distance." *British Journal of Psychology* 5 (1912): 87–118.

BURCKHARDT, JAKOB. *Der Cicerone.* 6th ed. Leipzig, 1893.

BURKE, KENNETH. "Freud and the Analysis of Poetry." *American Journal of Sociology,* 1939.

——— *The Philosophy of Literary Form,* 2d ed. Baton Rouge, La., 1967.

BUSH, MARSHALL. "The Problem of Form in the Psychoanalytic Theory of Art." *The Psychoanalytic Review,* Spring, 1967.

BYCHOWSKI, GUSTAV. "From Catharsis to Work of Art: The Making of an Artist." In GEORGE B. WILBUR and WERNER MUENSTERBERGER, eds., *Psychoanalysis and Culture.* New York, 1951.

CASSIRER, ERNST. *An Essay on Man.* New Haven, Conn., and London, 1944.

CAUDWELL, CHRISTOPHER. *Illusion and Reality.* London, 1937.

——— *Studies in a Dying Culture.* London, 1938.

CAZAUX, JEAN. *Surréalisme et psychologie.* Paris, 1938.

CHARCOT, JEAN MARTIN. "La Foi qui guérit." *Revue Hebdomadaire,* December 1892, pp. 112–32.

CHARCOT, JEAN MARTIN, and PAUL RICHER. *Les Démoniaques dans l'art.* Paris, 1887.

——— *Les Difformes et les malades dans l'art.* Paris, 1889.

DALBIEZ, ROLAND. *Psychoanalytical Method and the Doctrine of Freud.* Vol. 2. London, 1947.

DALI, SALVADOR. *Diary of a Genius (1952–63).* New York, 1965; London, 1966.

DALI, SALVADOR. *Secret Life of Salvador Dali.* New York, 1942; London, 1948.

DAVID, MICHEL. *La Psicanalisi nella cultura italiana.* Turin, 1966.

—— *Letteratura e Psicanalisi.* Milan, 1967.

DECAUDIN, MICHEL. *La Crise des valeurs symbolistes.* Toulouse, 1960.

DEUTSCH, HELENE. "Über Zufriedenheit, Glück und Ekstase." *Internationale Zeitschrift für Psa.* 13 (1927).

DEVEREUX, GEORGE. "Why Oedipus Killed Laius. A Note on the Complementary Oedipus Complex in Greek Drama." *International Journal of Psychoanalysis*, no. 2 (1953), pp. 1–10.

DOOLITTLE, HILDA [H.D.]. *Tribute to Freud.* New York, 1956.

DU BOIS-REYMOND, EMIL. "Naturwissenschaft und bildende Kunst." *Deutsche Rundschau* 65 (1890): 195–215.

DUNBAR, H. FLANDERS. *Symbolism in Mediaeval Thought.* New Haven, Conn., 1929.

EASTMAN, MAX. *The Enjoyment of Laughter.* New York, 1936; London, 1937.

—— *Heroes I Have Known.* New York, 1942.

—— "Mr.-er-er-Oh! What's his Name?" *Everybody's Magazine*, July 1915, pp. 95–103.

EISENSTEIN, SERGE. *The Film Sense.* New York, 1942; London, 1943.

EISSLER, K. R. *Leonardo da Vinci: Psychoanalytic Notes on the Enigma.* London, 1962.

ELIADE, MIRCEA. *Mephistopheles and the Androgyne.* New York, 1965. Published in Great Britain as *The Two and the One*, London, 1965.

ELLENBERGER, HENRI F. *The Discovery of the Unconscious.* New York and London, 1970.

EMPSON, WILLIAM. *Seven Types of Ambiguity.* New York, 1931; London, 1930.

ERIKSON, ERIK H. "The Dream Specimen in Psychoanalysis." *Journal of the American Psychoanalytic Association*, no. 1 (1954), pp. 5–56.

EXNER, SIGMUND R. VON. *Physiologisches und Pathologisches in den bildenden Künsten.* Vienna, 1889.

FECHNER, GUSTAV THEODOR. *Vorschule der Ästhetik.* 2 vols. Leipzig, 1876.

FELDMAN, A. BRONSON. "Betwixt Art, Revolution and Religion: A Chronicle of the Psychoanalytic Movement." In Otto Rank, Hanns Sachs et al., *Psychoanalysis as an Art and a Science. A Symposium.* Detroit, 1968.

—— "Zola and the Riddle of Sadism." *American Imago*, 13 (1956): 415–25.

FERENCZI, SANDOR. *Sex in Psychoanalysis.* London, 1950.

—— "Stages in the Development of the Sense of Reality." In *Contributions to Psychoanalysis.* Boston and London, 1916.

FISCHER, KUNO. *Über den Witz.* 2d ed. Heidelberg, 1889.

FLETCHER, ANGUS. *Allegory: The Theory of the Symbolic Mode.* Ithaca, New York, 1964.

FRANKL, VIKTOR. *Der unbewusste Gott.* Vienna, 1949.

FREUD, ANNA. *The Ego and the Mechanisms of Defense* (1936). 1st English ed., 1937.

FREUD, ERNST L., ed. *Sigmund Freud: Briefe 1873–1939.* Frankfurt, 1960.

FREUD, MARTIN. *Sigmund Freud: Man and Father.* New York, 1958; London, 1957.

FREUD, SIGMUND

(1895) *Studies on Hysteria. S.E. (Standard Edition),* vol. 2.

(1896) "Further Remarks on the Neuro-Psychoses of Defence." *S.E.,* 3.

(1900) *The Interpretation of Dreams. S.E.,* 4–5.

(1901) *The Psychopathology of Everyday Life. S.E.,* 6.

(1904) "Freud's Psycho-Analytic Procedure." *S.E.,* 7.

(1905a) *Jokes and Their Relation to the Unconscious. S.E.,* 8.

(1905b) *Three Essays on the Theory of Sexuality. S.E.,* 7.

(1905c) "Psychopathic Characters on the Stage." *S.E.,* 7.

(1907a) *Delusions and Dreams in Jensen's "Gradiva." S.E.,* 9.

(1907b) "Contribution to a Questionnaire on Reading." *S.E.,* 9.

(1908a) "Hysterical Phantasies and their Relation to Bisexuality." *S.E.,* 9.

(1908b) "On the Sexual Theories of Children." *S.E.,* 9.

(1908c) "Creative Writers (Poets) and Daydreaming." *S.E.,* 9.

(1910a) *Five Lectures on Psycho-Analysis. S.E.,* 11.

(1910b) "The Antithetical Meaning of Primal Words." *S.E.,* 11.

(1910c) "A Special Type of Choice of Object Made by Men." *S.E.,* 11.

(1910d) *Leonardo da Vinci and a Memory of his Childhood. S.E.,* 11.

(1911) "Formulations on the Two Principles of Mental Functioning." *S.E.,* 12.

(1912–13) *Totem and Taboo. S.E.,* 13.

(1913a) "The Theme of the Three Caskets." *S.E.,* 12.

(1913b) "The Claims of Psycho-Analysis to Scientific Interest." *S.E.,* 13.

(1914a) "The Moses of Michelangelo." *S.E.,* 13.

(1914b) "On Narcissism: An Introduction." *S.E.,* 14.

(1914c) "On the History of the Psycho-Analytic Movement." *S.E.,* 14.

(1916a) "Some Character-Types Met with in Psycho-Analytic Work." *S.E.,* 14.

FREUD, SIGMUND – *Contd.*

  (1916b) "A Mythological Parallel to a Visual Obsession." *S.E.*, 14.

  (1917a) *A General Introduction to Psychoanalysis.* *S.E.*, 15–16.

  (1917b) "A Childhood Recollection from 'Dichtung und Wahrheit'." *S.E.*, 17.

  (1919) "The Uncanny." *S.E.*, 17.

  (1920) *Beyond the Pleasure Principle.* *S.E.*, 18.

  (1921) *Group Psychology and the Analysis of the Ego.* *S.E.*, 18.

  (1922) "Medusa's Head." *S.E.*, 18.

  (1923a) *The Ego and the Id.* *S.E.*, 19.

  (1923b) "A Seventeenth Century Demonological Neurosis." *S.E.*, 19.

  (1924) "The Resistances to Psychoanalysis." *S.E.*, 19.

  (1925) *An Autobiographical Study.* *S.E.*, 20.

  (1926) "Address to the Society of B'nai Brith." *S.E.*, 20.

  (1927a) "A Postscript to my Paper on the *Moses* of Michelangelo." *S.E.*, 13.

  (1927b) *The Future of an Illusion.* *S.E.*, 21.

  (1928) "Dostoievsky and Parricide." *S.E.*, 21.

  (1930a) *Civilization and Its Discontents.* *S.E.*, 21.

  (1930b) "Address Delivered in the Goethe House at Frankfort." *S.E.*, 21.

  (1931) "Female Sexuality." *S.E.*, 21.

  (1932) *New Introductory Lectures on Psychoanalysis.* *S.E.*, 22.

  (1933) Preface to Marie Bonaparte's *Edgar Allan Poe.* *S.E.*, 22.

  (1935) "The Subtleties of a Faulty Action." *S.E.*, 22.

  (1937) "Constructions in Analysis." *S.E.*, 23.

  (1938) "A Comment on Anti-Semitism." *S.E.*, 23.

  (1939) *Moses and Monotheism.* *S.E.*, 23.

—— *The Origins of Psychoanalysis, Letters to Wilhelm Fliess . . . 1887–1902.* New York and London, 1954.

FRIEDMAN, PAUL. "The Nose. Some Psychological Reflections." *American Imago* 8 (1951): 337–50.

FROMM, ERICH. *The Forgotten Language.* New York, 1951; London, 1952.

FRY, ROGER. *The Artist and Psychoanalysis.* London, 1924.

FRYE, NORTHROP. *The Anatomy of Criticism.* Princeton, N.J., 1957.

FUCHS, EDUARD. *Geschichte der erotischen Kunst.* Berlin, 1908.

—— *Illustrierte Sittengeschichte.* 3 vols. Munich, 1909–12.

GALTON, FRANCIS. "Composite Portraits." *Journal of the Anthropological Institute* 8 (1878): 132–42.

GILBERT, KATHERINE S., and HELMUT KUHN. *A History of Esthetics.* Bloomington, Ill., 1953; London, 1956.

GOMBRICH, ERNST. "Freud's Aesthetics." *Encounter*, January 1966, pp. 30–40.

――― "Psychoanalysis and the History of Art." *International Journal of Psychoanalysis*, no. 4, 1954.

GREENBERG, CLEMENT. "Modernist Painting." *Arts Yearbook*, no. 4, 1961.

GRINSTEIN, ALEXANDER. *Sigmund Freud's Dreams*. New York, 1968.

――― "A Psychoanalytic Study of Schwind's 'The Dream of a Prisoner.'" *American Imago* 8 (1951): 65–91.

GRODDECK, GEORG. "Unconscious Symbolism in Language and Art" (1926). In *Exploring the Unconscious*. New York and London, 1950.

GROOS, KARL. *The Play of Man*. 1st ed. 1898.

――― "Das Spiel als Katharsis." *Zeitschrift für pädagogische Psychologie* 12 (1912).

HARTT, FREDERICK. *Michelangelo: The Complete Sculpture*. New York, 1968; London, 1969.

HATFIELD, HENRY. *Modern German Literature*. New York, 1967; London, 1966.

HELD, JULIUS S. *Rembrandt's Aristotle and Other Essays*. Princeton, N.J., 1969.

HESSE, HERMANN. *Briefe*. Berlin, 1951.

――― "Künstler und Psychoanalyse" (1918). In *Gesammelte Schriften*, vol. 7. Berlin, 1958.

――― "Über gute und schlechte Kritiker. Notizen zum Thema Dichtung und Kritik." In *Gesammelte Schriften*, vol. 7. Berlin, 1958.

HOFFMAN, FREDERICK J. *Freudianism and the Literary Mind*. 2d ed. Baton Rouge, La., 1957.

HOLLAND, NORMAN N. *The Dynamics of Literary Response*. New York, 1968.

HOME, H. J. "The Concept of Mind." *International Journal of Psychoanalysis* 47 (1966): 42–9.

HUXLEY, ALDOUS. "The Farcical History of Richard Greenow." *Limbo*, 1923.

――― *Mortal Coils*. London, 1920. Renamed *The Gioconda Smile*, 1922.

HYMAN, STANLEY EDGAR. *The Armed Vision*. New York, 1948.

――― *The Tangled Bank. Darwin, Marx, Frazer and Freud as Imaginative Writers*. New York, 1962.

JACOB, MAX. *L'Art poétique*. Paris, 1922.

JANET, PIERRE. *L'Automatisme psychologique: essais de psychologie expérimentale sur les formes inférieures de l'activité humaine*. Paris, 1889.

――― *Psychological Healing. A Historical and Clinical Study*. London, 1925.

JANSON, H. W. "The Right Arm of Michelangelo's 'Moses.' " In ANTJE KOSEGARTEN and PETER TIGLER, eds., *Festschrift Ulrich Middeldorf.* Berlin, 1968.

JEKELS, LUDWIG. "The Riddle of Shakespeare's 'Macbeth.' " In *Selected Papers.* London, 1952.

JENKS, WILLIAM A. *Vienna and the Young Hitler.* New York, 1960.

JENSEN, WILHELM. *Gradiva : Ein pompeianisches Phantasiestück.* Dresden, 1903. French edition translated by MARIE BONAPARTE, in *Délire et rêves dans un ouvrage littéraire : la Gradiva de Jensen.* Paris, 1931.

JOAD, C. E. M. *Decadence : A Philosophical Inquiry.* London, 1948.

JOHNSON, P. *Khruschev and the Arts.* Cambridge, Mass., 1965.

JONES, ERNEST. *Free Associations.* New York and London, 1959.

—— *Hamlet and Oedipus.* London, 1949.

—— *The Life and Work of Sigmund Freud.* 3 vols. New York and London, 1953, 1955, 1957.

—— "The Oedipus Complex as an Explanation of Hamlet's Mystery. A Study in Motive." *American Journal of Psychology*, January 1910.

—— "The Theory of Symbolism" (1916). In *Papers on Psychoanalysis.* 5th ed., 1948.

JUNG, CARL G. *Memories, Dreams, Reflections.* New York, 1961; London, 1963.

JUST, GOTTFRIED. *Ironie und Sentimentalität in den erzählenden Dichtungen Artur Schnitzlers.* Berlin, 1968.

KEYSERLING, HERMANN. "Encounters with Psychoanalysis" ("Begegnungen mit der Psychoanalyse"). *Merkur* 4 (1950): 1151–68.

KLEIN, MELANIE. "The Importance of Symbol-Formation in the Development of the Ego." *International Journal of Psychoanalysis* 11 (1930): 24–39.

—— "The Role of the School in Libidinal Development" (1923). In *Contributions to Psychoanalysis.* London, 1968.

KNIGHTS, L. C. "How Many Children Had Lady Macbeth?" In *Explorations.* London, 1951.

KOESTLER, ARTHUR. *Insight and Outlook.* New York and London, 1949.

KRIS, ERNST. *Psychoanalytic Explorations in Art.* New York, 1952; London, 1953.

KUBIE, LAWRENCE S. *Neurotic Distortion of the Creative Process.* Lawrence, Kansas, 1958.

LAFORGUE, RENÉ. "Ein Bild von Freud." *Zeitschrift für Psychotherapie und medizinische Psychotherapie* 4 (1954): 210–17.

LALO, CHARLES. *La Beauté et l'instinct sexuel.* Paris, 1922.

LANGER, SUSANNE K. *Philosophy in a New Key.* Cambridge, Mass., 1942.

LANGFELD, HERBERT S. *The Aesthetic Attitude*. New York, 1920.

LAUMONNIER, JEAN. *Le Freudisme, Exposé et Critique*. Paris, 1925.

LAWRENCE, D. H. *Fantasia of the Unconscious*. New York and London, 1930; 1st ed., 1922.

LENORMAND, HENRI RENÉ. *Confessions d'un auteur dramatique*. Paris, 1949.

LESSER, SIMON O. *Fiction and the Unconscious*. Boston, 1957; London, 1960.

LEVI, ALBERT WILLIAM. *Literature, Philosophy and Imagination*. Bloomington, Ind., 1963.

LEVIN, MEYER. "A New Fear in Writers." *Psychoanalysis*, no. 1 (1953), pp. 34–38.

LÉVI-STRAUSS, CLAUDE. *Structural Anthropology*. New York, 1963; London, 1968.

LIPPS, THEODOR. "Einfühlung, Innere Nachahmung." *Archiv für die gesamte Psychologie*, vol. 1, 1903.

———— *Raumästhetik und geometrische-optische Täuschungen*. Leipzig, 1897.

LOEWY, EMMANUEL. *The Rendering of Nature in Early Greek Art* (1900). New York and London, 1907.

MAEDER, ALPHONSE. *"Une Voie nouvelle en psychologie—Freud et son école."* *Caenobium*. Lugano, 1906.

MÂLE, ÉMILE. *L'Art religieux du XIIe siècle en France*. Paris, 1947.

MARCINOWSKI, J. "Gezeichnete Träume." *Zbl. Psychoanal.*, 2 (1912).

MARCUSE, HERBERT. *Eros and Civilization*. New York, 1955; London, 1969.

MARCUSE, LUDWIG. "Freud's Aesthetics." *Journal of Aesthetics and Art Criticism* 12 (1956): 16–17.

MEREZHKOVSKY, DMITRY S. *The Romance of Leonardo da Vinci*. New York and London, 1902.

MILLER, N. E., and J. DOLLARD. *Personality and Psychotherapy*. New York, 1950.

MILNER, MARION. *International Journal of Psychoanalysis* 23 (1952): 181–95.

MORRIS, CHARLES. *Signs, Language and Behavior*. New York, 1946.

MUENSTERBERGER, WARNER. "The Roots of Primitive Art." In G. B. WILBUR and W. MUENSTERBERGER, eds., *Psychoanalysis and Culture*. New York, 1951.

NUNBERG, HERMAN, and ERNEST FEDERN, eds., *Minutes of the Vienna Psychoanalytic Society*. Vol. 1 (1906–8), New York, 1962. Vol. 2 (1908–10), New York, 1967.

OBERNDORF, CLARENCE P. "Psychoanalysis in Literature and Its Therapeutic Value." *Psychoanalysis and the Social Sciences.* New York, 1947.

OGDEN, C. K., and I. A. RICHARDS. *The Meaning of Meaning.* New York and London, 1927.

OGDEN, CHARLES K., I. A. RICHARDS, and JAMES WOOD. *The Foundations of Aesthetics.* New York, 1925.

PANOFSKY, ERWIN. *Idea.* Leipzig, 1924. English ed., New York, 1970.

———— "The Neoplatonic Movement and Michelangelo." *Studies in Iconology.* New York, 1939.

PEARSON, KARL. *The Life, Letters and Labours of Francis Galton.* 3 vols. Cambridge, Mass., 1930; Cambridge, England, 1924.

PFISTER, OSKAR. *Der psychologische und biologische Untergrund expressionistischer Bilder.* English ed., New York, 1923; London, 1922.

———— "Die psychologische Enträtselung der religiösen Glossolalie und der automatischen Kryptographie." *Jb. psychoanal. und psychopath. Forsch.* 3 (1911–12).

PHILIPPSON, LUDWIG. *Israelitische Bibel.* 3 vols. 2d ed. Leipzig, 1858, 1859.

PHILIPSON, MORRIS. *Outline of a Jungian Aesthetic.* Evanston, Ill., 1963.

PHILLIPS, WILLIAM, ed. *Art and Psychoanalysis.* New York, 1957.

POULET, GEORGES. *Études sur le temps humain.* Paris, 1950.

———— *La Distance intérieure.* Paris, 1952.

PRAZ, MARIO. *The Romantic Agony.* 2d ed. New York and London, 1951.

RANK, OTTO. "Dreams and Creative Writing" and "Dreams and Myths." Included in *The Interpretation of Dreams,* 4th–7th eds., 1914–22.

———— *The Trauma of Birth.* Vienna, 1924; London, 1929.

RANK, OTTO, and HANNS SACHS. *The Significance of Psychoanalysis for the Mental Sciences.* New York, 1916.

RECOULY, RAYMOND. "A Visit to Freud." *The Outlook,* 5 September 1923, pp. 27–29.

REICH, WILHELM. *Reich Speaks of Freud.* M. HIGGINS and C. M. RAPHAEL, eds., New York, 1967.

REIK, THEODOR. "Freud and Jewish Wit." *Psychoanalysis,* no. 3 (1954), pp. 12–20.

———— *From 30 Years with Freud.* New York and London, 1942.

REINACH, SALOMON. *Cultes, Mythes et Religions,* vol. 4. Paris, 1912.

RICHARDS, I. A. *Coleridge on Imagination.* London, 1934.

RICOEUR, PAUL. *De l'Interprétation.* Paris, 1965. English ed., New York and London, 1970.

RIEFF, PHILIP. *Freud: The Mind of the Moralist.* New York, 1959; London, 1960.

RIESMAN, DAVID. "Themes of Work and Play in the Structure of Freud's Thought." *Psychiatry,* no. 1 (1950), pp. 1–16.

ROAZEN, PAUL. *Brother Animal.* New York, 1969; London, 1970.

ROBINSON, PAUL. *The Freudian Left.* New York, 1969. Published in Great Britain as *The Sexual Radicals.* London, 1970.

RORSCHACH, HERMANN. "Zur Symbolik der Schlange und der Kravatte." *Zeitblatt für Psychanalyse,* no. 2 (1912).

ROSENFELD, EVA M. "Dream and Vision. Some Remarks on Freud's Egyptian Bird Dream." *International Journal of Psychoanalysis* 37 (1956): 97–105.

––––– "Review of Eissler, Leonardo." In *International Journal of Psychoanalysis,* January 1963, pp. 113–15.

ROSENMAYR, LEOPOLD. *Sociology in Austria.* Graz, 1966.

ROSENTHAL, EARL E. "Michelangelo's Moses, *dal di sotto in sù.*" *Art Bulletin,* December 1964, pp. 544–50.

SACHS, HANNS. *Freud, Master and Friend.* Cambridge, Mass., 1944; London, 1945.

––––– *The Creative Unconscious.* Cambridge, Mass., 1942.

SANCTIS, SANTE DE. *La Conversione religiosa.* Bologna, 1924.

––––– *I sogni.* Turin, 1899.

SANOUILLET, MICHEL. *Dada à Paris.* Paris, 1965.

SAUL, LEON J. "The Feminine Significance of the Nose." *Psychoanalytic Quarterly,* January 1948.

SCHACHTEL, ERNEST G. *Metamorphosis.* New York, 1959; London, 1963.

SCHAPIRO, MEYER. "Leonardo and Freud: An Art Historical Study." *Journal of the History of Ideas,* April 1956.

––––– "Two Slips of Leonardo and a Slip of Freud." *Psychoanalysis,* Winter 1955–56.

SCHERNER, KARL A. *Das Leben des Traumes.* Berlin, 1861.

SCHNEIDER, DANIEL. *The Psychoanalyst and the Artist.* New York, 1950.

SCHORSKE, CARL E. "Politics and the Psyche in *fin-de-siècle* Vienna: Schnitzler and Hofmannsthal." *American Historical Review,* July 1961, pp. 930–46.

SEGAL, HANNA. "A Psychoanalytical Approach to Aesthetics." *International Journal of Psychoanalysis* 33 (1952): 196–207.

SELANDER, STEN. "Zwei Aufsätze über den Einflusz der Psychanalyse." *Dagens Nyheter,* 6 December 1931.

SERVADIO, EMILIO. "Il Surrealismo: Storia, dottrina, valutazione psico-analitica." *Psicoanalisi*, 1946.

SHAKOW, DAVID, and DAVID RAPAPORT. "The Influence of Freud on American Psychology," *Psychological Issues*. Vol. 4, no. 1. New York, 1964.

SHARPE, ELLA. "Certain Aspects of Sublimation and Delusion." *International Journal of Psychoanalysis* 11 (1930): 12–23.

SHATTUCK, ROGER. *The Banquet Years*. New York, 1958; London, 1959.

SILBERER, HERBERT. "Bericht über eine Methode, gewisse symbolische Halluzinations—Erscheinungen hervorzurufen und zu beobachten." *Jb. Psychoan. psychopath. Forsch.* Vol. 1, 1909. Vol. 3, 1912.

SLOCHOWER, HARRY. "Incest in 'The Brothers Karamazov.'" *American Imago* 16 (1959): 127–45.

SOKEL, WALTER H. *The Writer in Extremis*. Stanford, Conn., 1959.

SOURIAU, PAUL. *La Beauté rationnelle*. Paris, 1904.

SPECTOR, JACK J. "Freud and Duchamp: The *Mona Lisa* 'Exposed.'" *Artforum*, April 1968, pp. 54–56.

——— "The Method of Morelli and Its Relation to Freudian Psychoanalysis." *Diogenes*, no. 66 (1969), pp. 63–83.

STAROBINSKI, JEAN. "Freud, Breton et Myers." In MARC EIGELDINGER, ed., *André Breton*. Neuchâtel, 1970.

STEKEL, WILHELM. *Die Sprache des Traumes*. Wiesbaden, 1911.

STERBA, RICHARD. "The Problem of Art in Freud's Writings." *Psychoanalytic Quarterly* 9 (1940): 256–68.

STOKES, ADRIAN. "Form in Art: A Psychoanalytic Interpretation." *Journal of Aesthetics and Art Criticism*, no. 2 (1959).

——— *The Invitation in Art*. New York and London, 1965.

THIBAUDET, ALBERT. "Psychanalyse et littérature." *Nouvelle Revue française*, April 1921.

TRILLING, LIONEL. *Beyond Culture*. New York, 1955; London, 1966.

TROTSKY, LEON. *Literature and Revolution*. Ann Arbor, Mich., 1960.

VINCHON, JEAN. *L'Art et la folie*. Paris, 1924.

VISAN, TANCRÈDE DE. *L'Attitude du lyrisme contemporaine*. Paris, 1911.

VISCHER, FRIEDRICH THEODOR. *Kritische Gänge*. Stuttgart, 1873.

VOLKELT, JOHANNES. *Die Traum-Phantasie*. Stuttgart, 1875.

——— *System der Ästhetik*. 1905–14. Munich, 3 vols.

WEISS, J. "A Psychological Theory of Formal Beauty." *Psychoanalytic Quarterly*: 16 (1947): 391–400.

WHEELWRIGHT, PHILIP. "The Guilt of Oedipus." In *The Burning Fountain*. Bloomington, Ind., 1954; London, 1968.

WHYTE, LANCELOT LAW. *The Unconscious Before Freud*. New York, 1960; London, 1962.

WILSON, EDMUND. "The Historical Interpretation of Literature." In D. A. STAUFFER, ed., *The Intent of the Critic*. Princeton, 1941.

WITTELS, FRITZ. *Freud and His Time* (1930). New York, 1931; London, 1956.

WITTKOWER, RUDOLF and MARGOT. *Born Under Saturn*. London, 1963.

WOHLGEMUTH, ADOLPH. *A Critical Examination of Psychoanalysis*. New York and London, 1923.

WORTIS, JOSEPH. "Fragments of a Freudian Analysis." *The American Journal of Orthopsychiatry* 10 (1940).

WYSS, DIETER. *Depth Psychology*. London, 1966.

Index